SIE Exam Prep

2024-2025

Complete Review + 510 Questions and Detailed Answer Explanations for the FINRA Securities Industry Essentials Exam (6 Full-length Exams)

Printed in the United States of America

Table of Contents

Introduction

The Securities Industry Essentials (SIE) exam tests your knowledge of the securities industry. It is administered by the Financial Industry Regulatory Authority (FINRA) and is a prerequisite to the Series 7 and other series-level exams.

As a candidate, you will be expected to demonstrate knowledge of the securities industry, the structure and function of marketers, regulated and prohibited practices, securities products, and regulatory agencies and their functions.

The exam tests your knowledge of securities industry-related concepts through 85 multiple-choice questions based on the following four sections:

- **Overview of the Regulatory Framework** – This section covers topics like employee conduct and reportable events, regulatory requirements for associated persons, and FINRA bylaws.
- **Knowledge of Capital Markets** – This section covers agencies' market structure, regulatory entities, offerings, economic factors, and FINRA rules.
- **Understanding Trading, Customer Accounts, and Prohibited Activities** – This section covers trading settlement, compliance considerations, customer accounts, corporate actions, and prohibited activities.
- **Understanding Products and Their Risks** – This section covers product ownership, varying maturities, voting rights, packaged products, investment risks, hedge funds, and corresponding FINRA rules.

Aside from the topics covered in the above sections, you will also be tested on several FINRA and SEC laws and regulations.

How Is the Exam Administered?

The exam is administered on a computer. You can take the exam remotely or in a testing center.

The exam consists of 85 questions, ten of which are ungraded.

Since you will not be penalized for errors, you should attempt all the questions in the allotted time.

The exam is graded using a statistical adjustment process called "equating." This process accounts for slight variations in difficulty levels that may exist in the different sets of exams candidates receive. It also promotes fair grading.

Registration Process

To register, visit the official FINRA website, enter your identification information, enroll for the SIE exam, and schedule your exam.

The website features step-by-step instructions.

This study guide will walk you through everything you need to know and help you prepare for the exam.

Chapter 1: What Is Regulation?

The SEC is an independent federal government regulatory agency. Its primary purpose is to ensure adherence to the rules and regulations that the commission makes and enforces.

The SEC protects investors from fraudulent activities, ensures that the securities markets remain effective, and facilitates the capital formation required to support economic growth.

The laws and regulations of the SEC originate from the concept that all investors should have access to basic facts about investments.

Financial services firms, such as advisory firms, broker-dealers, and asset managers, must register with the SEC.

The SEC oversees national securities exchanges. These exchanges are regulated in part by entities such as the Municipal Securities Rulemaking Board (MSRB) and FINRA.

FINRA oversees brokerage firms and their associated persons, while the MSRB regulates the municipal securities market, including dealers, municipal advisers, and issuers. Within these exchanges, different entities work for firms, such as broker-dealers, branch officers, and principals.

We will expand on these concepts and highlight how capital markets work and how regulatory bodies streamline the activities of securities firms and brokers. We will also discuss investor protection against fraud.

Federal Reserve Board

The Federal Reserve, or the Fed, is the central banking system of the US. It was founded on December 23, 1913, to oversee the monetary system after a series of financial panics. Even though it operates within the government's framework, the Fed operates independently of direct political influence.

The Federal Reserve Act was passed:

- To stabilize prices.
- To maximize employment.
- To moderate long-term interest rates.

Structure of the Fed

The structure of the Fed has both public and private elements. It does not require public funding and derives its workflow, purpose, and authority from the Federal Reserve Act.

There are four primary components of the Fed:

- The Board of Governors.
- The Federal Open Market Committee.
- Twelve Regional Federal Reserve Banks.
- Member banks throughout the US.

The Federal Reserve System is made up of the Federal Reserve Board (FRB), which is appointed by the U.S. president and 12 regional Federal Reserve Banks. These regional banks supervise private commercial banks. These commercial banks act as chartered entities and hold a financial interest in their respective Federal Reserve Bank. Also, they can get involved when electing board members.

Monetary policy is established by the FOMC, a body that consists of the seven members of the Board of Governors and the twelve presidents of the regional Federal Reserve Banks. It is important to note that not all of the twelve presidents have a vote at any given time.

Five bank presidents are allowed to cast votes at any given time. The New York Federal Reserve Bank president retains the right to vote perpetually, while the others rotate through successive one-year intervals of voting eligibility.

The Department of the Treasury is an entity that is separate from the central bank and prints currency. Advisory councils are also in place to provide guidance, which makes the structure of the Federal Reserve unique among central banks.

Role and Responsibilities of the Fed

The duties of the Fed have increased over the years. One of its key responsibilities is supervising and regulating banks.

Some other current functions of the Fed include:

- Strengthening the US standing in the world economy.

- Maintaining a balance between the private interests of banks and the centralized responsibilities of the government, including supervising and regulating banking institutions and protecting the credit rights of consumers.
- Ensuring the financial system's stability and mitigating systemic risk within the financial markets.

Federal Deposit Insurance Corporation (FDIC)

Established in 1933, the FDIC is an independent agency created by Congress to foster stability within the financial system while concurrently upholding public confidence in its efficacy. It provides deposit insurance; oversees financial institutions to ensure their safety and soundness; facilitates the resolution of significant financial organizations; and administers receiverships.

As of 2023, the FDIC safeguards deposits by providing insurance coverage of up to $250,000 per individual depositor. To avail themselves of the FDIC's protective umbrella, financial institutions are required to become members of the organization.

The objective of the FDIC is to prevent scenarios like the Great Depression from occurring and to ensure that customer funds are secure. The organization extends its protection to checking and savings accounts, money market accounts, certificates of deposit (CDs), individual retirement accounts (IRAs), revocable/irrevocable trust accounts, and employee benefit plans.

The FDIC does not cover annuities, mutual funds, life insurance policies, bonds, or stocks.

State (Blue-Sky) Regulators

Blue-sky laws are anti-fraud regulations at the state level. They require issuers of securities to provide details of their offerings as a safeguard against securities fraud.

The laws vary from state to state but require sellers of new issues to provide in-depth financial details of the entities involved in every deal. This provides investors with verifiable information upon which they can base their investment decisions.

Blue-sky laws, which supplement federal securities regulations, typically require brokerage firms, investment advisers, and individual brokers offering securities in their states to obtain licenses.

These laws require that private investment funds register in their home state and every state where they conduct business.

Blue-sky laws are based on the Uniform Securities Act, which was originally drafted in 1956. Although it provides a framework for states to create their securities legislation, not all states have adopted it in its entirety, and the number of states that have adopted it can vary.

Subsequent legislation, such as the National Securities Markets Improvement Act of 1996, preempts blue-sky laws when they overlap with federal law.

North American Securities Administrators Association

The North American Securities Administrators Association (NASAA) is a group of securities regulators dedicated to safeguarding investors against fraudulent activities. Established in 1919 in Kansas, the organization comprises 67 securities administrators from various parts of North America.

NASAA comprises a group of regulators who are appointed, hired for career-based roles, or who come under the jurisdiction of their states' attorneys general. These individuals are responsible for licensing securities firms, investment professionals, and other tasks.

NASAA's mission is to protect clients who seek investment advice or deal with securities, working alongside complementary regulatory systems at the federal, state, and industry levels.

For instance, NASAA helps small businesses review financial offerings and provides guidance that helps them comply with state securities laws. It also provides valuable information to help businesses navigate regulatory landscapes and avoid major pitfalls and costly mistakes.

The Securities Act of 1933

The Great Stock Market crash of October 29, 1929, often referred to as 'Black Tuesday,' laid the foundation for the inception of the Securities Act of 1933. The law was passed to protect investors. It had two main goals:

- Establish laws against misrepresentation and fraudulent activities in the securities markets.
- Ensure transparency in financial statements to help investors make informed decisions.

Before the Securities Act of 1933, sales of securities were governed mainly by state laws. The legislation helped ensure complete disclosure by companies by registering them with the SEC.

Companies planning to go public must comply with the 1933 Act, commonly called the Truth in Securities law or the Federal Securities Act. This legislation mandates that investors receive financial information regarding securities offered for public sale.

Companies must make information easily accessible to potential investors before their initial public offering (IPO). The information includes:

- Description of the security being offered.
- Description of the company's business and properties.
- Financial statements that have been certified by independent accountants.

Securities Exchange Act of 1934

The primary objective of the Securities Exchange Act of 1934 (SEA) was to regulate securities trading in the secondary market after their issuance. Its purpose was to promote financial transparency and accuracy while reducing the incidence of fraudulent activities and market manipulation.

The secondary market is where trading occurs after a company issues assets. These assets include bonds, stocks, futures, and options.

The SEA established the SEC, which is tasked with enforcing the SEA and other securities laws.

The companies that are listed on stock exchanges have to comply with the SEA of 1934. Some compliance requirements include the following:

- Proxy solicitations.
- Company financial disclosures.
- Registration of any securities listed on stock exchanges.

Five commissioners lead the SEC. The president appoints them. The agency is divided into five major divisions:

- Division of trading and markets.

- Division of investment management.
- Division of corporation finance.
- Division of enforcement.
- Division of economic and risk analysis.

The SEC is vested with the authority to spearhead inquiries into suspected breaches of the SEA, such as insider trading, sale of unregistered stocks, misappropriation of clients' funds, market price manipulation, misrepresentation of financial information, and violation of broker-customer trust.

Investment Advisers Act of 1940

The Investment Advisers Act of 1940 is a federal statute established to oversee and govern the operations of investment advisers as defined by the law. This law is the primary basis for regulating investment advisers and is enforced by the US Securities and Exchange Commission (SEC).

The Act of 1940, like other significant financial regulations enacted in the 1930s and 1940s, was primarily driven by the stock market crash of 1929 and the severe consequences of the Great Depression.

The act prohibits advisers from engaging in front-running and churning practices. That means they are bound to provide accurate and complete information to ensure their clients' best interests and maintain the market's integrity.

The Investment Advisers Act provides several exclusions to the definition of an investment adviser. A person eligible for any exclusions is not subjected to any provisions of the act. The following are people or entities that are excluded from the act:

1. Banks and bank holding companies.
2. Lawyers, accountants, engineers, and teachers.
3. Brokers and dealers.
4. Publishers.
5. Government securities advisers.

6. Credit rating agencies.

7. Family offices.

Securities Investors Protection Act (SIPA)

Congress enacted SIPA in reaction to concerns about brokerage firm failures and to address potential impacts on investors.

The objective was to renew faith in the capital markets among investors and enhance the financial obligation prerequisites for registered brokers and dealers. Additionally, it aimed to assign the execution of various legislative goals to multiple bodies, including the SEC, self-regulating organizations within the securities industry, and the Securities Investor Protection Corporation (SIPC).

The SIPC is a nonprofit organization established by Congress to safeguard the customers of brokerage firms that become insolvent.

SIPC Coverage Examples

Under the SIPC's protection, cash and securities in an account are covered up to $500,000. However, it is crucial to remember that there is a limit of $250,000 for cash coverage. It is also worth noting that if an individual holds $500,000 in securities and $250,000 in cash, the combined amount will be covered, but only up to the $500,000 limit for securities and the $250,000 limit for cash.

SIPC insurance only applies when the SIPC intervenes, which happens when regulatory agencies refer to a broker-dealer failure resulting in loss of securities and cash.

When initiating the liquidation process, the SIPC appoints a trustee. This trustee can either be the SIPC itself or a lawyer. Their role is to oversee the liquidation of the firm's assets.

In certain situations, the SIPC may opt for an alternative approach by directly engaging with customers outside the court system. This can be done through a direct payment procedure, facilitating a more streamlined resolution process.

The SIPC extends its coverage to various investments classified as securities, including treasury stock, bonds, and stocks. These securities fall under "separate capacities," which encompass different categories of investment accounts. Here are a few examples:

- Joint accounts.

- Corporate accounts.
- Individual accounts.
- Trust accounts.
- Roth IRAs and traditional IRAs.
- Accounts held by a legal guardian or estate executor.

Other Federal Laws

Some other important federal laws will be discussed here briefly.

The Penny Stock Reform Act of 1990

Congress established the Penny Stock Reform Act of 1990 as part of the securities legislation that seeks to prevent fraud in non-exchange listed stocks, known as penny stocks.

A stock that trades below $5 per share is known as a penny stock.

These penny stocks are typically part of the broker-dealer market, which means they are traded through the over-the-counter (OTC) market. President George H.W. Bush signed the law on October 15, 1990. It aimed to address penny stock fraud after instances increased from the 1970s to the 1980s.

Small companies not meeting the listing requirements to trade on national exchanges usually issue penny stocks. For instance, the New York Stock Exchange (NYSE) mandates companies to have a certain minimum in outstanding equity shares and a specific market capitalization. The specific thresholds and criteria can vary and should be checked in the NYSE's official listing standards.

The Insider Trading and Securities Fraud Enforcement Act of 1988 (ITSFEA)

ITSFEA expanded the authority of the SEC to enforce insider trading laws, and amended the Securities Exchange Act.

Signed into law by President Ronald Reagan on November 19, 1988, the act aims to increase the liability penalties to all involved parties for insider trading.

There have been many cases of insider trading since 1988. For instance, Martha Stewart was accused by the SEC in 2003 of insider trading and obstruction of justice for her involvement in the ImClone case of 2001, and she served a five-month prison sentence as a result.

The Investment Company Act of 1940

Signed into law by President Franklin D. Roosevelt, the Investment Company Act of 1940 governs the formation and operations of investment companies and sets industry standards. Its chief aim is to safeguard investors by making them aware of the risks of purchasing and holding securities.

The Telephone Consumer Protection Act of 1991 (TCPA)

This act was enacted in response to consumer concerns about telemarketing. It was a response to complaints directed to the Federal Communications Commission (FCC) regarding the use of telephones for the solicitation of business.

TCPA limits the use of telemarketing, including artificial messages, text messages, fax machines, prerecorded messages, and autodialing systems.

Financial Industry Regulatory Authority (FINRA)

FINRA is a nongovernmental and independent organization that establishes and enforces rules governing broker-dealers and brokers in the US.

This self-regulatory organization safeguards the investing public against fraud and bad practices.

FINRA came into existence after the consolidation of the National Association of Securities Dealers (NASD). It was established by combining the regulatory, enforcement, and arbitration functions of the New York Stock Exchange. FINRA oversees over 3,400 brokerage firms, 617,550 registered securities representatives, and 152,000 branch offices as of 2020.

It has been authorized by Congress to protect the interests of investors. This section will highlight conduct rules and some other attributes of FINRA.

Conduct Rules

FINRA has many important rules, including:

- **Rule 2266** – SIPC Information – This rule requires SIPC member firms to provide written notice to customers about SIPC protections.
- **Rule 2269** – Disclosure of Participation or Interest in Primary or Secondary Distribution – This rule requires firms to disclose any participation or interest in a primary or secondary distribution of securities to customers.
- **Rule 5250** – Payments for Market Making – This rule prohibits firms from accepting payments from issuers or promoters of a security for acting as market makers in that security.

Uniform Practice Code (UPC)

The Uniform Practice Code is a set of rules that govern the activities of FINRA member firms, and ensures consistent practices in the securities industry. It standardizes practices, customs, trading techniques, and operational and settlement issues as much as possible.

Some topics covered by the UPC include:

- Trade terms.
- Payment and delivery procedures.
- Dividend and interest payments.
- Reclamations.
- Exchange of confirmations.

Code of Procedure (COP)

COP are FINRA's procedural rules. They oversee the disciplinary proceedings against FINRA member firms.

Municipal Securities Rulemaking Board (MSRB)

The Municipal Securities Rulemaking Board is a self-regulatory organization (SRO) overseen by a board of directors and four committees that manage various aspects of the organization's governance and operation.

The MSRB sets its own rules and standards, but the SEC supervises them. Different regulatory agencies enforce these rules:

a. FINRA and the SEC monitor broker-dealers.

b. Bank dealers fall under the jurisdiction of the Comptroller of the Currency, the FRB, or the FDIC.

Chicago Board Options Exchange (CBOE)

Inaugurated in 1973, the CBOE facilitates trading activities mainly in options and futures products. It does not trade US and European stocks or international foreign exchange products directly.

Despite its international presence, CBOE is not the largest stock exchange in Europe. It is one of the largest options exchanges in the United States and a prominent global market exchange for ETP trading.

Chapter 2: Market Participants and Market Structure

Financial markets impact how capitalist economies operate. In broad terms, financial markets are marketplaces where securities are traded. These securities include bonds, stocks, derivatives, and forex.

This chapter focuses on the role of market participants in these marketplaces and how the market structure works.

Participants and Their Roles

Investors

Investors, whether individuals or entities like mutual funds or firms, play a pivotal role in the financial ecosystem because they allocate capital with the anticipation of reaping financial rewards.

Investors can invest in mutual funds, bonds, stocks, ETFs, foreign exchange, precious metals like silver and gold, and real estate.

Types of investors found in the marketplace include:

- **Venture Capitalists** invest in start-ups and small businesses. They seek an equity stake in return for their investment and help grow the company to sell their stake for a profit. They focus on businesses already in early stages with growth potential.
- **Angel Capitalists** provide capital to entrepreneurs and start-ups when the risk is high, i.e., in the early stages. They do so once or on an ongoing basis.
- **Institutional Investors** are organizations that invest other people's money, such as mutual funds, pension funds, and hedge funds, buying large blocks of assets that can influence prices. They are typically large and sophisticated.
- **Personal Investors** invest their own capital in stocks, bonds, mutual funds, and ETFs, seeking higher returns than traditional savings accounts or CDs. They are not professional investors.

Broker-Dealers

The marketplace is a strange world to investors who hear industry jargon like "alpha," "beta," and "Sharpe ratio." Due to its complexity, investors and other participants often seek the assistance of a dealer or a broker.

Broker

A broker carries out orders for clients. They help investors buy and sell securities.

Dealers

While a broker executes trades for investors, a dealer executes trades for itself. The terms "dealer" and "principal" are often used interchangeably. When large financial firms trade using their own accounts, they act as dealers.

Industry regulators commonly refer to firms that handle transactions as "broker-dealers" since they typically act as both brokers and dealers. These broker-dealers play an essential role in financial markets as they provide the infrastructure that assists stock trading.

Some examples of broker-dealers include E-Trade, TD Ameritrade, and Charles Schwab.

Investment Advisers

Unlike a stockbroker or financial adviser, an investment adviser is a group or person that makes investment recommendations or carries out securities analysis. The term "investment advisers" was coined in the Investment Advisers Act of 1940.

The investment adviser's fiduciary duty is to prioritize clients' interests over their own.

Municipal Advisers

A municipal adviser is a financial expert who provides advice to municipal entities or individuals with financial obligations. Their expertise lies in municipal financial products and municipal securities issuance. This may include providing recommendations on the structure, terms, and timing of municipal transactions or products.

The role of a municipal adviser may change over time; the primary roles are:

- **Marketing of Bonds** – Creating suitable offering documents for the type of issuance and providing support with a bond rating.

- **Approach for Sale** – Assisting the issuer in determining the transaction's optimal sales method and selecting underwriters.
- **Project Feasibility** – Creating financing alternatives for the issuer's assessment, considering present and future capital requirements.
- **Selling of a Bond** – Compiling information and evaluating bond conditions on comparable bonds to assist in pricing.
- **After-sale** – Creating a closed deal with important information, option pricing calculations, and ongoing disclosure filings.

Issuers and Underwriters

Companies, organizations, or governments that sell securities to raise capital are known as issuers. Issuers hire underwriters, also called investment banks, to advertise and arrange the sale of securities.

Investors acquire securities in the primary market, overseen by the SEC.

Underwriters have a pivotal role since they assist issuers to mitigate business risks. They also contribute to sales-type activities. For instance, the underwriter may purchase entire IPO issues and sell it to investors.

An IPO is when a privately owned company offers to sell its shares for the first time on a public stock exchange.

Traders and Market Trustees

A 'board of directors' is a group of individuals appointed or elected to oversee an organization's management. They serve as the organization's governing body and safeguard stakeholders' interests in all management decisions.

Transfer Agents

A transfer agent is an institution, such as a company or bank, that a corporation designates to manage investor financial records and monitor account balances. It performs tasks like maintaining records of transactions, issuing and canceling certificates, managing investor correspondence, and resolving issues like lost or stolen certificates.

Moreover, transfer agents collaborate with registrars to ensure timely payment of interest and dividends to investors and send monthly investment statements to mutual fund shareholders.

Depositories and Clearing Corporations

Established in 1999, the Depository Trust and Clearing Corporation (DTCC) is a financial services company based in the US. Its primary services include clearing and settlement services for the financial markets.

The DTCC was created by merging two organizations, the Depository Trust Company (DTC) and the National Securities Clearing Corporation (NSCC), to streamline their functions. Currently, the NSCC operates as a subsidiary of the DTCC.

State and Local Governments

State and local governments have a considerable influence on markets. They regulate transactions, enforce property rights and contract law rules, stabilize markets, and provide institutional framework.

Governments do not typically seek to increase inflation rates for short-term economic uplift. Although inflation can decrease the real burden of debt, it can also have negative impacts such as eroding purchasing power.

Foreign Governments

Foreign governments impact cross-border commerce in the region by decreasing import and export duties and encouraging investment in international trade. When countries have disagreements, these arrangements might be terminated, or, more drastically, trade embargoes could be enforced, blocking trade altogether.

Types of Securities That Cause Issues

A security is a financial instrument that is negotiable, interchangeable, and holds some form of monetary value. It can represent ownership in a corporation through stocks, a creditor relationship with a corporation or government body through bonds, or the right to ownership through options.

We will discuss two types of securities that can pose issues.

Equity

Equity securities are financial instruments that represent ownership in an entity, such as a company, partnership, or trust. They are typically issued as capital stock shares, including common and preferred stock.

Equity securities also give the holder some control over the company through voting rights. In the event of bankruptcy, holders of equity securities only receive residual interest after all obligations to creditors have been paid. Additionally, payment-in-kind (PIK) typically refers to interest or dividends that are paid in the form of additional securities rather than in cash. Equity securities themselves are not typically described as 'payment-in-kind'.

CDOs and CMOs

Collateralized Mortgage Obligations (CMOs) and Collateralized Debt Obligations (CDOs) are types of investment vehicles that are used in the financial industry.

Collateralized Mortgage Obligations (CMOs):

- CMOs contain a pool of mortgages that are grouped together and sold as an investment.
- CMOs are sold by financial institutions as fixed income investments and offer regular payments.
- CMOs can be affected by factors such as prepayments, credit risk, and fluctuating interest rates.

Collateralized Debt Obligations (CDOs):

- CDOs are divided into tranches, each of which reflects a different level of risk. Senior tranches have the lowest risk because holders of these tranches will be paid first from the corresponding collateral in case the loan proceeds to default.
- CDOs are packaged and in turn rated by credit rating agencies. This allows Wall Street to sell them to investors.
- CDOs contain a range of loans such as car loans, credit cards, commercial loans, and even mortgages.

Debt

A debt security is a financial instrument that represents borrowed funds, with specific terms that outline the loan amount, interest rate, and repayment date.

Debt securities, such as government and corporate bonds, CDs, and collateralized securities (like CDOs and CMOs), typically provide the holder with regular interest payments and repayment of the principal loan amount. Holders of debt securities do not have voting rights but may have other contractual rights.

How Broker-Dealers Function

We discussed what broker-dealers represent and how the term is used in US securities regulations. Let us see how they function.

How a Broker Functions

A broker acts as an intermediary between sellers and buyers in a transaction.

When working for an agency, brokers will execute orders on behalf of clients and receive a commission for their services.

When working individually, brokers will execute buy and sell orders for clients to earn a commission.

How a Dealer Functions

Dealers buy and sell securities from their inventory and earn a profit when the sale price is higher than the purchase price.

The difference between the two prices is known as a markup or markdown.

Principal dealers trade securities from their inventory, which means they take the risk of the transaction. In contrast, a broker acts as a middleman who facilitates the buying and selling of securities without taking on the risk like principal dealers do.

The Structure of a Securities Firm

A large securities firm will typically have multiple departments, including:

Investment Banking (50%)

Investment banking is the largest department of a securities firm.

Investment banks issue new debt and equity securities for corporations. They also aid in selling securities and facilitate mergers, acquisitions, reorganizations, and broker trades for institutions and private investors.

Research (12.5%)

The research department helps support other departments by giving insight into data, salespeople, and underwriters. It helps traders with pricing and selling securities.

The research department typically has many experts, including technical analysts, economists, and research analysts.

The research department can be further divided into institutional and retail divisions.

Investment Management (12.5%)

The investment management department handles financial assets and other investments. It devises long-term and short-term strategies for disposing of and acquiring portfolio holdings.

The department aims to meet specific investment goals for clients. Some services provided by the department are stock selection, asset allocation, financial statement analysis, monitoring of existing investments, and portfolio strategy and implementation.

Sales and Trading (12.5%)

A firm's trading department will have separate divisions focused on trading stocks, bonds, or other financial instruments.

For example, the stock-trading department executes orders from institutional sales and retail staff.

Private Clients (12.5%)

Private clients are individuals or families with significant financial portfolios. This department directly deals with private clients and manages their money without third-party brokers and distributors.

Market Makers

Market makers are firms or individuals who quote two-sided markets in security. They provide bids and offers (also known as asks).

Market makers provide liquidity and depth to markets. Many are brokerage houses that provide trading services for investors to assist in keeping the financial markets liquid.

Institutional and Retail Investors

Institutional and retail investors have many similarities and some distinctions. Retail investors are individuals who invest their own capital at lower volumes and frequencies.

Retail investors primarily invest in:

- Bonds.
- Stocks.
- Retirement accounts.
- Cryptocurrency.

Institutional investors trade large volumes of securities on behalf of a collective group of shareholders. Although some institutional investors might be accredited investors, the two terms are not synonymous. Institutional investors typically work within organizations, such as pension funds, endowments, or insurance companies.

Institutional investors primarily invest in:

- Mutual funds.
- Hedge funds.
- Real estate.
- Stocks.

Qualified Institutional Buyers (QIBs)

QIBs are sophisticated investors who do not require the same level of regulatory protection as less sophisticated investors. To be a QIB, an entity must, in the aggregate, own and invest on a discretionary basis at least $100 million in securities of issuers not affiliated with the entity. For a registered broker or dealer, the threshold is $10 million.

QIBs are more actively involved in financial markets, often through frequent buying and trading, because they have more experience with complex financial products. Unlike accredited investors, who can be individuals, QIBs are always entities such as banks or insurance companies.

The Primary Market

The primary market is a source of new securities. It is facilitated by underwriting groups that consist of investment banks. Once the initial sale is completed, further trading is done on the secondary market. The primary market is not a physical place. However, it deals with processes like the IPO.

The main characteristic of a primary market is that securities are directly purchased from an issuer. All issues are subject to strict regulations before they are approved for sale to investors.

Secondary Markets

In secondary markets, securities are traded among investors after they are created in the primary market. Investors can buy and sell securities without the involvement of the issuing company.

Trading is overseen by a specialist market maker who maintains an orderly market in a specific stock with fair trading. The specialist also acts as an intermediary, who buys and sells securities for their own accounts when there is a shortage of buyers and sellers.

Types of secondary markets include auction and dealer markets.

Some examples of secondary markets include:

NYSE American and NYSE MKT

The NYSE American serves as a listing platform for small-cap companies, and offers investors an alternative to the larger companies listed on the NYSE. The NYSE MKT was formerly known as the American Stock Exchange (AMEX) and employs market makers to oversee securities trading. Floor brokers execute trades on behalf of clients on the exchange floor of the NYSE. The Intercontinental Exchange (ICE) is now the owner of both the NYSE and NYSE MKT.

Boston Stock Exchange (BSE)

The BSE is one of the oldest regional stock exchanges in the United States, dating back to its founding in 1834.

Chicago Stock Exchange (CHX)

Formerly known as the Midwest Stock Exchange, the CHX was founded in 1882. It offers trading in more than 3,000 stocks, including Nasdaq, NYSE Amex Equities, and NYSE.

Pacific Stock Exchange (PCX)

The PCX was founded in 1882. It ceased physical operations in 2002 and served as a regional stock exchange in California. Later, it merged with the Archipelago Exchange to form NYSE Arca, which now operates as an electronic trading platform.

Dealer-to-Dealer Markets

Dealer-to-Dealer markets are a financial arena where multiple dealers buy or sell specific securities or instruments at different quoted prices.

Nasdaq is an example of an equity dealer market.

Nasdaq

Nasdaq was the first electronic trading system for buying and selling securities. It opened on February 8, 1971, and now has an index of more than 3,700 stocks.

Non-exchange Issues

Non-exchange issues are securities that are not part of any organized exchanges, which makes them extremely low-priced and thinly traded.

They are traded OTC through dealer networks. The two most popular markets were the OTCBB and OTC Pink markets. FINRA officially ceased operations of the OTCBB on November 8, 2021.

Traders

Traders are people who purchase or sell assets in financial markets, either on their own behalf or on behalf of others.

Unlike investors, traders typically hold the asset for a shorter period.

Third Markets

The third market refers to trading by non-exchange member brokers/dealers and institutional investors of exchange-listed stocks. The third market is different from the primary market and the secondary market. Specifically, it allows for greater liquidity and efficiency during trading because it provides another venue for investors to buy and sell securities.

Securities that are not listed on conventional exchanges like the NYSE can be traded OTC, and they are subject to regulation by the SEC.

Fourth Markets

The fourth market is exclusive to institutional investors such as banks and hedge funds. Usually there is a greater level of regulation that is applied in this market. Also, larger amounts of funds are traded in a single transaction.

Dark Pools

Dark pools are private exchanges for trading securities that are not accessible to public investment. They exist to facilitate institutional investors' participation in block trading.

Dark pools allow large trades to proceed without affecting the market at large, but their lack of transparency creates potential conflicts of interest.

Clearing and Settlement Process

Clearing and settlement processes are often associated with trading securities rather than wire transfers. The financial institution of the sender forwards the payment instructions to an interbank clearing network. Typically, systems like the Clearing House Interbank Payments Systems (CHIPS) manage this process.

The settlement process, on the other hand, can be initiated by banks immediately or at a later time. Typically, payment systems like CHIPS transmit a final settlement wire transfer once the business day ends.

Clearing and settlement are distinct processes. Clearing primarily establishes the obligations of funds. In contrast, settlement involves the final exchange of funds between banks. During clearing, the obligations between the two parties are established and confirmed. Settlement may occur later, and involves the actual transfer of funds or securities between the two parties.

Fully Disclosed vs. Omnibus

Fully disclosed accounts disclose the complete identity of the account holder. These accounts are individually held and provide complete transparency and control to individual traders.

In contrast, omnibus accounts, utilized by futures commission merchants, facilitate managed trading for multiple individuals while ensuring their anonymity.

Depository Trust and Clearing Corporation (DTCC) and Options Clearing Corporation (OCC)

The DTCC handles securities worth trillions of dollars daily. It serves as a centralized clearinghouse for several exchanges and equity platforms, and facilitates the settlement of transactions between buyers and sellers of securities. It significantly contributes to centralizing, standardizing, streamlining, and automating the global financial markets.

For instance, suppose an investor instructs a broker to place an order, and the trade occurs on an exchange. In this instance, the transaction details would be relayed to the DTCC, of which NSCC (National Securities Clearing Corporation) is a subsidiary for clearing and settlement.

Prime Brokerage Accounts

Prime brokerage refers to a set of comprehensive services that investment banks and other financial institutions provide to hedge funds and large investment clients.

These clients might need securities or cash lending facilities. Such facilities assist them in executing netting to attain absolute returns.

Chapter 3: Economic Factors

Economic factors include elements that influence a country's economy and financial state. They are essential for understanding the principles of working and investing in business.

This chapter will cover economic factors and how they function, business cycles, and market capitalization.

What Is the Business Cycle?

A nation's economy goes through many expansions and contractions over time. The business cycle, or the economic cycle, is the natural fluctuation in a nation's economy.

Government regulations, gross domestic product (GDP), interest rates, global commerce, technological advancement, and consumer behavior all impact the business cycle. It influences jobs, salaries, costs, and profits within a country.

Each business cycle affects corporate earnings, profits, bonds, and stock prices. Understanding the business cycle is vital to understanding a company's workings and when to invest.

Every economy faces periods of rapid and stagnant growth. A period of rapid growth is called a boom, and a period of economic decline or negative growth is called a recession.

A business cycle length is the time it takes to complete a sequence of a boom and recession. This process has four stages.

Expansion

Expansion refers to the stage where businesses are prospering. They are building inventories and investing in stocks and infrastructure.

The employment rate is high, which raises income, per capita income, the GDP, and consumer spending.

The debtors are paying their debts, and the velocity of money supplied is high. This phase continues until the economy reaches its peak.

Peak

Peak is the second stage of the business cycle, where businesses have reached the pinnacle of their growth. The employment rate, income, and wages do not increase any further.

However, the demand for goods and services also stops growing, which causes an increase in prices and, ultimately, inflation.

Consumer spending decreases, and economic activity slows. Businesses become more cautious in their investments, and consumers lessen their spending.

Contraction

A contraction phase follows a peak. The economic growth in this phase slows, investing becomes cautious, and unemployment rises, which decreases income and consumer spending.

It is a tough time for people and businesses.

Trough

The economy's growth rate becomes negative, and the supply and demand of goods and services hit rock bottom.

The trough has the lowest national income and expenditure point in the cycle. However, it also marks the beginning of the next expansion phase. Businesses start to recover and invest in new endeavors, and the employment rate gradually increases and starts the next phase in the business cycle.

Economic Indications

Economic indicators are the signs that point to current and future economic performance. There are several types.

Leading Indicators

Leading indicators help forecast future economic activity. They help predict changes in economic performance before the economy starts to move in a particular direction.

Building Permits

The number of building permits issued for private housing plans is a leading economic indicator.

Manufacturers' New Orders, Consumer Goods, Non-defense Capital Goods

Manufacturers' new orders for consumer goods and non-defense capital goods are examples of leading economic indicators. The consumer goods produced by manufacturers are also leading indicators.

S&P 500 Index

The S&P 500 index is a widely recognized leading economic indicator. It is a stock market index that tracks the performance of the 500 leading companies listed on the stock exchange.

Initial Claims for Unemployment Insurance

Unemployment insurance claims are the benefits claimed by jobless citizens. The number of these initial claims can serve as a leading economic indicator. For example, a significant number of claims indicates a weak economy.

Interest Rate Spreads

Interest rate spread measures the difference between a long- and short-term interest rate. If the spread is wide, it indicates a higher growth for future economic conditions.

Coincident Indicators

These indicators increase and decrease with the current economy. In other words, they coincide.

The Index of Industrial Production

The number of products or services industries produce as an output. It is a coincidental indicator as it reflects the current state of the economy.

Employees on Nonagricultural Payrolls

People who are employed by non-agriculture industries, such as construction, manufacturing, and retail. The number of people employed in such industries is also a coincident indicator.

Disposable Personal Income

After the subtraction of taxes and the addition of transfer payments such as social security and welfare payments, individuals' total income is an indicator of the current economic state. It reflects the consumers' buying power.

Lagging Indicators

Lagging indicators are those factors observed to change after an economic shift in the business cycle. In other words, they lag behind the correlated economic change.

Some lagging indicators are unemployment, corporate profits, and labor costs.

Change in the Consumer Price Index

The consumer price index (CPI) is a measure of inflation or deflation. The average change in the price consumers are willing to pay for a service can be an excellent lagging economic indicator.

The Average Prime Rate

The prime rate is offered to customers who have high credit ratings. The average prime rates of banks also determine other kinds of loans, which is why it is a lagging indicator. It leaves a trail of how the economy will look over time.

The Average Duration of Unemployment

The period in which people are unemployed serves as a lagging indicator. The unemployment phase can indicate a fallen economy or a thriving economy about to fall. Both conditions are considered lagging indicators.

How to Measure Interest Rates

The interest rate represents the extra sum a lender levies on the borrower over and above the primary amount (the loaned sum). It is the most crucial element to consider in the lending and borrowing process.

The loan interest rate is noted yearly and called the annual percentage rate (APR). Here are some of the methods used to measure interest rates.

Prime Rate

The prime rate is the interest rate that banks charge their most creditworthy customers. If the prime rate increases, it often leads to an increase in interest rates for various types of loans and credit. The prime rate also affects the liquidity in financial markets. If the prime rate is low, liquidity increases.

Discount Rate

The discount rate is the interest rate the central bank charges all other banks. Discount rates and interest rates are directly related. Decreased discount rates encourage banks to borrow more from the Federal Reserve. This action can potentially increase the money supply and lower interest rates.

Federal Funds Rate

The federal funds rate describes the interest rate commercial banks charge each other for overnight lending and borrowing their extra reserves. The FOMC sets this rate according to their own understanding of economic factors.

If the federal funds rate increases, money becomes less readily available, and the short-term interest rate rises.

Call Money Rate

The call money rate is the interest banks charge brokers, who lend to investors to fund margin accounts.

This interest is not paid over a set amount of time but on demand.

Classifications of Stock

Classification of companies based on their stocks categorizes them by their financial condition. Here are some of the classifications of stock.

Cyclical

Cyclical stocks move with the economy. They perform well when the economy flourishes but decline when it is weak. Examples of cyclical stocks are companies that provide luxury products, such as the automotive industry and hospitality.

Defensive

These stocks are the least affected by the overall stock market. Defensive stocks tend to produce stable dividends throughout the year and are a more reliable option for investors. They include health care and staple products.

Procter & Gamble, Johnson & Johnson, Philip Morris International, and Coca-Cola are examples of well-established defensive stocks.

Growth

Growth stocks are stocks currently performing well in the stock market and are expected to grow faster in the future. These companies usually retain their earnings and reinvest in themselves rather than pay dividends to shareholders.

Examples of companies owning growth stocks are Amazon, Facebook, and Netflix.

Value

Value stocks are those whose current share price is less than their intrinsic value. These companies are often undervalued in the market, not necessarily new, and their share price is expected to increase.

They are often found in competitive industries such as the energy sector.

Market Capitalization of Stocks

The market capitalization of stocks refers to the total outstanding shares of a company. It is calculated by multiplying the value of a share by the total number of shares.

Listed below are some of the classifications of stocks based on market capitalization.

Nano-cap

Nano-cap is the smallest stock by market cap. They are stocks of companies with a market cap of $50 million or less.

Micro-cap

Micro-cap stocks have a market capitalization of $50 million to $300 million. These are also small companies with limited resources. These stocks are risky investments.

Small-cap

Stocks that have a market capitalization of $300 million to $2 billion are small-cap. These companies are yet to flourish, so their growth potential is high.

Examples of small-cap companies are Sinclair Broadcast Group and Jackson Financial.

Mid-cap

Mid-cap stocks have a market capitalization of $2 billion to $10 billion. These companies are well-established, have produced a considerable profit, and still have the potential to grow.

Examples of mid-cap stock companies are United States Steel Corp and Silicon Laboratories Inc.

Large-cap

Large-cap stocks have a market capitalization of above $10 billion. These companies are well-known and well-established. They have a long history of success. Therefore, they offer low risk.

Such companies include Adobe Inc., Airbnb, Chipotle, and Netflix.

Monetary and Fiscal Policy

The concept of monetary policy pertains to measures implemented by the central bank to impact the quantity of credit and money circulating within an economy. An example of a monetary policy is the utilization of interest rates to manipulate the dynamics of money supply and demand to influence the broader economic landscape.

A fiscal policy encompasses the government's actions concerning taxation and expenditure. Fiscal and monetary policies are used to control economic activity over time.

Tax reductions, increased public spending, and a large budget deficit are all components of an expansionary fiscal policy.

Tools of the Fed

The Fed has several tools to implement monetary policy and maintain a stable and healthy economy.

Regulation T

Regulation T is the Fed's tool to control credit extensions made by securities brokers and dealers. Its most well-known use is to control the margin requirements for stocks purchased on margin.

For example, if investors want to buy $10,000 worth of stock with a 50% margin requirement, they must advance $5,000 before they can borrow the other $5,000.

Discount Rate

The Fed uses this tool to implement monetary policies by adjusting the interest rates it charges banks.

For example, if the Fed increases the discount rate, the amount of money in circulation will be reduced, which can help lessen inflation.

Reserve Requirement

The reserve requirement is a regulation about the amount of money commercial banks can hold in their reserves as liquid assets. This tool enables the Fed to manage how much money the banks can lend.

For example, if the reserve requirement increases, it leads to banks lending less money as more money needs to be in the reserves.

Federal Open Market Committee (FOMC)

The Federal Open Market Committee (FOMC) is a committee of the Federal Reserve System. US law allows the FOMC to regulate the country's open market operations.

This committee makes important decisions about interest rates and the expansion of the US money supply. For example, to boost the economy, the FOMC can buy government securities to lower interest rates.

Actions of the FOMC

The FOMC regulates the sale of treasury securities and the flow of credit to banks. The FOMC meets eight times throughout the fiscal year, approximately every six weeks. It makes any necessary adjustments, most notably to the discount and federal funds rates.

It also conducts open market operations and quantitative easing.

International Economic Factors

The international economic environment refers to global factors beyond a specific organization's control but can potentially impact how businesses conduct their operations.

Some of these factors are as follows:

Balance of Payments

The balance of payments (BOP) records all international financial transactions made by a country's residents, including government, businesses, and individuals. It is an important global economic factor as it keeps track of all the trade of goods and services the US makes with other countries.

GDP and GNP

The GDP and gross national product (GNP) evaluate the scope of an economy's activity. GNP tracks all economic activity carried out by businesses and citizens of a nation, regardless of location.

In contrast, GDP measures productivity and economic activities within a nation's borders.

For example, a high GDP is attractive for foreign investment, and a high GNP means that US companies with divisions in other countries are making high profits.

Exchange Rates

The rate at which one currency is exchanged for another is known as the exchange rate.

For example, the exchange rate between the US dollar and the Euro is an important international economic factor because it determines the price of trade in goods or services between the US and European countries that use the Euro.

Foreign Exchange

Trading one currency for another during the trade of goods or services between two countries is called foreign exchange. It is an important factor in the global economy.

For example, if a company imports goods from Japan, it must convert dollars to Japanese yen.

The Balance Sheet

A balance sheet provides a snapshot of the company's financial position at a specific moment. It lists a company's assets (inventory, equipment, and cash) and liabilities (debts and loans).

The balance sheet also shows the shareholders' equity, which represents the owners' investment in the company. The key idea is that the total value of the assets should equal the combined value of the liabilities and shareholders' equity, which ensures a balanced equation.

Balance sheets provide the foundation for calculating investor return rates and a company's capital structure. They include the following:

Current Assets and Liabilities

Current assets, or possessions of a company, have the potential to generate future revenue. In contrast, current liabilities are the amount the company owes to another party.

For example, liquid cash is an asset, but payable amounts are liabilities.

Fixed Assets

A fixed asset is a tangible piece of property a company owns for the long term and used to generate wealth—for example, land, buildings, and machinery.

Long-term Liabilities

Long-term liabilities are the debts of a company that are due beyond a year. Mortgage loans, bonds, and lease liabilities are examples of long-term liabilities.

Intangibles

Non-physical assets are called intangibles. They include goodwill, brand recognition, and intellectual property, like patents, trademarks, and copyrights.

Shareholders' Equity

The amount a company's owners have invested in their business is known as shareholders' equity. Shareholders' equity includes common stock, preferred stock, and retained earnings.

The Income Statement

An income statement is a financial document that summarizes a company's revenue and expenses. It determines the profitability or loss incurred by the company during a specified time frame.

The income statement covers the following aspects:

Revenue

Revenue is the money brought in by normal business operations. For example, sales, service revenues, fees earned, and interest income.

Gross Profit

Gross profit is the amount obtained by subtracting the cost of production from the revenue. For example, if the revenue earned by a company is $100,000 and the cost of goods sold is $40,000, then the gross profit will be $60,000.

Operating Income

Operating income is the adjusted revenue of a business after subtracting all operating costs and depreciation. The costs paid to maintain the operation of the business are known as operating expenses.

For example, if a company's gross profit is $60,000 and the operating expense is $15,000, the operating income will be $45,000.

Earnings Before Interest and Taxes (EBIT)

Earnings before interest and taxes (EBIT) shows a company's profit and considers all revenues and costs without interest and income tax. It measures how successfully a business generates profits over a given time frame.

EBIT = Revenue - COGS - Operating Expenses

For example, if the revenue earned by a company is $100,000, the COGS is $25,000, the operating expenses are $15,000, then the EBIT will be:

$100,000 - $25,000 - $15,000 = $60,000.

Taxable Income

Taxable income describes the basis on which an income tax system charges tax. In other words, the amount of income that the government will tax.

This includes wages, salaries, bonuses, and tips.

Net Income or Loss

Net income or loss is calculated by subtracting all the expenses, interest, and taxes from the revenue. If the amount is positive, it is a profit, and a loss is negative.

For example, if a company made a revenue of $100,000 with expenses worth $80,000 and interest and taxes of $5,000, the net income would be $15,000.

Key Economic Terms

These are some of the terms required to understand an economy.

Consumer Price Index

The consumer price index (CPI) represents the average fluctuation in prices consumers pay for various goods and services. It serves as a key metric for measuring inflation rates and evaluating the efficacy of government policies.

Inflation

Inflation refers to the upward movement of prices for goods and services within a specific time frame, typically a year. It occurs due to various factors, which include rising production costs that increase prices.

Inflation has been associated with reduced purchasing power of money and can lead to various economic disruptions if left unchecked.

Deflation

A decline in the price of goods and services over a specific period characterizes deflation. Factors like increased supply and decreased demand can contribute to deflation.

As a result of deflation, the purchasing power of a particular currency tends to rise. However, it is important to note that the benefits of deflation are realized when prices are falling while income levels are increasing.

Chapter 4: Types of Offering

Companies often raise capital through offerings. Companies can choose from a few types of offerings depending on the type of company and the amount of capital required. Each offering comes with benefits and risks.

Types of Financing Transactions

Financing transactions are how a company or an individual obtains capital for business ventures. The following are several types of financing transactions and their various benefits and risks.

Let's take a look at several types.

Public Offerings

A public offering enables a company or corporation to offer securities like stocks or bonds to the public to generate capital.

Private Offerings (Reg. D)

Private offerings are offered to a small pool of investors and are not open to the general public.

Regulation D is a provision of the U.S. securities laws that allows companies to sell their securities even if the securities are not registered with the SEC. It is often used by smaller companies to raise capital. It also helps gather capital quickly.

What Are Underwriting Commitments?

Large financial institutions like banks, insurance companies, and investment houses provide underwriting services. Underwriters agree to buy specific securities from a firm at a set price. The underwriter then resells the securities to other investors at a higher price.

An underwriting commitment refers to the liability of the underwriter. Firm underwriting commitments make the underwriter liable for any unsold shares, but it also helps firms raise capital quickly.

Types of Underwriting Commitments

There are several types of underwriting commitments, such as:

1. Firm Commitment

A firm commitment denotes a contractual agreement between the underwriters and the issuer. This agreement mandates that the underwriters purchase all the securities directly from the issuer, regardless of their ability to sell them to their customers.

In simpler terms, the underwriters take on the risk and promise to buy the securities from the issuer, which ensures the issuer receives the funds they need.

2. Best Efforts

In best efforts underwriting, the underwriter promises to try and sell most of the company's securities to investors. However, in this type of underwriting, the underwriter is not liable for any unsold securities.

3. Best Efforts All-or-None

Best efforts all-or-none is an underwriting agreement in which underwriters must put their best efforts into selling all of a company's securities to investors. All-or-none offerings require the entire offering to sell for the deal to close.

4. Best Efforts Mini-Maxi

A mini-maxi agreement is a form of best-efforts underwriting active only when a predetermined minimum number of securities is successfully sold.

Once this minimum threshold is reached, the underwriter can sell the securities up to the maximum amount outlined in the offering's terms. However, the deal cannot be closed if the underwriter fails to meet the minimum sales requirement.

5. Standby

In a standby underwriting agreement, the underwriter commits to buying any shares that the public doesn't subscribe to during an issuance, like a rights offering. Afterward, the underwriter can either keep or sell these remaining shares.

Underwriting Issues

During the process of underwriting, specific issues may arise. The two most common ones are:

1. Shelf Registration

A shelf registration statement allows a company to register many securities with the SEC. The company can then sell those securities whenever the economy's condition is favorable. However, the company is not bound to sell them all at once.

A shelf offering enables the issuing company to capitalize on favorable market conditions by entering the securities market at the opportune moment.

2. Market-out Clause

A market-out clause is a stipulation included in an underwriting agreement that grants the underwriter the freedom to terminate the agreement without facing any penalties. This clause can be invoked due to factors such as deteriorating market conditions or challenges experienced by the underwriter in selling the company's stocks.

What Is the Primary Market?

The primary market refers to a market where securities are issued for the first time, such as an IPO. An IPO allows investors to buy securities directly from the company, facilitated by the financial institution that performed the initial underwriting for the offering. It occurs when a private company issues stock to the public for the first time.

The primary market involves several people, such as the following:

- **Issuer** –an investment company or a domestic or foreign government that creates, registers, and sells securities to fund its ongoing operations.
- **Underwriting Manager** – typically an investment banker who manages all the underwriting activities involved in the offerings, which can include purchasing unsold shares if the required number of shares are not sold to the public.
- **Syndicate** – a group whose members sell shares to applicants by working with underwriters. They play a vital role for the issuing company during the IPO. Syndicate members should only be chosen after conducting in-depth research.
- **Selling Group** – dealers and financial firms responsible for marketing or selling new or second-issued securities. These groups of people usually receive a commission on every security they sell.

What Is the Underwriting Spread?

When companies want to raise money by selling securities, they often work with an underwriter (usually an investment banker) to help them with the process. The underwriter will buy the securities from the company and then sell them to the public for a profit.

The difference between the price underwriters pay to buy the securities from the company, and the price at which they sell them to the public is known as the underwriting spread.

This spread represents the compensation underwriters receive for taking on the risk of buying the securities and doing all the work involved in marketing and distributing to potential buyers.

The manager oversees the underwriting process and assumes the liability associated with the sale of the securities. For this role, the manager receives a portion of the underwriting spread, which usually ranges from one to eight percent.

The underwriters or the syndicate members also receive a part of the underwriting spread in return for their services in the underwriting process. The spread ranges from one-half to two percent.

A concession is part of the spread paid to the selling group for their service of selling the securities to the investors. Their percentage is usually smaller than that of the underwriters.

The Registration Process

Registration is when a company files required documents with the SEC before an IPO. This process is divided into three periods.

Pre-registration Period

This is the time frame before the issuer submits registration documentation. Throughout this period, the issuer collects data about the firm and its financial records. However, it is strictly prohibited from making any offers to sell securities.

Issuers begin searching for underwriters and consult them about marketing their IPO. Law firms draft and file the SEC documents.

Cooling-off Period

The cooling-off period is the interval from when a registration statement is lodged to its enforcement date. In this phase, which lasts a minimum of twenty days, the SEC studies the registration statement, and sales of securities are not permitted.

Post-registration Period

The post-registration period is from the date the registration statement has been "declared effective" by the SEC. During this period, the company and the underwriters will meet to price the offering.

After that, the issuer and the managing underwriters write and execute the underwriting agreement. This period can extend for one year or more. During this period, the SEC and the investors must be informed of the company's financial developments.

After-Market Prospectus Requirements

Legal requirements that must be fulfilled when a company offers its securities to the public are called after-market prospectus requirements. They give investors important information about the company, its operations, and its securities, which helps them decide whether to invest in the company.

The following are common after-market prospectus requirements.

Non-listed IPO

A non-listed company is not listed on the stock exchange. The prospectus for these companies' IPOs should be filed within ninety days of the offering.

Non-listed, Follow-on Offering

A non-listed, follow-on offering refers to an offering made by a company that is not listed on the stock exchange but has already made an IPO and is now issuing additional securities to the public to raise more capital.

For a non-listed, follow-on offering, a prospectus must be filed within forty days of the offering.

Security IPO on an Exchange

For a company issuing its shares to the public for the first time by listing them with the NYSE or the Nasdaq, the prospectus must be filed with the authorities within twenty-five days of the offering.

Follow-on Offering Listed on an Exchange

An exchange-listed, follow-on offering refers to an offering made by a company already registered with the NYSE or the Nasdaq and is issuing additional securities. For such companies, specific prospectus requirements are stipulated by the Securities and Exchange Commission (SEC).

Types of Prospectuses

A prospectus is a formal document required by and filed with the SEC. It provides details about an investment offering to the public and is filed for offerings of securities like stocks, bonds, and mutual funds.

The following are the different types of prospectuses.

Statutory Prospectus

The statutory prospectus is a detailed document filed with a regulatory authority such as the SEC before an offering occurs. It contains all the relevant information about the company, its operation, financial condition, and securities.

Preliminary Prospectus

A preliminary prospectus, or a red herring, contains information about the issuer's company. It is made to brief prospective investors about a company's operations and financial position.

The preliminary prospectus can also be considered an initial version of the final prospectus and is issued before the final prospectus.

Summary Prospectus

A summary prospectus is the disclosure document provided to investors by companies before or at the time of the sale of securities. It contains pertinent information, such as a summary of the company's background and financial information.

It is a shorter version of the statutory prospectus and is intended to give investors a quick and easy look into the company.

Free-writing Prospectus

A free-writing prospectus contains details not mentioned in the registration statement but must be known by potential investors.

What Are Exempt Securities?

Exempt securities do not have to be registered with regulatory authorities like the SEC under federal securities laws.

The issuer of these securities is not required to register them with the SEC under federal securities laws, but there might be other regulations they need to adhere to when selling them. Usually, these securities are sold to private agencies instead of the public.

The following are types of exempt securities.

Government and Agency Securities

Government securities are loans investors make to government agencies or federally backed private corporations.

Because the government backs them, these securities are considered exempt.

Municipal Securities

A municipal security is launched by state or local administrations or their established bodies, like agencies and special districts. These securities are not required to register with respective agencies.

Securities Issued by Banks

Filing requirements do not apply to securities issued by banks or insurance companies, as the regulations set forth by the SEC aim to safeguard investors who may have limited expertise in making informed choices. Banks and insurance companies are not classified as accredited investors. Instead, they are institutions with their own set of regulations. Accredited investors are individuals or entities that meet certain financial criteria set by the SEC.

Securities Issued by Nonprofit Organizations

Securities issued by nonprofit organizations are exempt because they are not in business to make a profit but to help society as a whole and are typically endorsed by the local or federal government. They include securities issued by universities and hospitals.

Short-term Corporate Debt

Debt securities are exempted from registration with the regulatory authorities if they have a maturity of no more than 270 days.

Specific requirements must be fulfilled to be exempted, such as issuing the securities to qualified institutional buyers.

Securities Issued by Small Business Investment Companies

Private investment companies issue securities to finance small businesses for which there are no registration requirements. However, certain conditions must be met, such as having a maximum leverage ratio of 2:1.

What Are Exempt Transactions?

An exempt transaction is not required to be registered with any regulatory body, provided the number of securities issued is negligible compared to the issuer's operations.

Exempt transactions are usually made when only a few securities and investors are involved.

What Is Regulation D?

Regulation D states that any offer to sell securities must be registered with a regulatory body, usually the SEC. If the securities are not registered, they must meet a requirement that exempts them from any registration.

Private Placement

Offerings exempt from the SEC's registration requirements under Regulation D of the Securities Act are often called private placements. A private placement is an investment round that offers securities to private investors such as friends and family, accredited investors, and institutional investors.

There are three exemptions available to conduct a private placement:

1. Rule 504 allows certain issuers to offer and sell up to $10 million of securities in twelve months. These securities can be sold to as many investors as needed, and the issuer is not subject to specific disclosure requirements.

2. Rule 506(b) states that the securities offered can only be bought by accredited investors and up to thirty-five unaccredited investors to qualify for registration exemption.

3. Rule 506(c) allows the issuer to offer securities to unlimited accredited investors, provided their accredited status is verified.

Issuing GO and Revenue Bonds

A general obligation (GO) bond is a municipal bond supported by the issuer's reliability and ability to collect taxes from the residents.

State law sets the grounds for local governments to issue general obligation bonds. The taxation amount of a particular GO bond can be limited or unlimited.

GO bonds act as a means for municipal administrations to garner capital for essentials such as highways, public spaces, apparatus, and overpasses. Unlike revenue bonds, which are backed by the revenue from specific projects like toll highways, GO bonds are backed by the full faith and credit of the issuing municipality.

Revenue bonds are project-specific and are not financed by tax dollars. Revenue bonds depend upon the project revenue they will be used to fund. In contrast, GO bonds rely entirely on the issuing municipality.

Competitive vs. Negotiated Sale

The underwriter is the party that sells and distributes a company's securities to potential investors. There are two ways for an underwriter to purchase securities and offer them to investors: competitive and negotiated sale.

In a competitive sale, the issuer advertises the securities for sale, and details the terms of the sale and the securities being offered. Multiple underwriting firms submit bids, and the securities are typically awarded to the underwriter with the best terms. Investors do not directly bid on the securities in this process.

During a negotiated sale, the underwriter is chosen by the issuer. The underwriter then determines which investors to sell the securities. The terms of the contract are negotiated to meet the investor's demands and the issuer's needs.

The final security pricing may also be established after underwriters seek customer indication of interest. This process is called presale.

Municipal Documents/Information

Municipal documents convey relevant legal information to investors during the issue of municipal securities. These securities are issued by the state or local governments or entities they create, such as authorities and special districts.

These documents include the following:

Official Statement

An official statement describes the essential terms of the bonds. It typically provides the most detailed description of the terms and features of the company's securities, financial condition, and the risks involved.

Legal Opinion

A legal opinion is an official document written by a lawyer or a law firm in which the issuer's securities are legally analyzed to be valid. It is usually a part of the official statement.

New Issue Confirmation

A new issue confirmation is a written summary of the transaction details of the purchase or sale of new securities delivered to investors. It includes information about the number of securities issued, the interest rate, and the maturity date.

Committee on Uniform Securities Identification Procedures (CUSIP)

A CUSIP is a nine-character alphanumeric code that uniquely identifies and tracks North American securities throughout their life cycle.

Electronic Municipal Market Access (EMMA)

The Electronic Municipal Market Access (EMMA) system, operated by the Municipal Securities Rulemaking Board, is the source of municipal securities details and related financial data.

The system's website offers interactive tools for investors, municipal entities, and others. It also provides objective municipal market information.

Rules Essential to Security Offerings

The following are essential rules to keep in mind when making offerings.

What Is Rule 144?

Rule 144 provides an exemption and permits the sale of restricted or controlled securities to the public if several conditions are fulfilled, which include how long the securities are held, how they are sold, and the amount that can be sold at any one time.

Restricted securities are purchased from the issuing company in unregistered, private sales. Usually, they are provided to investors through private placement offerings.

In contrast, control securities are held by an affiliate of the issuing business. An affiliate is a person who shares control with the issuer, such as an executive officer, a director, or a significant shareholder.

Some factors that affect the execution of Rule 144 are the holding period, current public information, trading volume formula, ordinary brokerage transactions, and filing a notice of proposed sale with the SEC.

What Is Rule 144A?

Rule 144A is an SEC regulation that permits the resale of privately placed securities to Qualified Institutional Buyers (QIBs).

Rule 506 allows the issuing of large quantities of securities in private placements. However, Rule 144A allows investors to sell the purchased securities from the issuer to a larger group of prospective investors, which makes private placements much more attractive.

What Is Rule 145?

Rule 145, an SEC regulation, deems that exchanges of securities in certain business combinations, including mergers, acquisitions, and reclassifications, involve an offer and sale that would require registration under the Securities Act unless an exemption is available.

A reclassification replaces one security with another, except in events like changes in par value, stock splits, or reverse stock splits. In contrast, a merger or consolidation occurs when a company's securities are transformed into or swapped for the securities of another company.

Rules 147 and 147A

Rule 147 allows a company to raise funds without registering with the SEC. It is also known as the safe harbor rule. This rule is most commonly applied to small companies that raise funds locally without any expensive fees for registering with the SEC.

Some conditions that need to be met under Rule 147 are that the company, including its issuer, proceeds of the offering, and purchasers of the securities must be in the same state.

The SEC created a new offering exemption in 2016 called Rule 147A. This rule permits the offering of securities to out-of-state residents. Rule 147A also applies to issuers of securities located out of state.

Rule 147A exempts the owner and the business from being in the same state. Now, the securities can be advertised online, such as through crowdfunding, where they can be easily accessible by out-of-state investors.

Chapter 5: Equity Securities

Equity securities represent an ownership interest (common and preferred stock) in a trust or company. They are issued on a specific date at a specific price, and some come with voting rights while others do not.

There are two types of equity securities, as described below:

Common Stock – These shares represent ownership in the company. These have a claim to any residual cash, and their liability is limited.

Preferred Stock – These shares represent a higher claim on the earnings and assets of a company. Preferred stockholders usually have limited or no voting rights but receive dividends before common shareholders, and these dividends are often fixed.

What Are Corporations?

A corporation is a business organization that operates as a legal entity separate from its owners and which the law treats as an individual. It can own property, can fire or hire its own workforce, and can sue independently.

To create a corporation, articles of incorporation are needed. A corporate charter or certificate of incorporation is a document filed with a state to create a corporation. Filing the charter or certification is the legal action required to structure a new company as a corporation, and each state has its own set of rules regarding the process.

In simple terms, a certificate of incorporation is a birth certificate for the company or corporation. In many jurisdictions, the registrar of companies grants the certificate after all the requirements have been met. However, in some states, it may be a different entity that grants the certificate.

The corporate charter includes all the details regarding the company, such as its structure, governance, operations, and objectives.

How Corporations Raise Money

Companies raise money using two methods.

Debt Financing Through Bonds

The term "debt financing" refers to raising funds through borrowing, which can include issuing bonds, taking out loans, or other forms of borrowing. It is an alternative to other external financing methods, such as bank loans, etc. Debt financing occurs when a company sells fixed-income products, such as bills, bonds, or notes.

An advantage of debt financing is that the shareholders' control is not affected, and they retain full control of the company. A disadvantage is that the company has to pay fixed charges even if it is not doing well financially.

Equity Financing Through Stock

Equity financing is when a corporation gets funds by selling ownership in the company in the form of shares. There is no promise of interest or a fixed return. It is less risky for the corporation than debt financing.

Plus, it allows investors to reinvest the cash generated by profitable ventures back into the company. Dividends do not have to be paid unless specified by the board.

However, dividends are not tax-deductible, and issuing stock dilutes the ownership of the company.

Issuing Stock

A stock issue is when a company offers securities (in the form of stock) to raise funds from investors. The company sets the number of shares it is authorized to issue in its articles of incorporation.

Once that's done, an initial public offering (IPO) in which shares of the company are sold to investors is offered.

Shares Repurchased by Corporations

A share buyback is when a corporation repurchases its own shares. Companies buy back shares to reduce their capital by canceling the repurchased stock. This reduces the number of outstanding shares and increases the value of the remaining shares.

There are several reasons why companies buy back their own stock. These include the following:

- Consolidation of ownership.
- Preservation of stock prices.

- Augmentation of financial ratios.
- Reduction in capital cost.

Common Stock Ownership Rights

Common stock is a security that represents an ownership interest in a company, which can be public or private. It gives voting rights and offers the possibility of sharing in the company's success through dividend payouts.

Common shareholders are granted the following rights.

Right to Inspect Corporate Documents

Shareholders have the right to investigate the company's administrative and financial records. However, they have to specifically request to review governing documents or financial statements.

Evidence of Ownership

Stock certificates are documents that show a shareholder's ownership in a company. They provide information, such as the purchase date, the number of shares owned, an ID number, and the signatures of the parties involved.

Transfer of Ownership

A transfer of ownership means that stockholders can usually sell their shares without any restriction from the company unless they are subject to restrictions, such as lock-up periods or insider trading regulations. The corporation does not participate in the transfer of ownership rights after the original sale.

Participation in Corporate Earning

Common stock owners can profit from the capital appreciation of securities as they retain partial ownership of the company. They share in the gains if the company produces a profit.

Types of Voting Methods

There are two methods of voting.

Statutory Voting

An investor who owns common stock has one vote per share. This allows the investors to cast votes based on their number of shares. For example, an investor with 20 shares has the power to cast 20 votes to elect directors at the annual meeting.

Cumulative Voting

Cumulative voting means the number of shares is multiplied by the number of director seats available. The shareholder can use these votes to vote for one director or split them among several seats.

Restricted Securities

Restricted securities are acquired privately in an unregistered manner from the issuing company or an affiliate of the issuer. They are protected by lock-up agreements and cannot be transferred by the holder until certain conditions are met.

A lock-up agreement is used to ensure that company insiders do not sell their shares for a set period of time. Lock-up periods usually last between 90 and 180 days. Once this duration is over, most trading restrictions are removed.

Lock-up agreements protect investors against excessive selling pressure from insiders. They are often accompanied by an investment letter that ensures newly issued securities won't be immediately sold.

An investment letter is a letter of intent between the issuer of new securities and the buyer when these securities are acquired privately. It includes details of the investment, the purpose, and the terms of the investment.

The letter establishes that the securities are being bought for a minimum duration of time and are not for resale. It is signed by the sender and sent to the potential investor.

Restricted vs. Controlled Stock: Rule 144

Rule 144 outlines the regulations that govern the trading of securities by significant shareholders. The rule provides an exception and permits the reselling of restricted or controlled securities if certain prerequisites are in place.

The rule also includes details about the following:

- The restricted period.
- The number of securities sold.
- The way in which the securities are sold.

Restricted Stock

Restricted stock includes the shares issued to the employees in a company as part of their pay, but it cannot be fully transferred until certain terms and conditions have been met. This is one way that the employer grants company shares to its employees.

There are two types of restricted stock.

Restricted Stock Units

This is an agreement an employer makes to grant a given number of shares to an employee at a predetermined time in the future.

Restricted Stock Awards

This is a grant of company stock in which the recipient's rights in the stock are restricted until shares are vested or there is a lapse in the restrictions. The restricted period is referred to as the vesting period.

Controlled Stocks

Controlled stock refers to equity shares owned by major shareholders of a publicly held company. This stock is held by a business affiliate rather than an employee of the company.

Sale of Restricted and Controlled Stocks: Rule 144

Rule 144 gives insight into the sale of restricted and controlled stocks.

Restricted Stock

The holding period of restricted stock when held by a non-affiliate is 6 months. There are no sale restrictions after the period is over.

Controlled Stock (Registered) Held by an Affiliate

The holding period of controlled stock when held by an affiliate is 6 months. After the period is over, sale limitations still apply.

What Are American Depositary Receipts (ADRs)?

An American depositary receipt (ADR) is a certificate that represents a specific number of shares of a foreign company's stock. It is issued by a depositary bank.

Once an ADR is sold, supply and demand determine its subsequent price, like with any ordinary share.

Types of ADRs

There are two types of ADRs.

Sponsored ADR

With a sponsored ADR, a legal association is established between the ADR and a foreign company, where the foreign company assumes the expenses related to issuing the security. Here are some examples of sponsored ADRs.

- Toyotal Motor Corporation
- Nokia Corporation
- Tencent Holding Limited

Unsponsored ADRs

Unsponsored ADRs are issued by a depository bank without the involvement or participation of a foreign company. They are traded on the OTC market, not on a stock exchange, and are level-one ADRs.

They do not comply with regulatory reporting.

Types of Stocks

There are various types of stocks.

Blue Chip Stock

Blue chip stocks are shares of large companies with well-known brands and successful track records. A company must have the following to be considered a blue chip stock:

- Dependable business model.
- Proven track record.
- Industry leadership.
- Regular increase in its payouts.
- History of delivering strong returns.

Some examples include Coca-Cola, Walmart, and Disney.

Growth Stock

A growth stock is a share in a company that's anticipated to grow at a significant rate, usually above the average growth rate of the market. These stocks generally do not pay dividends and yield higher-than-average returns in the long term.

Companies with growth stock include Amazon, United Rentals, SolarEdge Technologies, etc.

Income Stock

Income stocks offer regular and steady income, mostly in the form of dividends over a period of time, with low exposure to risks. These stocks usually offer a high yield, have a high switching rate with low capital investment, and dividends can be paid in cash.

However, income stocks are expensive compared to other stocks, and the dividend income is taxable. Some examples of industries with income stock include healthcare, utilities, and telecommunication.

Defensive Stock

Defensive stocks provide stable earnings and consistent returns, even in an economic crisis. Contrary to offering reduced dividends, decreased revenue, and lower consumer confidence, these stocks often offer reliable dividends, are less susceptible to market fluctuations, and maintain performance during downturns.

Industries with defensive stocks include consumer staples and healthcare sectors.

Cyclical Stock

A cyclical stock is a stock whose price is affected by changes in the economy. Cyclical stocks are associated with industries that are sensitive to economic cycles, such as automobiles, airlines, and luxury goods.

These stocks have high volatility, a high-risk factor, and a high return profile.

What Is Preferred Stock?

Preferred stock offers dividend payments prior to common stock and a higher claim to assets in the event of liquidation. It does not come with voting rights but is superior to common stock in terms of dividend payment.

This type of stock can be converted to common stock.

Types of Preferred Stock

There are several types of preferred stock.

Noncumulative

Noncumulative preferred shares are those in which the dividend does not accumulate. If a dividend is to be paid, it must be paid to noncumulative preferred shareholders at a set rate before any dividend is paid to common shareholders.

Shareholders are not entitled to have any arrears carried forward if there is insufficient profit.

Cumulative

Cumulative preferred shares accumulate dividends each year until they are paid. Shareholders must receive all dividends in arrears before common stockholders get any dividends.

Cumulative preferred shares may carry higher prices due to their cumulative dividend feature, but it's not accurate to claim they are always more expensive than any other stock on the market. Stock prices vary widely based on a multitude of factors, that include the company's performance, overall market conditions, and investor sentiment.

For example:

Dividend accumulation	**Year 1**	**Year 2**	**Year 3**
Accrue	$20,000	$20,000	$20,000
Paid	$10,000	0	0
Cumulating	$10,000	$30,000	$50,000

The table above shows how cumulative preferred stock works.

Callable

Callable preferred stock is a type of stock in which the issuer has the right to call in or redeem the stock at a preset price after a set period of time. The investors have an assurance of a premium price at the time of the call.

Callable preferred stock allows the issuing company the right to redeem shares after a certain period of time. However, the lack of voting rights is a general feature of most preferred stocks and not just callable stocks. Callable stock also brings down the cost of capital.

Plus, investors receive steady and higher returns from callable preferred shares and get preference in case of dividends and repayment.

However, companies need to keep a stockpile of cash ready in case there is a call for shares.

Participating Stock

Participating stock comes with a provision stating that preferred shareholders have to share additional dividends with common shareholders.

Participating preferred stocks can either be fully participating or partially participating. The former share equally with common shareholders, while the latter share extra dividends, but the participation is limited to a fixed rate or amount per share.

Convertible Preferred Stock

Convertible preferred stock is a type of preferred share that gives the stockholder the option to convert it into a specified number of common stock shares. These shares give an investor a stream of income.

What Are Preemptive Rights?

Preemptive rights are contractual rights that allow existing shareholders to purchase additional shares before the company offers them to other investors during a new round of financing. Simply put, it is the right of first refusal and includes the following:

Shareholders' Right to Maintain Percentage Ownership

These rights allow stockholders to maintain their percentage of ownership of the shares. Percentage ownership is determined by dividing the number of shares a shareholder owns by the number of outstanding shares.

Discount

A discount is the amount that the share price is lower than the net asset value, expressed as a percentage. Shares often trade at a price different from the value of the underlying net asset.

A discount on a stock occurs when its market price is lower than its intrinsic or perceived value. The actual difference between a higher par value and a lower price is the discount. It's used to incentivize investors to purchase stocks.

Short Term

Short-term trading involves stocks that are traded on a frequent basis. These assets are not held by investors for long periods. The company details change over time, but at this moment, some examples include Trident, NBCC, Brightcom Group, etc.

Usually, the holding period is less than one fiscal year. Short-term trading is considered riskier than others.

Tradable

Tradable shares are fully paid and duly issued. They increase the ability of shareholders to diversify their investments. They also help companies raise as much capital as needed.

Corporations with free tradable shares are open or public companies, and corporations with restricted tradability are considered private or closed.

What Are Warrants?

A warrant is a derivative issued by a company that gives buyers the right to purchase a company's stock at a certain price before an expiration date.

There are two types of warrants:

- **Put Warrant** – A put warrant allows holders to sell the underlying security at a fixed price.
- **Call Warrant** – A call warrant allows investors to purchase the intrinsic asset or shares of common stock at a fixed price.

Warrants have fixed prices and have no voting rights or dividends. Although some warrants might not be listed on a stock exchange, many warrants are in fact listed and traded on exchanges. The price of a warrant at issuance is not necessarily above the market price. It depends on various factors, including the terms of the warrant and market conditions.

Miscellaneous Equity Rules

Let's take a look at miscellaneous equity rules.

FINRA 2261

FINRA rule 2261 directs the disclosure of financial information to customers. Under this rule, members are obligated to make important information available to customers and other members in the members' most recent balance sheet.

Specifically, this rule states that a member must make their financial information available at the request of a customer. Their balance sheet should also be open for inspection by customers.

SEC Rule 10b-18

Rule 10b-18 is intended to reduce the liability for companies when they repurchase common stock. It is considered a "safe harbor," which is a provision to eliminate legal liabilities in certain situations.

Chapter 6: An Introduction to Debt Instruments

A debt instrument is a written agreement or formal promise that allows the issuer to generate capital by vowing to pay back the lender according to the stipulations of the agreement.

So, a debt instrument is a tool that any entity can use to raise capital. It is an intangible financial asset in the form of loans, bonds, leases, or other forms of agreements between a lender and borrower.

There are two types of debt instruments:

- **Long Term** – These include bonds, mortgages, and long-term loans.
- **Medium or Short Term** – These include working loans, treasury bills, and short-term loans.

What Are Bonds?

A bond is a fixed-yield financial tool that characterizes credit extended by an investor to a debtor, generally governmental or commercial entities.

Governments and corporations issue bonds to raise funds. When someone buys a bond, they are essentially lending money to the issuer. In return, the issuer commits to repay the amount on a predetermined date and also to make regular interest payments, typically twice a year.

Simply put, the investor agrees to give the corporation a certain amount of money for a specific period of time. In exchange, the investor receives interest payments.

Term and Serial Maturities

In general, bonds may be classified as term bonds or as serial bonds.

Term Bonds

Term bonds, the predominant form of bonds, require repayment of the principal sum at a single maturity date.

To guarantee liquidity for repayment at maturity, the borrower conscientiously allocates funds to what is commonly referred to as a sinking fund.

By definition, a sinking fund is an investment pool specifically designated to earmark monetary reserves that will be used to settle the debt as it comes due and payable.

Serial Bonds

Serial bonds require payments in installments over a period of time, maybe years. This makes it easier for the borrower to meet bond obligations as they become due.

What Is a Zero-Coupon Bond?

A zero-coupon bond is a type of security where the holder does not receive interest. However, this type of bond trades at a deep discount, which means the investor receives a profit at maturity. These are the simplest bonds in the market.

An example is treasury bills. They are considered zero-coupon government bonds with a maturity of up to one year.

Issued

Zero-coupon bonds eliminate reinvestment risk. They also ensure fixed returns, so they're a good choice for people who prefer long-term investments and earning a lump sum.

Maturity

Bond maturity represents a point in time where the holder of the bond will receive a return that includes interest. For example, a 15-year bond will mature in 15 years, and the holder will receive the principal at that time. Long-term zero-coupon bonds have a maturity date of ten to fifteen years.

Interest

The interest earned from zero-coupon bonds is typically subject to tax. These bonds do not distribute regular interest payments. Rather, the interest accumulates semi-annually at a predetermined rate.

The disparity between the acquisition cost and the nominal value equates to the interest earned on the bond. Upon maturity, the bondholder receives the par value of the bond in addition to the compounded interest.

Carrying Value

The carrying value of a bond is its face value adjusted for any premium or discount. It can be calculated as the face value plus the premium or the face value minus the discount.

The following formula is commonly used to calculate the carrying value:

Bonds payable + premium on bonds – discount on bonds = carrying value of a bond.

How It Trades

Some bonds are traded publicly through exchanges, while others are traded OTC between large broker-dealers.

Investors can buy or sell marketable bonds from each other, but bond dealers usually conduct the trading. In bond trading, the goal is to take a spread between the price at which the bonds are bought and the price at which they are sold. The spread allows bond dealers to generate a profit or loss.

Reinvestment Risk

Bonds pay periodic interest, but there is the risk that these payments will have to be reinvested at a lower rate. This risk is known as reinvestment risk. Bonds with a longer maturity period are at greater reinvestment risk. Callable bonds are also at greater reinvestment risk because they are redeemed when the interest rate declines.

Who Are They Suitable For?

Zero-coupon bonds are popular because they give investors a fixed nominal value in the distant future. As these bonds do not pay periodic interest, they are better for people who prefer long-term investments and want to earn a lump sum.

Why Do Bond Prices Fluctuate From Par?

Bond prices fluctuate because they depend on the income provided by coupon payments related to interest rates. A bond below par means that its price is currently below its face value, and this happens when any of the following conditions are met:

- An increase in interest rates.
- A decrease in the credit rating of the issuer.

- An excess of supply over demand.

After a bond is issued, it can be traded in the secondary market. This is where the fluctuation begins, and it depends on the factors mentioned above. Another influential factor is that the yield of the bond represents the annual return on the bond's price.

What Is the Interest-Rate Risk?

The interest-rate risk is the risk that arises for bond owners when there is fluctuation in interest rates in the market. It is the potential that any change in the overall interest rate will reduce the value of a bond.

A bond's dependency on the interest-rate risk is related to the sensitivity of that bond's price to fluctuation. The sensitivity depends on two things:

- The maturity time of the bond.
- The coupon rate of the bond.

What Is Credit Risk?

Credit risk is the possibility of a loss that may result from a borrower's failure to repay a loan or failure to meet the contractual obligations. The main causes of credit risk in banks or the attributes used to gauge an applicant's credit risk include the following:

- Conditions of the contract.
- Collateral payment.
- Character of the applicant.
- Capital.
- Capacity.

There are three types of credit risk:

- Credit default risk.
- Concentration risk.
- Country risk.

An example of credit risk is when a homeowner stops making mortgage payments.

What Are Credit Rating Companies?

A credit rating company or agency assigns credit ratings and rates a debtor's ability to repay a debt by making timely payments of principal and interest. It also calculates default risk.

Standard and Poor's

Standard & Poor's is one of the largest credit rating companies in the world. It provides financial market intelligence, which includes credit ratings, indices, and research on stocks, bonds, and commodities.

The company assigns letter grades to businesses and countries, and the debt they issue is on a scale from AAA to D. This lettering indicates the investment risk.

Fitch Ratings

Fitch Ratings is a credit rating agency that provides forward-looking credit opinions. It rates the viability of investments relative to the likelihood of default and uses a letter system to grade investment risk.

Moody's Investor Service

Moody's Investor Service provides investors with credit ratings, risk analysis, and research on bonds and other debt instruments. It also provides international data research on bonds issued by governments and non-government entities.

What Are Credit Ratings?

A credit rating is an assessment tool that determines the fiscal responsibility of a borrower, either in relation to a specific debt or more generally. This judgment is formed by scrutinizing the history of borrowing and repaying debts of an individual or organization.

Credit ratings are from AAA to D, with AAA being the highest. In contrast, credit scores generally range from 300 to 850 and fit into these categories:

- Poor.
- Fair.

- Good.
- Very good.
- Excellent.

Investment Grade – S&P/Fitch/Moody's

As mentioned above, credit ratings show an entity's credit or default risk. The letter system is used to grade the credit risk. Investment grades are from AAA to BBB- in the S&P and Fitch Rating.

Moody's Investor Service considers the lowest investment grade as Baa3.

Investment grades allow money to be loaned and investments to be made. A grade lower than this is considered a speculative grade.

The advantage of the grading system is that it gives investors an idea of the credit risk of a bond, so there is less chance of them losing their funds.

Speculative Grade – S&P/Fitch/Moody's

S&P and Fitch consider BB+ to D speculative grades, while for Moody's, speculative grades are from Ba1 to C.

A speculative grade carries substantial credit risk, and indicates a higher risk that issuers may not meet their obligations.

Coupon Rates and Bond Pricing

The coupon rate is the interest rate an issuer agrees to pay every year on a fixed-income security. The coupon rate is typically applied to an annual basis, but interest payments can be made semi-annually, quarterly, or at other intervals, depending on the terms of the bond. The following is the formula for calculating the coupon rate:

*Coupon = Coupon rate x par value or coupon rate = Coupon/par value.*The coupon rate quantifies the proportion of interest an investor will periodically earn from the entity that issues the bond. Upon acquisition, a bond's rate of return at maturity and its coupon rate are equivalent. The term "yield-to-maturity" denotes the complete profit expected on a bond provided the bond is retained until its maturity date.

For example, if an individual has a ten-year $2,000 bond with a coupon rate of 10%, the person will get $200 annually for ten years, irrespective of the bond's price in the market.

The bond price will rise if a coupon is higher than the prevailing interest rate. If the coupon is lower, the bond price will fall. So, bond prices are inversely proportional to interest rates, as explained above.

Pricing of Government Securities

Government securities are financial instruments issued by the government to finance its activities, essential infrastructure, and defense projects. They typically have the following features:

- They have low default risk.
- Interest is often exempt from local or state taxes.
- They are issued at par value.

The price of a government security, like any other financial instrument, keeps fluctuating in the secondary market. It is determined by the demand and supply of securities, the changes in interest rates in the economy, inflation, and liquidity.

Government bond prices are affected by the following factors:

- Credit rating.
- Inflation.
- Interest rates.
- Supply and demand.
- Maturity time.

What Are Bond Yields?

Bond yield represents the return an investor receives annually. It is usually mentioned as a percentage of the overall capital that an investor has put in the market.

Bond yields are inversely related to bond prices. As one rises, the other falls. The formula used for calculating the bond yield is as follows:

Current yield = annual coupon payment/bond price.

There are different types of yields, as described below.

Normal Yield

A normal yield or an up-sloped curve indicates that yields rise on a long-term bond. A normal curve starts with a low yield for bonds with a short maturity period and then gradually increases for bonds with a longer maturity period.

This curve is observed in times of economic expansion when there is a rise in inflation and economic growth.

Current Yield

Current yield is the ratio of the interest rate payable on a bond to the actual market price of the bond represented as a percentage. Here's a formula for calculating the current yield:

Current yield = annual cash inflow/market price.

Unlike the coupon rate/coupon yield, the current yield fluctuates with changes in the market price.

Yield to Maturity

Yield to maturity is the promised compound rate of return received from a bond purchased at the current market price and then held until its maturity. The formula is given below:

$$YTM= C+ (FV - PV/\ t)/\ (FV + PV/\ 2).$$

Here,

C = Coupon or interest payment.

FV = The security's face value.

PV = The security's present value.

t = Years to reach maturity.

Retiring Debt Before Maturity

Retiring debt before maturity, also known as early extinguishment of debt, happens when a long-term debt of a company is retired before maturity. There are two common ways to do so.

Call Provision

A call provision is a clause embedded in the contractual agreement governing a bond or any similar fixed-income instrument that grants the issuer the prerogative to repurchase and subsequently retire the debt security.

In such instances, if the current interest rates fall below the interest rate of a bond, the issuer has the option to exercise a call provision and call the bond back. This primarily benefits the issuer, as they can refinance the debt at a lower interest rate. Bondholders receive the face value of the bond but may lose out on future interest income, especially if they cannot find a similar investment with the same return. Moreover, it enables the bond issuer to retire the bond before its scheduled maturity by paying a penalty or premium to the bondholders.

There are several types of call provisions:

- **Optional** – The bond can be called whenever the issuer feels like calling it.
- **Sinking Fund** – This is when an issuer redeems a specific number of bonds on a set schedule.
- **Extraordinary** – This is when an issuer redeems the bonds when certain conditions have been met.
- **Mandatory** – This is when an issuer specifies the circumstances when they might call the bond.

Put Provision

A bond featuring a put provision gives the bond owner the right to cash it in at its face value at a predetermined time before its maturity date. This action might be appealing to investors if there's an increase in interest rates subsequent to the bond's issuance.

Bonds with a put provision aren't prevalent. They protect bondholders from default risk and ensure they have the option to sell the bond at a higher value.

What Are Convertible Debentures?

A convertible debenture is a form of financial debt obligation that is issued by a corporate entity. It can be converted into shares after a predetermined duration. These financial instruments can be considered loans or unsecured bonds, and usually do not have tangible collateral.

A convertible bond offers investors the security of a debt instrument along with the high growth potential of an equity investment. Additionally, these bonds typically have lower interest rates compared to other debt instruments. The average length of a convertible bond can range between several years to perpetuity. These bonds are issued by companies as a flexible form of financing and provide the potential for conversion to equity in the future.

There are two types of convertible debentures:

- **Fully Convertible** – The whole value of these debentures can be converted into equity shares.
- **Partly Convertible** – Only a part of these debentures is eligible for conversion into equity shares.

For instance, a company raises $1,000,000 in convertible debt from an investor with the following conversion privileges:

- The loan can be converted into 20,000 common shares in the company.
- The price is $50 per share within two years.

What Is the Conversion Parity Price?

The conversion parity price is the effective price an investor has paid for the conversion of a company's bonds into shares. It is important because until they reach this price, there is no benefit in converting bonds into shares.

The formula for parity price is as follows:

> *Parity price = Market price of convertible bond/number of shares received upon conversion (conversion ratio).*
>
> *Conversion ratio = Par value of bond/price of equity issued upon conversion.*

Chapter 7: Types of Debt Instruments

A debt instrument is a tool used by an entity or corporation to raise its capital. It is also defined as a written contract or assurance that enables the issuer to raise funds by making a promise to repay the lender according to set terms and conditions.

Debt instruments are considered financial assets and can be in the form of loans, bonds, or leases. There are two types of debt instruments, long- and short-term.

Long-term debt instruments include debentures, bonds, mortgages, and long-term loans. Medium- and short-term debt instruments include working capital loans and treasury bills.

Treasury Debt Overview

The US Treasury publishes the debt information in its monthly statement. The US has the world's largest economy and highest national debt, which has increased annually for the past 10 years.

The biggest holder of intragovernmental US debt is Social Security, which holds a significant amount in treasury notes and bonds. Foreign debt holders include Japan, China, and the UK.

T-Bills, T-Notes, and T-Bonds

Let's look at T-bills, T-bonds, and T-notes.

Treasury Bills

Treasury bills (T-bills) are short-term government debt obligations backed by the Treasury Department with a maturity of one year or less. They are money market instruments to finance the short-term government requirements.

T-bills are issued at a discounted price of the face value. They are intended to meet temporary liquidity shortfalls and their maximum validity is 364 days from the issue date. These bills can be traded in the secondary market.

Treasury Notes

Treasury notes (T-notes) are tradeable obligations of the government that provide steady interest rates and terms of two to ten years. They can be purchased from the government through either a competitive or noncompetitive bidding process.

The Bureau of the Fiscal Service is responsible for the administration of public debt. It oversees the issuance of various Treasury securities, including Treasury notes, bills, and bonds.

Treasury notes are issued in maturities of two, three, five, seven, and 10 years. They are popular forms of investment due to a large secondary market. Interest payments are made every six months.

Treasury Bonds

Treasury bonds (T-bonds) are fixed-rate government debt securities with a maturity range between 10 and 30 years. They earn periodic interest until their maturity.

Treasury bonds can be purchased from banks, brokers, the bond market, and the government. They are considered risk-free government-issued securities. The income received via these bonds is taxed only at the federal level.

Investors do not have a required holding period for T-bonds before they can be sold in the secondary market.

T- Notes vs. T- Bills vs. T- Bonds

The primary differences among these notes are presented in the following table:

Bill Type	Denomination	Issuer	Interest	Maturity
T-bills	$1,000 to $5 million	Government (in bids)	No interest till maturity	<52 weeks (a year)
T-bonds	$100	US Treasury (in monthly auctions)	3.41% for 10 years	10 to 30 years
T-notes	$100	The Bureau of Fiscal Service	>0.125%	<10 years

Pricing of Government Securities

Government securities are sovereign obligations of the government. They include central government and state government securities, T-bills, and government-guaranteed bonds.

These securities are issued at face value, with no default risk and ample liquidity in the market. Their maturity period is one to 30 years, and interests are paid biannually at a fixed rate. Government securities are repaid at par on their expiry.

Treasury Inflation-Protected Securities (TIPS)

Treasury inflation-protected securities (TIPS) are marketable treasury securities that match their principal value and interest payments to protect against inflation. They are issued by the government and indexed to inflation.

TIPS are an attractive option for investors as they offer a guaranteed return. They are issued in terms of five-, 10- and 30-year maturity levels. The minimum number of units issued is $100. TIPS are acquired through competitive auction.

However, TIPS have a unique interest rate risk. During deflation, investors can lose the interest earned. This interest is also taxable and must be paid every six months until maturity. There is no required holding period, so investors can generally buy and sell TIPS in the secondary market at any time after purchase.

Despite their high-risk rate, TIPS are low-risk bonds with low inflation risk. They help protect purchasing power and the principal amount from depreciation.

Here's an example of how a 10-year TIPS bond with a 3% rate of return works:

Suppose an investor buys a 10-year TIPS bond with a face value of $1,000 and a 3% coupon rate.

If inflation is 2% over the next year, the face value of the bond will be adjusted to $1,020 (the original $1,000 plus 2% inflation).

The coupon payment for the first year will be $30.60 (3% of the adjusted principal of $1,020).

If inflation is 3% over the second year, the face value of the bond will be adjusted to $1,050.60 ($1,020 plus 3% inflation).

The coupon payment for the second year will be $31.52 (3% of the adjusted principal of $1,050.60).

This process continues for the remaining eight years of the bond's term, with the coupon payment amount increasing or decreasing based on the adjusted principal value.

T-STRIPS

STRIPS stands for "Separate Trading of Registered Interest and Principal Securities." T-STRIPS are bonds in which the principal and coupon payments are traded as separate securities. Each is considered a zero-coupon security that matures separately with only one payment.

The holders of T-STRIPS do not receive coupon payments. T-STRIPS provide an alternative to more traditional bonds for investors who rely on definite amounts of money coming due at a specific date.

Some of the important features of T-STRIPS include:

- They are purchased from brokerages and institutions, not the government.
- The final payoff is at the maturity of the bond.
- The difference between the purchase price and the par value is the return earned.
- They are also referred to as pure discount bonds, treasury zero-coupon bonds.
- They have maturities as long as 30 years.
- They carry interest rate risk and inflation risk.
- They have an inverse relation to the interest rate.

The advantage of T-STRIPS is that financial institutions can create default risk-free securities because they are backed by the government. T-STRIPS are safe investment options.

Bidding at Auctions

An auction is a transaction where potential buyers engage in competitive bidding to acquire an asset. It serves as a public sale mechanism where property is sold to the highest bidder.

The primary objective is to secure the most favorable financial outcome for the property owner and foster an environment of open and equitable competition among the bidders. Auctions play a significant role in the US economy. Their exact contribution to the GDP is hard to quantify as they intertwine with various sectors.

The auction process is as follows:

- The seller establishes the initial quantity of shares or securities available for sale, along with the opening price.
- The auction commences with the starting price and can either ascend as bids are placed and shares are sought or descend in the case of a Dutch auction.
- The auction concludes when the final bidder accepts the prevailing price.

- The last or lowest bid determines the offering price for all shares.

An auction can be conducted live or online. Some types of auctions include:

- Absolute.
- Reserve.
- Minimum bid.
- Multi-parcel.
- Sealed bid.

Agency Securities

An agency security is a debt obligation issued by a US government-sponsored enterprise (GSE) or other federal related entity.

Agency securities are issued by GSEs, which include the Federal National Mortgage Association (FNMA), Federal Home Loan Bank, Federal Home Loan Mortgage Corporation (FHLMC), and Student Loan Marketing Association (SLMA).

Federal agency bonds and GSE bonds pay more than US treasury bonds. Most, but not all, agency securities are exempt from state and local taxes. They are subject to interest rate risks.

There are two types of agency securities, GSE and federal government agency securities.

GSE

Government-sponsored enterprises (GSEs) are quasi-governmental entities established to enhance the flow of credit to specific sectors of the American economy. They are federally chartered corporations but are privately owned by shareholders. These bonds carry a credit and default risk as they are not explicitly backed by the full faith and credit of the U.S. government.

The yield of GSEs is high. Some companies issue no-coupon discount notes to meet their short-term financing needs, These discount notes have maturities that range from 24 hours to a year. They result in a loss for the investing agency when sold before their maturity date. Discount bonds are also subject to capital gains taxes when sold or redeemed.

Federal Government Agency Securities

Federal government agency securities are issued by the Federal Housing Administration (FHA) and Small Business Administration (SBA). The most common issuer is the Government National Mortgage Association (GNMA). Federal agency securities are fully backed by the US government.

These bonds provide regular interest payments to the investors. When the bond matures, the bondholder receives its full face value. These are callable bonds and the issuing agency can redeem them before the maturity date.

Other Loan Types and Systems

Let's look at other loan types and systems.

Farming Loans (FFCB)

The Federal Farm Credit Banks, also known as the Farm Credit System, comprise a widespread network of cooperative financial institutions owned by their borrowers. While these institutions have a government-sponsored mandate to support rural and agricultural businesses, their debt doesn't carry a full faith and credit guarantee from the US government.

The primary objective of this system is to provide dependable and consistent credit and financial services to rural communities and the agriculture sector. A 2021 census found 44% of the total farm business debt in the United States was financed by the Farm Credit System.

Several institutions are involved with the Farm Credit System, including:

- Banks for Cooperatives.
- Federal Land Banks.
- Production Credit Association.
- Federal Intermediate Credit Banks.

The Farm Credit Administration consists of the following:

- Federal Farm Credit Board.
- Governor.

- Staff.

The Federal Land Banks specialize in providing farmers with long-term real estate loans. The Federal Intermediate Credit Banks focus on discounting short-term loans issued by commercial banks.

The Production Credit Association offers farmers short- and intermediate-term loans.

Mortgage-Backed Securities

Mortgage-backed securities are considered collateral to an asset and secured by a bundle of home loans. They generate cash from debt, such as loans and credit card balances.

The process includes the aggregation of mortgages and their subsequent sale to a group who then turns them into an investable security.

For example, an individual wants to purchase a house for $400,000. He contacts his bank and funds the purchase of his house with a 30-year mortgage at an interest rate of 3%. For the next 30 years, the homeowner will pay the principal payment and the interest. The bank can then sell the principal and interest money to an investor.

Municipal Bonds and Their Issuers

A municipal bond is a fixed-income debt security issued by a governmental entity to fund public projects. Municipal bonds are tax-exempt, but they are not the same as private activity bonds. Private activity bonds are issued for the benefit of private entities, even though the issuance is done by a governmental entity.

Municipal bonds allow investors to lend money to local governments to fund daily operations as well as public works projects, such as road construction, improvements to schools and hospitals, etc.

Issued by states, school districts, transit authorities, local governments, and cities, municipal bonds have no federal taxes imposed upon the earned interest. Their capital expenditures include:

- Highways.
- Bridges.

- Schools.
- Parks.

An example of municipal bond construction is the Golden Gate Bridge.

There are two primary types of municipal bonds: revenue bonds and general obligation bonds.

Revenue

Revenue bonds help finance projects. The bond issuers make a commitment to the bondholders that the future revenues generated by the project will be utilized for repayment.

The funds required for interest payments, and the eventual return of the principal amount, are sourced from the project's specifically designated revenues. For instance, if a bond is used to finance the construction of a new toll road, the revenue generated from the tolls collected becomes the primary source for repaying the bondholders.

Revenue bonds rely on the steady stream of income generated by the designated project itself. This ensures that the financial obligations to bondholders are met through the generated revenue.

General Bond Obligation

General obligation bonds are issued by states, counties, and special districts. They are secured by tax revenue and backed by the full faith and credit of the issuer. Taxes are used to pay back principal and interest.

Some of the disadvantages of municipal bonds are:

- They provide minimal protection against inflation.
- The fixed income cannot keep pace with the increase in living costs.
- Bond prices may fluctuate with changes in market interest rates (i.e., when interest rates rise, the bond value typically declines).
- There is a limited market.
- Tax-free bonds can seldom be purchased directly for less than $5,000.
- Bid-ask spreads are large, which affects the investors' total return.

Types of Revenue Bonds

A revenue bond is a type of municipal bond. Repayment of the obligation is primarily guaranteed by the operating revenues of an entity. The most common examples include water and sewer bonds issued to finance the construction and improvement of sanitation or water utility services.

There are various types of revenue bonds.

Transportation Revenue

Transportation revenue primarily comes from transit fares, tolls, and other user fees related to transportation services. These revenues primarily come from carrying passengers and freight.

Transportation revenue is divided into three categories:

- **Own-Source Revenue** – This is revenue accrued from transportation-specific taxes and tariffs applied directly to transportation related activities. This includes fuel taxes, property taxes, income or corporate taxes, vehicle license fees, violation tickets, fines. and investment income.

- **Revenue Directed to Other Uses** – This includes funds that are raised from transportation related activities but used to finance programs unrelated to transportation services. For example, receipts from fuel taxes may be directed to the general fund for other uses.

- **Supporting Revenue** – This includes funds that are collected from non-transportation related activities but are dedicated to supporting transportation programs. An example might be receipts received by the state from sales or property taxes to finance transportation projects.

Special Tax

A special tax bond is repaid through revenues derived from taxes imposed on existing activities or assets. It has characteristics of both general obligation and revenue bonds. This renders it a hybrid security.

Holders of these securities receive periodic interest payments from the issuer until the bond reaches maturity. At this point, the principal amount is slated for repayment.

Special assessment taxes are used to repay special assessment bonds. These bonds are issued by the government to fund diverse community projects, such as highway construction, the development of sewage systems, and the establishment of healthcare facilities.

Special Assessment

A special assessment bond relies on revenue generated from an incremental tax imposed directly on residents who benefit from a specific project.

For instance, the construction of a new freeway prompts the issuance of a special assessment bond. In this scenario, residents close to the proposed road will experience a rise in property taxes because they will use the road in the future. This increase in taxes funds the interest payments on the special assessment bond. Financial responsibility is effectively distributed across the community that stands to benefit from the proposed development.

Double-Barreled

A double-barreled bond is a type of municipal bond where the repayment of interest and principal is guaranteed by two separate entities.

Specifically, these bonds rely on the revenue generated by a designated project as well as the financial capacity of the bond issuer and its taxing authority. Often referred to as combination bonds, they encompass both a revenue pledge and a general obligation commitment.

A double-barreled bond derives its support from two sources: the revenue generated by the project being financed and local government backing. If the project's revenue falls short, the issuer steps in to fulfill the payment obligations made to the bondholders and investors.

This mitigates the risk of default associated with the bond. However, it is worth noting that this comes at the expense of a lower interest rate.

Moral Obligation

A moral obligation bond is a revenue bond issued by a municipality or local government that includes a moral, but non-legally binding commitment to avoid default risk on payments. The moral obligation comes into play when revenues from the project being financed are insufficient to cover bond payments. In such cases, the government is morally, but not legally, obligated to appropriate funds to make up the shortfall.

Moral obligation bonds are not backed by the full faith, credit, and taxing power of the issuing entity, unlike general obligation bonds. Instead, moral obligation bonds have a secondary or moral pledge by the governmental entity to seek appropriation to service the debt upon insufficient project revenue. However, there is no legal obligation. These bonds are created as an added security to non-GO debt and have tax exemption benefits.

Private Activity

Private activity bonds (PABs) allow a private entity to secure funding for a variety of projects, which may include highways and freight transfer. These bonds are issued by a conduit on behalf of the private entity.

By utilizing PABs, private sponsors can take advantage of favorable interest rates provided by tax-exempt municipal bonds at lower borrowing costs.

The federal government has passed PAB legislation, which implies support of private-sector investment in transportation infrastructure.

The local or state government issues private activity bonds, and these funds go to private projects designed for public benefit. The financed projects contribute to the repayment of the funds initially acquired.

There are four types of PABs:

- **Exempt Facility Bonds** – Exempt facility bonds finance projects such as water or sewer facilities, airports, and residential rental properties.
- **Qualified Mortgage Bonds** – Qualified mortgage bonds provide finances to first-time home buyers through low interest mortgage loans.
- **Qualified 501(c)(3) Bonds** – These bonds provide financial aid to nonprofit organization and access to tax-exempt finances for eligible projects.
- **Qualified Redevelopment Bonds** – These bonds fund redevelopment efforts in economically distressed areas.

Industrial Development Bonds (IDBs)

IDBs are tax-exempt securities issued by government agencies to provide money for acquisition, construction, manufacturing, rehabilitation, and processing facilities for private sector companies.

IDBs are also known as industrial revenue bonds. They are organized by the state or the local government and are common due to their low cost.

There are two types of IDBs, small-issue and exempt-facility.

- **Small-Issue IDBs** – These are about $1 million in size but can be extended up to $10 million.
- **Exempt-Facility IDBs** – These have no size limit but must be used for specific businesses.

The benefits of using IDBs include:

- Federal tax exemption.
- Low interest rates for private businesses.
- Multipurpose use of funds availed.
- Economic growth.
- Encouragement of employment and business.

Municipal Notes

A municipal note is a short-term debt that is issued by state and local governments. This note is used to provide interim financing before longer-term bonds are issued or if irregular cash flows need to be covered. They offer a fixed income with a maturity period of one year or less. Most municipal notes are also tax-exempt at the federal or state level.

Municipal notes include tax anticipation notes (TAN), bond anticipation notes (BAN), revenue anticipation notes (RAN), construction loan notes (CLN) and tax and revenue anticipation notes (TRAN).

Tax Anticipation Notes (TANs)

A tax anticipation note is a short-term debt security issued by a state or local government to raise money for a public project. This debt is repaid with future tax collections.

TANs allow borrowing at a reduced interest rate for periods under a year. These notes mature within a year, typically around the time annual taxes are due.

These notes are offered to buyers at a discounted rate and when the note reaches maturity, the buyer receives the interest. The payments are usually made from a refined revenue source. TANs are considered a safe choice for investors, as they offer a low rate of return and tax-exempt interest.

Revenue Anticipation Notes (RANs)

Revenue anticipation notes represent a type of short-term debt commonly utilized by government issuers. They are typically repaid within a one-year time frame using revenue generated from a specific, named source.

RANs are similar to a type of municipal bond where the government borrows funds to finance a project and subsequently repays lenders with the revenue generated by that project.

Like other types of municipal bonds, RANs enjoy federal tax-exempt status. Local governments issue these notes when they need to bridge the gap between tax revenues and immediate expenses.

Government repayment of a RAN is sourced from various revenue streams that are specific to each project. These revenue sources may include increased rates, sales revenue, or other applicable sources. Examples of such projects might encompass renovations and improvements to recreation centers.

Grant Anticipation Notes (GANs)

GANs are used for short-term municipal financing. They are issued with the expectation of receiving grants, which usually come from the federal government or its agencies. These notes are typically issued by municipalities or public entities, not state banks, with the intent to provide immediate cash for expenses related to projects like the maintenance or construction of highways.

There is no guarantee that the state will receive the anticipated funding. However, if the grant is awarded, it is utilized to repay the bond.

Ratings for Municipal Notes

There are three major rating agencies for municipal notes:

- Moody's Investor Service.

- S&P Global Ratings.
- Fitch Ratings.

Investors can easily determine the investment risk for a particular municipal note by consulting these company ratings.

Moody's investor service assigns three potential ratings to municipal notes:

- MIG 1 (best quality).
- MIG 2 (high quality).
- MIG 3 (adequate quality).

S&P, on the other hand, uses a four-tiered rating system:

- SP-1+.
- SP-1.
- SP-2.
- SP-3 (risky).

Municipal Bond Underwriting

Municipal bond underwriting is the process of purchasing a new issue of municipal securities from the issuing entity and reselling them to investors. The underwriter, usually an investment bank, provides the necessary funds to the municipality by buying the new bonds which are to be repaid in the future. The underwriter then sells these bonds to investors.

The bonds' interest payout and yield rate are established prior to their sale in the primary market. This furnishes the issuer with the necessary capital at the minimum feasible expense.

There are two types of municipal bond underwriting deals, competitive and negotiated.

Competitive

During a competitive sale, multiple underwriters or groups of underwriters participate by submitting bids to the issuers. These bids provide recommendations regarding the coupons and yields at which the new bonds can be sold. The submission of bids can be made through various means, including hand delivery, fax, or online platforms.

The issuer selects the entity that presents the most competitive offer with the lowest cost. The chosen entity then takes on the responsibility of selling the new bonds to investors at the proposed values. Issuers can anticipate receiving five separate bids, on average. Dependent factors include size, credit quality, and prevailing market conditions.

Competitive underwriting deals commonly involve AAA insurance and consist of general obligations. They are particularly well-suited for stable bond markets.

Negotiated

Through this type of sale, an underwriter or group of underwriters negotiates directly with the issuer to discuss the interest rate and other specifications regarding the selling of the bond. Negotiated deals are designed to minimize the cost of the bond for the issuer and still be attractive enough for the investors to buy.

The underwriter provides the issuer with a purchase price, while the public is offered the securities at the offering price. The spread, the difference between these two prices, is paid by the issuer. When selecting underwriters to handle a new issue, they typically go through a request for proposal process.

Negotiated underwriting deals can be intricate, as they are sensitive to even minor fluctuations in interest rates. Furthermore, these deals may not have a robust investor demand. This makes them more suitable for a bond market characterized by volatility.

Corporate Bonds

Corporate bonds are securities issued by a corporation. They represent a promise to pay bondholders a fixed amount of money (the bond's principal/face value) at a future date, along with periodic payments of interest called coupons.

The coupon interest rate is the percentage of a bond's par value that must be paid annually.

Types of Corporate Bonds

Corporate bonds are divided into two major categories, secured and unsecured.

Secured Bonds

Secured corporate bonds offer specific collateral, such as property or assets owned by the company, as security for the bond. In case of an incident, the bondholders have the legal right to claim the collateral.

An example of a secured corporate bond is a mortgage bond, which can be collateralized by assets such as property or equipment.

These bonds are the best option for investors who wish to avoid the default risk of bonds, as the collateral serves as a guarantee. The interest rate is low due to low risk. Secured bonds can be issued by both small and large companies.

Secured bonds are further classified into three categories:

1. **Mortgage Bonds** – Mortgage bonds pledge specific property. If the company defaults on the bonds, the bondholders may take the property as collateral without any legal repercussions.

2. **Equipment Trust Certificates** – Equipment trust certificates permit a company to acquire and derive benefits from an asset while making incremental payments over a duration. These certificates are commonly employed by railway and trucking enterprises.

   The certificate holders own the equipment and lease it to the company. The interest and principal are paid by the trustee (the institution responsible for the investor's interests).

3. **Collateral Trust Bonds** – Collateral trust bonds include the debt that is secured with financial collateral. This is applied to companies with no real property to pledge.

Unsecured Bonds

Unsecured bonds, also known as debentures, are not backed by any specific asset or collateral. Instead, they are backed by the general creditworthiness and reputation of the issuing company. These bonds are considered relatively risky as there is no specific asset to recover in case the issuer defaults. The interest rates on these bonds are typically higher to compensate for the increased risk of default.

These bonds are generally used by established firms or well-known companies. Thus, repayment is based on the ability of the issuer to generate revenue and pay interest on schedule.

Examples of unsecured bonds include notes and corporate bonds, but not treasury bills. Unsecured bonds are divided further into two categories, debentures and subordinated debentures.

Debentures

Debentures are debt instruments that can be used by governments, companies, and organizations for the purpose of issuing a loan. They contain a contract for repayment of the principal amount on or before a specified date. Payment of interest is set at a fixed rate until the principal sum is repaid.

Debentures are used to raise the debt finance, and debenture holders are considered the creditors of the company.

Debentures are more flexible than loans as they offer greater choice regarding maturity, interest rate, security, and repayment. When a company intends to raise a loan amount from the public, it issues debentures.

Subordinated Debentures

Subordinated debentures are unsecured loans or bonds that rank below other securities with respect to asset claims or borrower earnings. If the borrower fails to repay, then the lender of the subordinated debt receives payment only after all other unsubordinated debts are paid.

By comparison, this debt has a higher risk level because it carries low credit ratings and a greater rate of interest (13% to 25%). Subordinate debt is useful for small companies that may not have access to other, more secure forms of debt because of their low credibility.

A subordinated debenture ranks below other debts in case of liquidation or bankruptcy. In the hierarchy of creditors, subordinated debenture holders only receive payment after all senior debt is paid.

Liquidation Proceedings

Liquidation is a process by which a company is brought to its end. The assets and property of the company are redistributed to the creditors and owners.

The main causes of liquidation include:

- Inability to pay debts.
- Liabilities that exceed the company's total assets.
- Minimal prospects.
- Inability of directors to cope with the pressure of the trading market.

There are three types of liquidation.

1. **Creditors' Voluntary Liquidation** – A creditors' voluntary liquidation (CVL) provides a mechanism for directors or owners to close an insolvent company. In this process, an appointed liquidator takes charge and oversees the realization of company assets. The proceeds from asset realization are then distributed to the creditors. Ultimately, the company is formally closed through the CVL procedure. The primary purpose of initiating a CVL is to voluntarily declare the company's insolvency before creditors pursue legal action against it.
2. **Members' Voluntary Liquidation** – Members' voluntary liquidation occurs when a company is solvent and can pay all its liabilities. The dissolution occurs with consent. Owners want to close the business because its main purpose or goal has been achieved.
3. **Compulsory Liquidation** – Compulsory liquidation is also known as forced liquidation. In this case, the creditors appeal to the court to dissolve the firm, as they believe that the company is unable to pay its debts.

The process of liquidation is:

- Appointment of the liquidator.
- Announcement of liquidation and call for claim submissions and valuer appointments.
- Verification and acceptance of claims.
- Preparation of asset memoranda and other reports.
- Formation of liquidation estate with inclusions and exclusions.
- Sale of assets.
- Distribution of assets.

- Dissolution of the corporate debtor.

Secured Creditors

Secured creditors hold a lien on their debtor's property. This allows the property to be sold to satisfy the debt upon default.

Secured creditors have a security interest in the company's assets, such as a mortgage. They typically have priority over unsecured creditors, but preferential debts might take precedence in certain jurisdictions. Therefore, they can repossess the company's assets to discharge their secured debts.

For example, in the event of a borrower defaulting on their payments, a secured creditor has the lawful authority to seize the borrower's assets, liquidate them, and utilize the proceeds to settle any outstanding debts.

Administrative Expense Claims

Administrative expense claims require bankruptcy court approval. These reflect the actual and necessary costs of preserving the bankruptcy estate after the bankruptcy petition filing.

Some examples of administrative expense claims are rent, utilities, supplies, equipment, insurance policies, benefits, and legal counsel.

General Creditors

A general creditor is a person or organization that lends money without a secured interest in the borrower's assets. If the loan is not paid back, the creditor does not have the right to directly seize specific assets as collateral.

A general creditor must file a proof of claim in bankruptcy court. In the case of liquidation of an unsecured property, the liquidated assets are distributed among the creditors.

Subordinated Creditors

A subordinated creditor is an individual or company ranked below senior creditors in claiming debts from a debtor. Subordinated creditors only get paid after all senior creditors have been settled.

Preferred Stockholders

Preferred stockholders enjoy priority of a company's earnings. This entitles them to receive dividends ahead of common shareholders or others.

Preferred stock represents a distinct class of shares that grants holders more privileges compared to common stock. This includes higher dividend distributions and a greater share in assets during liquidation proceedings.

It's important to note that preferred stockholders typically do not possess voting rights within the company. The dividends they receive can either be cumulative or non-cumulative in nature.

Stockholders

A common stockholder has purchased at least one common share of a company. The common stockholders are the last in line of priority of company asset distribution.

Common stockholders have voting rights, but they are not prioritized regarding the right to dividends or assets in the case of the firm's liquidation. They can appreciate equity ownership.

Common stock is typically calculated as part of total equity. It usually includes the initial capital paid by investors, plus any retained earnings. The exact formula can vary depending on the specifics of the company's equity structure and accounting methods.

Types of Corporate Bonds

Other types of corporate bonds include:

Income Bonds

The principal value of an income bond is promised, and interest or coupon payments are contingent upon the issuer's income. The interest is promised but only paid if the issuer earns sufficient income. Interest is paid to creditors as the issuer receives income, defined by the specifications of the note or bond.

Interest payments on these bonds are not fixed; they vary according to the earnings of the company. These bonds are typically issued during a corporate debt restructuring.

Income bonds are beneficial for the issuing company in its attempt to raise its capital. Failure to pay interest does not result in default.

Eurodollar Bonds

Eurodollar bonds pay interest and principal in US dollars and are issued outside the US. These bonds are internationally traded and can be issued by various entities, including US corporations. These securities allow buyers to benefit from variations in currency exchange rates.

Initially, Eurodollar implied that the accounts were held in Europe, but with the passage of time, it expanded to US dollar accounts held anywhere outside the United States.

Yankee Bonds

Yankee bonds refer to those bonds that are issued by a non-US entity in the United States and are traded in US dollars. For example, if a Swedish company issues bonds in the United States, the bonds would be known as Yankee bonds.

According to the Securities Act of 1933, these bonds must first be registered with the SEC before they can be sold in the market.

Yankee bonds are frequently released in multiple segments, with each issuance potentially reaching a substantial amount of up to $1 billion. These bonds typically undergo evaluation by credit rating agencies, and coupon payments to foreign investors are not subject to withholding tax.

The secondary market for Yankee bonds tends to exhibit higher liquidity compared to Eurobonds; this results in tighter bid-ask spreads.

Eurobonds

A Eurobond is an international bond that is denominated in a currency different from the country where it is issued. These are also known as external bonds.

Eurobonds are classified based on the currency of their issuance. The advantage of investing in a Eurobond is that it allows opportunities for overseas investments without leaving one's home country. They are quite affordable, with a small denomination, and possess high liquidity. Additionally, Eurobonds offer extended durations and increased flexibility.

The main disadvantage of these bonds is the vulnerability to political and economic risks within each country. They are also susceptible to exchange rate fluctuations and are not regulated in their home country.

Money Market Instruments

The money market covers trading of significant quantities of short-term debt instruments, such as commercial paper or overnight reserves. It is widely regarded as an excellent avenue for investing in highly liquid assets.

The money market is heavily regulated by various federal bodies, including the Federal Reserve, Office of the Comptroller of the Currency (OCC), and the Securities and Exchange Commission (SEC), among others. The exact level and type of regulation depends on the specific type of instrument and entities involved, such as:

- Interbank loans.
- Money market mutual funds.
- Commercial paper.
- Treasury bills.
- Short-lived mortgage and asset-backed securities.
- Foreign exchange swaps.
- Municipal notes.
- Deposit certificates.
- Eurodollar deposits.
- Repurchase agreements.

Chapter 8: Packaged Products

"Packaged products" is a term that includes long-term insurance contracts, units, or shares in collective investment schemes. It can also refer to a life policy, a unit in a regulated collective investment scheme, or an interest in an investment trust saving scheme. They are also referred to as packaged retail investment and insurance products (PRIIPs).

Types of Investment Companies

An investment company is an entity that is engaged in holding, managing, and investing securities. These companies are regulated by the SEC. All investment companies are registered under the Investment Company Act of 1940.

The investment company serves as a financial intermediary that pools funds from individual investors and uses those funds to invest in a variety of securities. This allows investors to diversify their investments and gain exposure to a broader range of assets.

An investment company has the following characteristics:

- It contains multiple investments.
- There is more than one investor investing in the company at present.
- The ownership interests are in the form of equity or partnerships.
- The way these investments are managed can vary depending on the investment strategy, type of security, and other factors. Some investments may be managed on a cost basis or using other valuation methods.

There are three main types of investment companies: management investment companies (which can be further divided into diversified and non-diversified), unit investment trusts, and face-amount certificate companies.

Management Investment Companies

A management investment company manages publicly issued fund shares and has two types:

- **Open-end Companies** – Open-end companies issue shares that are sold directly to investors. The shares are not bought or sold on a stock exchange.

- **Closed-end Companies** – Closed-end companies issue a fixed number of shares that are bought and sold on a stock exchange.

Unit Investment Trusts (UIT)

A UIT is an investment company that provides a portfolio with a fixed set of securities for a specific period of time. This financial company can buy or hold a group of securities and make them available to investors as redeemable units.

Some characteristics of UITs are listed below:

- These investments have access to a specified asset class and have targeted exposure.
- Many investors combine their funds, but unlike mutual funds, UITs are not actively managed by a manager.
- Securities are bought and sold directly from the company that issues them.
- Securities can also be bought from the secondary market.
- Securities are issued via an initial public offering.
- Securities have a stated expiration date.
- Securities are not actively traded.

Face-amount Certificate Company

Face-amount certificate companies offer investors a certificate of investment, along with fixed debt securities, commonly referred to as FACs, that require the issuer to make fixed payments at a future date.

A FAC represents a contractual agreement between an issuer and an investor, where the issuer commits to making predetermined payments on a specified future date. In return, the investor provides funds to the issuer, either through regular installments or as a lump sum payment, known as a fully paid face amount certificate.

It's worth noting that these companies do not receive any tax advantages.

Diversified Investment Companies

Diversified investment companies usually invest in multiple assets, and also in separate securities within each category. An example is mutual funds. Diversification is not only about venturing into new market segments, but also about spreading the risk across a variety of investments.

Here are a few reasons companies opt to diversify:

- For growth in business.
- To ensure the maximum utilization of their resources.
- To avoid unattractive industry practices being pushed by competitors.

Non-diversified Investment Companies

Non-diversified investment firms allocate their funds to a particular asset type or sector, or to a limited number of securities within each sector.

Prospectus

A prospectus is a formal document required by and filed with the SEC that provides details about an investment offering to the public.

The investment company releases the prospectus to inform the public and investors of the various securities that are available. These files include descriptions of mutual funds, stocks, and other investments offered by the company.

A prospectus usually includes detailed information about the investment, including its history, objectives, risk factors, management, and financial statements.

Investment Objectives

Investment objectives state what the client wants to achieve with the investments. They are a set of goals that determine an investor's financial portfolio.

There are two types of investment objectives, primary objectives and secondary objectives:

Primary objectives:

1. Safety of principal.
2. Income or dividends.

3. Growth or capital gains.

Secondary objectives:

1. Liquidity of assets and marketability.
2. Tax minimization.

Risk Disclosure

Risk disclosure is necessary when working with stocks, investments, bonds, and anything that is related to financial markets.

High-quality disclosures improve transparency because they provide investors and other participants with a better understanding of the company's risk exposure and risk management practices.

A risk disclosure document should include:

- Risk summaries in case of long disclosures.
- Material risk disclosure.
- Relevant risk headings.
- Inconsistent compliance.
- Appropriate disclosure volume.
- Generic risk headings.

Performance Information

Investment performance information is collected systematically. This allows potential investors to make judgments about achievements related to objectives, plans, or intentions. Performance information is an important part of performance management.

Performance management is the process of making sure that certain objectives and activities meet the organization's goals in an efficient manner. This can be applied broadly to the entire company or focused on a single employee.

In this scenario, performance information about a corporation or institution helps the investors in deciding whether they want to invest in a certain company or not, based on the information they have about its past performance and future prospects.

Sales Charge Disclosure

A sales charge is a commission that is paid to the financial intermediary in a mutual fund, such as a broker, advisor, or financial planner. This fee is compensation to the salesperson and is expressed as a percentage of the investment value.

Sales charge disclosure is a document that gives general background information about sales charges, expenses, management fees, waivers, etc. Fund companies typically provide comprehensive disclosure of their sales charges in their prospectus.

When dealing with mutual funds, the sales charge is known as "load," which can be charged upfront at the time of the purchase (i.e. front-end load) or when the shares are sold (i.e. back-end load). Sales charges are not included in the net expense ratio.

Operating Expenses Disclosure

An operating expense is an expense a business sustains through its normal operations. It is also defined as the cost that is associated with the maintenance and administration of a business on a daily basis.

When it comes to mutual funds or other investment vehicles, the operating expense ratio measures the percentage of the fund's assets that are used for administrative and other operating expenses.

These expenses range from an employee's pay to something as simple as ink used for printing. These include rent, utilities, advertising, inventory, property tax, etc.

OpEX is the abbreviation used to denote operating expenses. The importance of its disclosure is that it highlights the level of cost that a corporation has to make to generate revenue.

Class Comparison

Fund class comparison includes the descriptions that distinguish one class of fund shares from another within the same fund.

Breakpoint

When mutual funds charge front-end sales fees and offer discounts for larger investments, the specific investment thresholds at which these discounts apply are known as breakpoints.

In simpler terms, a breakpoint sale refers to the purchase of a mutual fund at a predetermined dollar amount that qualifies the investor for a lower sales fee tier. These sales provide investors with discounts based on their investment levels, which are determined by the fund company.

Breakpoint discounts may start at levels like $25,000, but the specific amounts and breakpoints vary by fund. The fees and breakpoints are outlined in detail in the company's prospectus and are agreed upon by intermediaries. FINRA closely monitors these breakpoint sales to prevent any criminal practices.

Exchange Privileges

Exchange privilege is an opportunity for a mutual fund shareholder to exchange the investment fund with another within the same fund family. This way, the investors can take advantage of the changes in the market.

For example, an investor can exchange ownership of a fund that has underperformed for a fund within the same family that is expected to perform better. The advantages of exchange privileges are:

- It allows shareholders to exchange their shares if the company undergoes a reorganization, with the new shares being of more value.
- It allows the shareholders to exchange their shares for shares in another fund in case the first fund is liquidated. This is beneficial as it gives the shareholders an opportunity to maintain their investment in a similar product.

There are also some disadvantages:

- It creates a sense of entitlement among shareholders and also raises expectations, which might result in disappointment.
- It can be costly and time-consuming for the company to entertain many requests for exchanges.

Mutual Fund Structure

A mutual fund is a collective investment that pools money from different investors and invests that money in equities, bonds, and securities. This money from the mutual fund is invested by professional fund managers.

There are three types of mutual funds: open-end funds, unit investment trusts, and closed-end funds.

Mutual funds have a three-tier structure:

Tier 1: Fund Sponsor – A person or entity that can set up a mutual fund to earn money through fund management. An associate company manages the investment of the fund. A fund sponsor must have at least some experience in financial services and must have a sound financial track record during those years.

Tier 2: Trust and Trustees – These form the second layer of mutual funds. A trust is created by the fund sponsor in favor of the trustees through a document called a trust deed. The trustees are answerable to the investors. They have a critical role to play in ensuring the mutual fund's compliance with regulatory requirements and fiduciary standards.

Tier 3: Asset Management Company (AMC) – This forms the third layer of mutual funds. An AMC is responsible for the creation and management of a variety of mutual fund schemes that are designed to meet the varying risk tolerance and investment objectives of investors, and to respond to market conditions. AMCs act as fund managers or investment managers, as they are responsible for all fund-related activities.

Other components in the structure of mutual funds include custodians, RTAs (Registrar and Transfer Agents), auditors, and brokers.

There are three types of mutual funds.

- Open-end funds.
- Unit investment trusts.
- Closed-end funds.

Board of Directors

A board of directors is an executive committee that supervises the activities of an organization, such as a business, a nonprofit organization, or a government agency.

The board of directors is an elected panel in a company that represents the company's shareholders. The board typically includes positions such as a chairman, executives and non-executive directors, and sometimes the CEO and vice president.

The benefit of having such panels is that they are helpful in coming up with a strategy for addressing issues.

The disadvantages include power imbalances, which can lead to discord among the directors.

To form a board of directors, the following must be considered:

- The number of board members and their designation.
- The payment methods and frequency.
- The process of the election of board members.
- Any term limits.
- Fair and equal treatment of people despite their stake in the company.

Investment Advisors

Registered investment advisors are professionals or firms that provide advice on securities to clients, and are registered with the SEC or state securities regulators. They may manage large sums of money, but this is not a requirement for their registration or operation.

An investment advisor should have the following characteristics:

- Analytical thinking.
- Business skills.
- Good interpersonal communication skills.
- Research skills.
- Empathy.

Transfer Agents and Custodian Banks

Transfer agents are entities appointed by a corporation or mutual fund to maintain records of investors and account balances, manage changes in share ownership, and distribute dividends if applicable.

For example, a transfer agent can be a financial company, trust company, bank, or any individual. Some other responsibilities of a transfer agent are listed below:

- Handling voting rights.
- Organizing company events.
- Acting as a liaison.
- Providing support services.
- Issuing certificates to show a change in ownership.

A custodian is a financial institution responsible for securely holding customers' securities to protect them from theft or loss. Their role is to act on behalf of trading members (brokers) by safely storing the securities.

Custodians can hold securities in physical or electronic form. Their primary function is to safeguard the assets of their customers. There are fees for providing this service.

The use of a custodian is considered beneficial as it allows both investors and fund and asset managers to concentrate on their area of expertise while managing investments. Also, the safekeeping of assets helps to reduce the market and counterparty risk. It also provides an opportunity for the custodian to generate fees and income from asset servicing activities.

Principal Underwriter

Underwriting involves an individual or institution assuming financial risk in exchange for compensation. An underwriter is a party that accepts the risk in return for payment of an insurance premium or other forms of consideration.

A principal underwriter is involved in the initial distribution of mutual fund shares, in a contractual relationship with the investment company issuing the fund shares. This is not necessarily a direct relationship with an affiliated individual of the issuer. This type of underwriter takes independent or collaborative action to establish an underwriting syndicate and is entitled to a higher commission rate or greater profit compared to other underwriters.

An underwriting agreement is a legally binding contract that establishes the relationship between an underwriting group or syndicate consisting of investment bankers and the issuing corporation of a new securities offering.

The primary role of underwriters is to evaluate the level of risk associated with the issuer's business. Through underwriting, they determine appropriate premium rates and loan borrowing rates and create a market for securities with accurate pricing based on risk assessment. This process facilitates fair pricing and enables the issuance of securities in the market.

Mutual Fund Complex

A mutual fund complex is a group of mutual funds managed by the same investment company or fund family. It provides a broad range of fund options under a single management company.

The benefit of a mutual fund complex is that it contains separate funds, which are focused on various aspects of the financial market. The biggest advantage of a mutual fund complex is diversification, as often individual investors do not have adequate funds to buy the wide range of securities that are offered by a group of mutual funds.

Investors have a choice to select from a diverse range of funds and can choose the one that aligns with their investing strategy. In some cases, investors are allowed to exchange shares in one fund with shares from another fund within the same complex. There is a single mutual fund family statement that outlines all investments within the family.

Net Asset Value (NAV)

The NAV of an investment company is the company's total assets minus its liabilities. For example, if an investment company has securities and other assets worth $200 million and liabilities of $10 million, the NAV of that company is $190 million.

NAV is calculated using this formula:

NAV = (Fund assets – fund liabilities)/total number of shares

A fund's NAV is not a reflection of the fund's cost. It represents the per-share value of the fund's assets after deducting its liabilities. Comparing NAVs between different funds does not provide meaningful insights about their cost or value.

Calculating the Sales Charge

When investors purchase front-end or redeem back-end load shares in a mutual fund, they pay a sales charge rate. This sales charge compensates financial intermediaries and is often expressed as a percentage of the investment.

For example, if the sales charge percentage is 4.3% and $8,000 is invested, the result is $344. Sometimes it is called the POP (public offering price). The formula for sales charge percentage is:

$$\text{Sales charge percentage} = (POP - NAV)/ POP \times 100$$

Calculating POP

The POP is the price at which new issues of stock are offered to the public by an underwriter.

The POP is the sum of the net asset value and the sales charge an investor must pay to invest. The formula is given below:

$$POP = NAV + SC$$

No-Load Funds

A no-load fund is a mutual fund in which shares are sold without commission or sales charge. This is only possible as the shares are directly distributed by the investment company and not through a secondary party.

No-load funds are preferred by some investors because they do not carry a sales charge, potentially reducing the cost of investment. However, it is not accurate to say that they universally offer higher returns. Some no-load funds may charge other fees, such as 12b-1 fees, which are used to cover costs associated with marketing and distribution. Sometimes no-load funds charge fees that are not sales charges, such as operating expenses.

The disadvantage is that as the transactions are made individually, there is a lack of professional guidance and advice about other options.

Mutual Fund Expense Ratio

The expense ratio is a measure of how much of a fund's assets are used for administrative and other operating expenses. It reflects how much a mutual fund pays for portfolio management, administration, marketing and other expenditures.

The expense ratio is represented as a percentage. A good expense ratio is around 0.5% to 0.75%. If an expense ratio is 1.5% or higher, it is considered to be detrimental to the overall health of the mutal fund. The mutual fund expense ratio is usually higher than the ETF expense ratio.

The expense ratio of a fund is the fund's total annual operating expense divided by its average net assets. The formula is given below:

Expense ratio = Total fund operating expenses/average net assets

For example, if the total annual expense for a fund with average net assets of $100 is $0.50, the expense ratio is 0.50%. This value is determined by dividing $0.50 by $100 and then multiplying by 100 to get the percentage.

Classes of Shares

A share class or share classification differentiates the various types of shares in company share capital. It is common for even small businesses to have different share classes.

The reasons for this system include various factors, such as the ability to vary dividends paid to different shareholders and to create different levels of voting.

The different classes of shares are described in detail below.

Class A

A Class A share refers to a share classification of common or preferred stock that has greater benefits in terms of dividends, asset sales and/or voting rights compared to other classes.

Class A has the most voting power. It has some trading restrictions, as these shares are sometimes not allowed to be traded, only converted.

Class A shares have a higher priority for dividends and profit. They can be more expensive than Class B or Class C shares or are often not available to the general population.

Class B

Class B shares are a classification of common stock.

Class B shares are bought and sold on the public exchange platform. They do not have any trading restrictions. As to their voting power, one share is equivalent to one vote.

There is no preferential treatment when it comes to the division of profits or dividends.

Class C

Class C shares are a class of mutual fund shares characterized by a level load that includes annual charges for servicing, distribution and fund marketing set at a fixed percentage.

Class C mutual fund shares often carry no front-end sales charge but do have ongoing fees such as 12b-1 fees. These shares typically do not carry voting rights and are not given to employees as compensation packages. The price of Class C shares is not necessarily related to the price of Class A shares. The main difference lies in their fee structures.

These shares are usually not available for trading. When it comes to dividing profits or dividends, these shares are like Class B shares, where there is an equal share.

Sales Charges

As mentioned above, a sales charge is a commission paid by investors on an investment in a mutual fund to the financial intermediary, i.e., a broker, manager, etc.

Front-end Load

The front-end load is the fee charged with each purchase, reducing the funds actually invested initially. This fee is around 5% to 6%. These mutual funds are made up of Class A shares.

For example, if an individual has invested $10,000 in a fund that has a front-end load of 5%, the amount deducted as the load would be 5% of $10,000, which is $500. The investment that goes into the fund would therefore be $9,500 ($10,000 - $500).

Contingent Deferred Sales Charges

Contingent deferred sales charges (CDSC) are a type of back-end load and the amount of charges depend on the length of time the investor holds their shares. Class B shares typically have a CDSC.

For example, if an investor liquidates $100,000 of an investment subject to a CDSC of 4%, they will pay $4,000 as a sales charge.

Level Load

A level load refers to a consistent fee that investors pay for the purchase of mutual fund shares, calculated as a fixed percentage over the course of the year. These shares are identified as Class C shares.

12b-1 Fees

This is the fee paid out of the mutual fund to cover the costs of marketing and selling mutual fund shares. The 12b-1 fees can range from 0.25% to 1% of the annual asset value.

The exact fee structure depends on the specific mutual fund. Class A shares usually carry a front-end load and may have lower 12b-1 fees compared to other share classes. Class B shares entail a contingent deferred sales load charge alongside a substantial 12b-1 fee.

Methods to Decrease Sales Charges

Listed below are the ways shareholders can reduce the sales charge on their investments in shares:

Breakpoints

A breakpoint signifies the investment thresholds necessary to qualify for a reduced sales load.

It represents the minimum amount of money required for an investor to purchase a significant number of shares in a mutual fund in order to be eligible for a reduction in sales charges.

Letter of Intent (LOI)

An LOI is a declaration in which shareholders indicate their intention to invest a predetermined sum of money in one or more Class A share accounts within a 13-month time frame. Although it expresses intent, it's not always legally binding in the same way as a contract.

Here are some key aspects of an LOI.

- Shareholders must submit a written request, which should include a list of the account numbers they wish to link. This request can be in the form of a letter, an application form or an account service form.
- When purchasing securities under the letter of intent, shareholders will be eligible for the breakpoint and reduced sales charges applicable at the time of the purchase.
- If shareholders are unable to fulfill the agreement, a portion of the LOI amount, typically up to 5%, will be held in escrow. These escrowed shares will still be eligible for dividend and capital gain distribution. Once the contractual obligations are met, the escrow status will be lifted.
- In the 11th month of the LOI, a reminder letter will be sent to shareholders if the agreement has not yet been fulfilled.
- Any purchases made within 90 days prior to the commencement of the LOI will count toward fulfilling the contractual obligations.

By committing to invest a specific sum of money, investors become eligible for a reduced sales charge on all applicable purchases outlined in the LOI.

Rights of Accumulation (ROAs)

Shareholders have the opportunity to connect their Class A, B or C accounts to reach a breakpoint for a Class A purchase through ROAs.

ROAs enable mutual fund shareholders to benefit from reduced sales commission charges when the total number of mutual funds purchased, combined with the existing holdings, meets the rights of accumulation breakpoint.

ROAs require eligible accounts and a written request. The combined account values are considered for reaching a breakpoint. The current value of all linked accounts is based on the POP and not the NAV.

Dollar Cost Averaging (DCA)

DCA is an investment technique used to mitigate price risk when acquiring mutual funds, ETFs or stocks. Rather than purchasing shares at a single price point, investors systematically buy smaller amounts of shares at regular intervals, regardless of the current price.

The key benefit of dollar cost averaging is its ability to reduce investment risk and preserve capital. By spreading out investments over time, it safeguards funds and offers flexibility in managing an investment portfolio.

The formula for calculating DCA is:

DCA = total investment cost/total number of shares

Redeem Mutual Fund Shares

Mutual funds' investments can be redeemed at any time. To redeem funds, investors must submit a redemption request form to the fund company or its transfer agent. The form must be filled out with details such as the holder's name, the number of units up for redemption, etc.

This process can be handled by the investor individually, or a broker or distributor can be involved. A mutual fund company must pay redemption proceeds to the shareholder within seven days of the filed request.

One downside to redeeming mutual fund shares is that, depending on market conditions and the specific terms of the mutual fund, early redemption might result in the investors receiving less than the initial investment amount. Moreover, they might have to re-invest the redeemed funds at less favorable terms.

The redemption fee is a shareholder fee that some funds charge when the investor redeems mutual fund shares.

Withdrawal Plans

A withdrawal plan is a financial plan that allows shareholders to withdraw their money from a mutual fund or any other investment account at predetermined intervals. These sorts of plans are usually used during retirement.

A systematic withdrawal plan is a phased mode of redemption from a mutual fund investment, such as monthly, biannually or annually. According to SWP, a shareholder can partially withdraw money and potentially continue to earn returns on the remaining investment.

Withdrawals are subject to tax deductions. Listed below are a few important strategies for withdrawal plans.

Fixed-dollar Amount

In a fixed-dollar amount strategy, retirees determine how much money they need to withdraw each year and then reassess the amount after a few years.

The withdrawal can be lowered in the future to match a lower portfolio value or could be raised if the investments have increased in value.

For example, a retiree may plan to withdraw $40,000 annually and then reassess this amount after a period of five years.

Fixed Time

Some retirees take out a fixed-dollar amount over a fixed period. The payments may be monthly, quarterly, biannually or annually. This is also called the systematic withdrawal plan.

Fixed Number of Shares

Mutual funds can continuously issue and redeem shares based on demand. However, a closed-end fund issues a fixed number of shares through an initial public offering (IPO) and does not continuously issue new shares or redeem outstanding shares as open-end mutual funds do. Although this isn't a withdrawal plan, a closed-end fund can be a valuable part of a retiree's investment portfolio due to its potential for regular cash flow.

Closed-end funds are generally designed for regular cash flow as these offer a higher potential distribution, and the average yield for fixed income is 6.2%, which is much higher than T-notes.

A closed-end fund can be used as a complement to generate high, steady income for retirees.

Sales Practice Violations

A sales practice violation is the failure of a FINRA broker firm and its financial advisors to comply with FINRA sales practice rules and regulations. Broker corporation misconduct can be characterized by different actions and, in some cases, may lead to legal action.

Sales practice violations include:

- Unsuitable investment advice.
- Breach of fiduciary duty.
- Negligence.
- Excessive trading.
- Misrepresentation of material facts or their omission.
- Unauthorized trading.
- Securities concentration.
- Mutual fund sales violation.
- Variable annuity fraud.
- Failure to supervise.
- Conflicts of interest.
- Private placements.
- Investment fraud.
- Private securities transaction.

Other Types of Investment Companies

Unit Investment Trust (UIT) Company

A UIT is a type of investment vehicle similar to a mutual fund, where funds from multiple investors are pooled with the aim of achieving a specific return. However, unlike mutual funds, UITs are managed by trustees rather than a fund manager, and have a fixed portfolio of assets that generally does not change over the life of the UIT.

A UIT operates as an investment company with a predetermined portfolio of redeemable units, including bonds and stocks, which are offered to investors for a specified period of time.

Investing in unit trusts offers several advantages. It provides investors with access to a diversified portfolio of securities, which helps mitigate the risk of financial loss. The securities within the unit trust portfolio remain fixed, ensuring stability.

Additionally, unit trusts offer benefits such as low initial investment costs, high liquidity, broad diversification and professional management.

Closed- or Open-end Funds

A closed-end fund is a mutual fund variant that raises capital for the company by issuing a predetermined number of shares in a single IPO.

In contrast, an open-end fund is a collective investment scheme that allows for the issuance and redemption of shares at any time. It does not impose restrictions on the transfer of shares.

The major differences between open- and closed-end funds are outlined below.

Parameter	Open-end Mutual Fund	Closed-end Mutual Fund
Buying period	Buy-in or buy-out anytime	Only buy-in during a specific period
Investment period	No fixed maturity date	3 to 5 years
Listing	No listing of SE	Listed on recognized SE
Liquidity	The fund is the liquidity provider.	The stock market is a liquidity provider.
Fund size	Flexible	Fixed
Pricing	NAV/ number of shares	Depends on the supply and demand of shares
Number of shares	No limit	Limited and fixed

Chapter 9: Variable Contracts and Municipal Fund Securities

Variable contracts, also known as variable annuities or variable life insurance policies, are contracts where the payout to the investor is dependent on the performance of an underlying portfolio of investments, often comprised of mutual funds.

Investment companies provide these services, and the value and benefit of the investments depend upon the investment experience and the types of accounts the investment company holds. Investors use variable contracts as a long-term investment.

Municipal securities refer to debt securities that are issued by local or state governments in order to fund public projects. Municipal fund securities are a subset of municipal securities that are specifically structured as a pool of investments. The interest income these securities generate is often exempt from federal, and sometimes state and local, taxes.

Investors use municipal fund securities to earn tax-exempt income. Each investment product comes with a different set of rewards and risks. So, investors need to choose the best option according to their situation.

Types of Annuities

An annuity is a contract between an investor and an insurance company. The investor can invest a certain amount with the insurance company, and the company will return that amount in a series of payments each year.

There are several types of annuities.

Fixed

Fixed annuities include fixed payments on an investment. For example, insurance companies invest in a low-risk project and guarantee a fixed payment to annuity holders each year, regardless of economic conditions.

A retired individual might invest in an ongoing project through an insurance company. That individual will receive a fixed rate of return on the investment at the end of each year.

At the end of a specified time period, the individual can either renew the annuity or cash out the investment. This method will provide a stable income stream.

Variable

Variable annuities are investment contracts that provide a variable rate of return on investment (ROI). These annuities do not provide a fixed rate of return on investment, but the amount returned can be larger than the amount in fixed annuities.

Moreover, variable annuities come with higher expenses, fees, and risks. Investors usually opt for such options when they can afford the risks balanced with a potentially high return.

Separate Accounts and Subaccounts

Insurance companies have general accounts linked to life insurance products and separate accounts for holding assets backed by variable annuities and investments of the policyholders.

Having separate accounts ensures that each policyholder has a secure, legally distinct account from the insurance company in case of any financial difficulty.

Subaccounts are accounts within a larger account. They help investors manage different types of investments and have different management fees. Either banks or investment companies keep these subaccounts.

Companies use subaccounts to keep track of the withdrawal and deposits from each department. Similarly, investment companies use subaccounts to keep track of their return on each investment for each individual.

Returns on investment depend on the investment product the subaccount holds and how the investment is performing in the market.

Annuity Phases

The process of investment in annuities is carried out in two phases.

Phase 1

The first phase is the accumulation phase, where the investor makes deposits into the annuity. This can be referred to as the phase where people save money or build up cash value for a long-term retirement plan.

The accumulation phase usually begins during people's mid-20s when they start working. Financial experts believe that the earlier the accumulation phase begins in an individual's life, the better and longer the return will be in the next phase.

Most annuities provide no immediate income benefits in the accumulation phase. During this phase, the annuity company then invests the contributions on the investor's behalf. Any returns are added to the value of the annuity. The value will naturally depend upon the condition of the underlying investments in the market.

Some contracts, however, do guarantee a minimum interest rate on the investment during the accumulation phase. This means the ROI will not drop below a certain level regardless of market conditions.

Another way of receiving benefits during the accumulation phase is through contracts that provide loans or partial withdrawals. However, these come with certain expenses and fees that might depreciate the value of the annuity over time.

If the annuity owner dies when the annuity is in the accumulation phase, the benefit to that point minus fees and other management charges is paid to the deceased's beneficiary. The beneficiary can receive the benefit as a lump-sum payment or over a period of time as specified in the contract.

Tax on an annuity after the owner's death is also a factor to be considered. Taxes may vary depending on the age at which the owner died or other circumstances. It is best to consult a tax consultant to analyze the terms and conditions of the entire annuity contract.

Phase 2

The second annuity phase is called the annuitization phase. During this period, the investment is converted into regular income payments. Depending on the type of contract, the payment could be a series of payments or a lump sum.

For fixed annuities, the owner will receive a set payment at each interval for the duration of the contract. The economic conditions of the market are not considered for fixed annuities.

However, the payment for variable annuities depends entirely on the performance of the investment and fluctuates based on the performance of the investments.

During this phase, if the owner makes an early withdrawal, there might be penalties. These depend on the conditions in the contract.

Some contracts also offer certain benefits, such as death or minimum withdrawal benefits. It is best to negotiate the terms and conditions according to your needs before signing the annuity contract.

Taxes are also charged in the withdrawal phase. The amount of tax will depend on the type of annuity and the distribution option chosen.

Payout Options

A payout option is a withdrawal during the distribution phase of the contract. Different annuity contracts offer different features, numbers of payments, duration of payments, and methods of payments.

Let's look at important payout options.

Straight Life Annuity

A straight life annuity provides a stable income stream to the owner over fixed periods during the time of the contract. It is an income plan that provides benefit payments throughout the life of the owner. It does not provide continuing payments to the beneficiaries after the owner's death.

The only factor that distinguishes a straight life annuity from others is that the payment amount is based on the annuity holder's life expectancy. When the owner dies, none of the benefits are given to the spouse or heir or any other beneficiary.

A straight life annuity is usually a good option for people without partners or family who are not concerned with leaving anything behind for any beneficiaries.

If the owner of an annuity dies and there is still an amount left in the payment plan of the straight life annuity, that amount is usually kept by the insurance company or the annuity provider.

Life Annuity with a Certain Period

A life annuity with a certain period (ten, fifteen, or twenty years) guarantees payment for the entirety of the owner's life. If the owner dies before that specific period, the annuity is passed to the beneficiary. This type of annuity provides both a lifetime income plan and passes the benefits to the beneficiaries in case of death during the specified period.

For example, an individual purchases an annuity for fifteen years. He has made periodic deposits and during the withdrawal phase starts receiving regular payments. If the owner dies after ten years of receiving payments, the beneficiary will receive the payments left for the remaining five years. However, if the owner outlives the fifteen years, payments will continue for as long as the annuitant lives.

The payments for a life annuity with a certain period might be less than for a straight life annuity, given that there's a guaranteed period during which payments will be made, even if the annuitant dies.

A life annuity with a certain period is a good option for people who are interested in a stable income stream and who want to make sure that their beneficiaries will receive some sort of payment after their death.

Joint and Last Survivor Annuity

A joint and last survivor annuity provides a payment option for two individuals, usually a married couple. The payments will continue as long as one of the spouses is alive. If one spouse outlives the other, the payments will not stop, but they may decrease, depending on the specifics of the annuity contract.

This annuity is a good option for couples who want to lead a comfortable retirement life. It will ensure a steady stream of income throughout their lives. The payments might be less compared to a straight life annuity.

Joint and last survivor annuities provide payments for retired couples who want to provide for one another, but it can also provide payments to a third party or beneficiary after the death of both spouses.

Unit Refund Life Annuity

A unit refund life annuity is a payment option that provides benefits throughout an owner's lifetime. This annuity also guarantees a minimum payout amount to the beneficiaries.

If the owner dies before receiving the payment equal to the initial investment, the balance remaining will be paid to the beneficiaries.

For example, a woman invests $500,000 in a unit refund life annuity, but before she can receive the $500,000 in total payments, she dies. Now, the remaining total payments up to $500,000 will be given to her beneficiary.

Annuity Charges and Expenses

Different annuity types come with different expenses. Usually, expenses on annuities include surrender charges, mortality and expense charges, rider fees, and administrative charges.

More complicated investment products have higher charges compared to straightforward investments. For example, a fixed annuity with simple terms and conditions has a smaller fee than a variable annuity. It is important to understand all these charges before choosing an annuity plan.

Surrender charges are incurred if the owner withdraws more than the scheduled payment amount. Annuity contracts usually have a certain period at the beginning called the surrender-fee period. Surrender charges usually allow an owner to withdraw up to 10% of the annuity value without a fee each year, but the exact terms may vary from contract to contract.

Mortality and expense charges compensate the insurance company for the death benefits or the risk they provide. They can range from 0.5% to 1.5% of the policy each year.

Some annuities provide death benefits to beneficiaries, which are covered by the riders' fee that insurance companies charge the owners beforehand.

The administrative fee is the amount insurance companies charge to cover the administrative and management charges of the annuity contract. Usually, it is about 0.3% of the value of an annuity contract.

Qualified vs. Non-Qualified Annuity

Qualified and non-qualified refer to whether taxes are paid before or after withdrawals.

In qualified annuities, pretax dollars fund the contributions. Taxes are paid when funds are withdrawn.

In non-qualified annuities, post-tax dollars fund the contributions. So, the deposited money grows tax-deferred. Only profits on the investments will be taxed when money is withdrawn.

Equity-Indexed Annuities (EIAs)

Equity-indexed annuities (EIAs) are a type of fixed annuity where the interest rate is based on the performance of an S&P 500-style stock index. They offer higher potential returns than traditional fixed annuities.

EIAs offer a minimum guaranteed interest rate and additional interest in case the underlying index performs well in the market. The additional interest is calculated using a formula that considers the rise of the interest rate over a specified period of time.

Some of the interest for equity-indexed annuities is the guaranteed minimum interest rate, which is usually 1–3% of the premium payment. Additional interest depends on the performance of the specified equities index.

Equity-indexed annuities provide a potential for a larger return on investment compared to traditional fixed annuities. However, the return is usually less than variable annuities. However, the risk factor of variable annuities is reduced in equity-indexed annuities.

Annuity Suitability Issues

Annuities are complex investment products and are not suitable for every individual. People usually choose annuity options according to their current financial condition, risk tolerance, future goals, etc. It is important to consider all these factors before choosing an annuity plan.

An annuity usually comes with high charges. The charges, such as sales commissions and surrender charges, are not only incurred at the beginning of the contract, but also in the form of annual maintenance fees, mortality and expense risk charges, etc. These charges are in addition to the taxes applicable during the accumulation or withdrawal phase.

Another issue most people face is the potential for illiquidity. An annuity is not a good option for people looking for immediate access to funds. They are specifically designed as a long-term investment, and withdrawing more than the permitted amount will incur certain charges.

Annuities are also not for people looking for high-return payments or for high-risk tolerance. Certain annuities offer high risk and ROI, but most of them offer a return that's periodic and predictable and usually not large.

Municipal Fund Securities

State or local government issue municipal fund securities. These securities give investors a tax-advantaged income. Some examples of municipal fund securities follow.

Local Government Investment Pools (LGIPs)

Local government investment pools (LGIPs) are investment pools local or state governments create and manage to invest their cash.

LGIPs invest in high-quality short-term debt securities, which offer investors a chance for higher return payments with comparatively lower risks. Local government investment pools (LGIPs) mostly invest in short-term securities. They do not include mutual funds, hedge funds, ETFs, pension funds, or unit investment trusts.

Prepaid Tuition Plans

State governments back prepaid tuition plans that offer tax-advantaged income and growth. These are college savings plans that save for education expenses to pay tuition at colleges and universities.

Direct-Sold

Direct-sold 529 plans are college savings plans that the plan sponsor, such as a state or financial institution, sell directly to the investor. Investors are then responsible for managing investments through their plans' online account portal.

529 ABLE (529A) Plans

State governments sponsor 529 ABLE (529A) plans, which are tax-preferred savings plans for the disabled.

These plans help meet the qualified disability expenses of eligible individuals, which may include education, housing, transportation, employment training, assistive technology, and personal support services.

An individual who becomes disabled before the age of 26 is entitled to these benefits.

Chapter 10: Alternative Investments

Alternative investments include exchange-traded funds (ETFs), exchange-traded notes (ETNs), and real estate investment trusts (REITs).

ETFs vs. Index Funds

ETFs are baskets of assets that are traded like securities. Index funds are a type of mutual fund that provides a passive investment strategy. In this strategy, the fund is designed to track the performance of a specific index, and the investor's money is invested in the fund, not directly in the index. However, ETFs can be bought and sold at any time during the day at the current market price, while index funds can only be traded at the end of the day at the NAV price.

Moreover, ETFs are traded on the stock exchange like individual stocks. So, when investors sell an ETF, they sell it to another investor rather than back to the fund company. However, the tax implications depend on several factors, including the investor's tax bracket and the length of time the investment was held, not just the structure of the ETF.

Inverse and Leveraged ETFs

Inverse ETFs offer returns that are opposite to the performance of a specific asset. They employ various strategies and derivatives to move against the market's underlying index. For instance, if an inverse ETF tracks the S&P 500 index, it will yield a positive return when the index drops and a negative return when the index rises.

Leveraged ETFs amplify the returns of an investment. They work just like ETFs, where they track the securities of an underlying asset, but the return of the index is leveraged by two or three.

Inverse and leveraged ETFs utilize derivatives like futures contracts to achieve their objectives. These contracts allow the holder to buy or sell a security at a predetermined price at a set date in the future. Inverse ETFs aim to profit from a decline in the market, and if the market does decline, they aim to generate returns that mirror the percentage decline.

Exchange-Traded Notes (ETNs)

ETNs are debt securities that track an underlying index of securities. Investors purchase ETNs from a financial institution that promises to pay them the return of an underlying index after the fees and commissions have been deducted. Unlike ETFs, ETNs do not own an underlying basket of assets. Instead, they are unsecured debt notes that are issued by a financial institution and promise to pay a return linked to a specific market index. But like ETFs, they are traded on the stock market at any time during market hours.

Real Estate Investment Trusts (REIT)

Real estate investment trusts (REITs) are investment vehicles that pool money from investors. These investors earn a dividend through the trust's ownership and operation of income-producing real estate buildings, such as office buildings, shopping centers, hotels, and apartment complexes, without having to buy, manage, or finance any properties themselves.

There are several types of REITs.

Mortgage/Debt

Mortgage or debt REITs are companies that loan money to real estate owners. Loans are either in the form of direct mortgages or by buying mortgage-backed securities that are sold to investors. Investors generate earnings using the net interest margin, which is when they charge higher interest on the loans they give.

Equity

Equity REITs are involved in physical real estate and earn income through rents or the sale of properties. Investors usually invest in specific properties, such as residential, retail, or industrial.

Hybrid

Hybrid REITs invest in both real estate properties (like equity REITs) and mortgages or mortgage-backed securities (like mortgage REITs). Hybrid REITs aim to provide investors with a balance of income (from the mortgage side) and growth potential (from the equity side), though the stability of these returns cannot be guaranteed.

Method of Offering REITs

REITs can be offered in several different forms.

Registered, Exchange-Listed, and Publicly Traded (Liquid)

These REITs are registered with the SEC. They are also listed on the stock exchange and can be publicly traded by investors in the stock market, like individual stocks. These REITs are considered liquid, as investors can trade them at any time during market hours.

Registered but Not Exchange-Listed (Non-Traded)

These REITs are registered with the SEC but are not listed on the stock exchange. They are considered non-traded because they are not exchange-listed and are sold and bought through a broker or a financial advisor to an investor.

Unregistered; Offered Through a Private Placement (Illiquid)

These REITs are not registered with the SEC. The only way they are bought and sold is through a private sale to a specific group of investors. They are considered illiquid because there is no specific market for these REITs, and potential buyers cannot be easily found.

What Are Limited Partnerships?

Limited partnerships consist of two or more partners—general and limited—who own a particular business entity. The general partner manages the business and is liable for the company's financial obligations, including debts and litigation. The limited partner contributes to the business's capital but is not liable for the company's financial obligations. The partners receive a share of the profits that the business makes according to their agreed-upon shares in the business.

Limited partners invest in the business while keeping their liabilities limited to their investment in the business, which means their personal assets are typically protected from the partnership's creditors in case of a lawsuit or bankruptcy. So, the limited partner will only be held liable for their investment in the business, not the partnership's debts or other obligations.

Disadvantages of Limited Partnerships

Limited partnerships also come with certain disadvantages.

Illiquidity

The investments involved in limited partnerships are typically illiquid, which means they cannot be bought and sold on the public market. Partners in a limited partnership may not be able to easily sell their interests when they want or at the price they want, as the partnership agreement or lack of a secondary market could limit their options.

Lack of Control

Limited partners are not involved in the management and the operations of the business, and as a result, they have limited or no control over the business. This could lead to conflicts between general and limited partners.

Increased Tax Complexity

Tax is applied to the limited partnership following the flow-through of income, which can be complex. Investors usually hire tax professionals to help navigate tax rules and obligations in a limited partnership.

Call to Contribute Additional Funds

If the business requires some additional capital, the general partner may ask the limited partner to contribute additional capital. This can be troublesome for the limited partner if they are not expecting additional capital calls.

Real Estate Programs

Real estate programs offer different investment opportunities to investors. Each comes with a unique set of goals and risks.

Raw Land

Investors invest in underdeveloped raw land. They usually buy a piece of land in hopes that its value will increase over time. While this can often happen for residential and commercial development land, it's not guaranteed and depends on several factors including location, market conditions, and regulatory approval for development.

New Construction

Investors may invest in a building that is currently under construction. They can do so by providing funding for the construction and receiving returns from the project once it is functioning.

Existing

Investing in properties that are fully constructed and developed, such as residential, commercial, or industrial properties, is called investing in an existing property.

Oil and Gas Programs

Types of oil and gas investments include exploratory, developmental, balanced, and income.

Exploratory

An exploratory program refers to an investment program that seeks new oil and gas reserves. This investment involves higher risk because there is no guarantee that an oil or gas reserve will be found. However, if it is found, the return on investment is high.

Developmental

Development programs refer to the development of already existing reserves of oil and gas, such as the drilling, production, and processing of oil and gas. They involve lower risk as the reserves are already discovered.

Balanced

A balanced investment invests in both exploratory and development programs so that the risk and rewards are balanced.

Income

These investments put capital into the production of oil and gas wells that are already generating revenue. Investing in these programs provides investors with a stable income stream.

A Risk Summary of a Direct Participation Program (DPP) Investment

A DPP provides investors with a partnership interest in ventures that are related to real estate, energy, or equipment leasing assets.

In a DPP, investors become limited partners, sharing in the income, tax benefits, and potential capital gains of the business venture. This happens through the structure of the DPP itself, which is a form of business entity. However, DPP investments carry risks.

Illiquid Nature and Potential Loss of Capital

DPP investments are risky due to their illiquid nature. The investments cannot be easily traded on the stock exchange.

Investors are also required to hold the investment for a specific period before they can sell. This can further lead to a loss of capital.

Unpredictable Income

DPP investment returns are unpredictable. They may offer a high return or none. It depends on the performance of the asset, which is in some cases difficult to predict. Therefore, DPP investments may not always provide a regular, stable income stream. The predictability of the income can depend on the nature of the asset and market conditions.

Rising Operating Costs

Certain factors can unexpectedly cause an increase in operating costs, such as inflation, the use of new technology, maintenance, and repair. These rising costs can decrease the return on investment.

Investor Considerations

Some common investor considerations include the following.

Investor Certification

An accredited investor is usually defined by specific financial criteria, such as income or net worth, which allows them to invest in securities that may not be registered with the SEC and are considered to have a higher risk profile.

Plus, an accredited investor can invest in securities that are not registered with the SEC. This provides access to unique investments and a chance for higher returns.

Discretionary Accounts

An investor opens a discretionary account with an authorized broker. The broker then has the authority to buy and sell securities on the investor's behalf. The investor and the broker sign a discretionary disclosure that includes the client's (the investor) specific restrictions or preferences for investing style or themes, which the broker must follow.

Discretionary accounts charge high fees, and there is the possibility of negative performance of investments.

Chapter 11: Understanding Option Fundamentals

An option contract provides the holder the right, but not the obligation, to buy or sell an underlying asset at a predetermined price within a specified period. This contract grants the potential buyer the right, but not the obligation, to purchase the property at a predetermined price within a specified period. During this period, the seller cannot offer the property to any other potential buyer.

The buyer is not bound to purchase the property. He or she is given an option to decide whether to purchase during a period specified in the contract. If, at the end of this period, the potential buyer refuses to buy the property, the seller can open the offer to other buyers.

Types of Contracts

There are several types of options contracts.

Put

A put option is a contractual agreement that provides the investor the privilege to sell the underlying asset at a predetermined strike price.

When a put option is acquired, the buyer holds a bearish view, and anticipates a future decline in the price of the underlying asset. If the asset's market value drops below the strike price, the buyer can exercise the put option and sell the asset at the higher strike price.

However, if the price of the underlying asset increases, the buyer may lose money.

Call

A call option is a type of contract that grants the purchaser the right to buy an asset at a set price known as the "strike price."

When acquiring the asset, the buyer holds an optimistic view of its future price increase and demonstrates a bullish sentiment. The buyer exercises the call option by purchasing the asset at the strike price and subsequently selling it at a higher price to generate a profit.

However, if the asset's price decreases over time, the buyer may incur a loss.

Equity Option

An equity option, a specific type of option contract, provides its holder with the right but not the obligation to buy (call option) or sell (put option) the shares of a company's stock at a predetermined price known as the strike price. This right can be exercised before or on the expiration date of the contract.

Investors utilize equity options to mitigate risk and potentially generate profits based on their anticipated market valuation of the underlying asset.

In the Money vs. Out of the Money

"In the money" (ITM) and "out of the money" (OTM) are terms used in options trading to compare the current market price of an asset and the strike price of the underlying asset.

ITM is when the current price of the underlying asset is advantageous for the holder of an option. In the case of a call option, this means that the current market price of the asset is higher than the strike price specified in the option contract. Conversely, for a put option, being ITM implies that the current price of the asset is lower than the strike price. In both cases, being ITM indicates a favorable position for the option holder.

OTM refers to a situation that is not favorable to the option holder. For a call option holder, the current price will be lower than the strike price, and for a put contract, the current price will be higher than the strike price.

There is another term, "at-the-money" (ATM), which is a situation where the market price is equal to the strike price. The market price has yet to move above or below the strike price, which will determine if it is in the money or out of the money.

Long and Short Calls

A long call option is exercised when an investor buys a call option and gives the holder the right but not the obligation to buy the underlying asset at the strike price on or before the expiration date. The holder profits if the market price of the underlying asset rises above the strike price.

In contrast, a short call option is the opposite of a long call and is where the seller (writer) is obligated to sell the underlying asset at the fixed strike price if the buyer decides to exercise the option. In writing a short call, the investor expects the market price of the asset to fall or stay the same, and by selling the option, they collect the premium and intend to profit if the option is not exercised.

Break-Even Point

The break-even point for a call option is located where the price of the underlying asset equals the sum of the strike price and the premium that is paid for the option. For a put option, the break-even point is the strike price minus the premium paid. At these points, the option holder neither makes a profit nor suffers a loss.

For example, if an investor buys a call option with a strike price of $87 and a premium of $3, then the break-even point would be $90. If the strike price of the underlying asset rises above $90 before the expiration date, then the investor will earn a profit.

What Is Speculation?

Speculators take on higher risks in hopes of getting higher returns. They also adopt certain strategies to ensure they earn a huge profit.

For example, if an investor believes that the price of crude oil is expected to increase soon, they will buy a futures contract on crude oil. If the price does increase, they can now sell it at a higher price and earn a profit.

But it can also cause a huge loss if the price of crude oil decreases in the future.

What Is Hedging?

Hedging is a strategy investors use to protect their existing investments from adverse market conditions. They try to reduce the risk of loss as much as possible.

For example, a farmer realizes that the price of a crop is about to drop. So, he sells futures contracts on the crop. By doing so, he locks in the price of the crop and reduces his exposure to market fluctuation.

Life of an Option

The life of an option contract can be divided into three stages.

Expire Worthless

The option may become valueless if it is not acted upon by the holder prior to the expiry date. In the event that the market value of the underlying asset does not align with the holder's prediction by the time of expiration, the holder does not have to implement the option.

The option then expires, and the holder will lose the premium paid to purchase the option.

Exercised

Exercising the contract means the holder has the right to buy or sell the underlying asset at the strike price. Depending on the market value of the asset and the strike price, the holder may earn a profit or incur a loss.

If it is a call option, the holder buys the asset at the strike price, and if it is a put option, the holder sells at the strike price.

Liquidated

The investor may choose to liquidate the option before the expiration date. This means selling the option in the market before it expires. This is usually done to earn a profit or avoid a loss.

If the investor liquidates the option, the value will then depend on the underlying asset's price and the remaining time until expiration.

Liquidate, Trade, and Closeout

Liquidating an investment refers to converting an asset into cash. For example, if an investment has continuously been performing poorly, the investor might liquidate the investment to avoid further losses.

Trading is buying and selling securities to make a profit. For example, an investor might buy a security whose price is expected to increase soon, keep it for some time, and then sell it once the price increases.

Investors close out investments by terminating or settling them. This is usually done to manage profits and losses or avoid risks.

Options Clearing Corporation (OCC) and Options Trading

The Options Clearing Corporation (OCC) is the world's largest clearing organization that works under the SEC to provide clearing and settlement services for options. It provides services, such as clearing and settlement, risk management, exercise and assignment, and regulatory compliance.

Moreover, the OCC acts as a middleman between the buyer and the seller. When an options contract is traded on the stock exchange, the OCC acts as the buyer to the seller and as a seller to the buyer. This reduces the risk of counterparty default and ensures that trades are settled efficiently.

Exercising an Equity Option

Exercising an equity option is when option holders use their right to buy or sell the underlying equity at the strike price, which depends on whether the option is a call or put option.

First, the investor must determine the option's expiration date, which is the last date the option can be exercised. Then, the strike price is determined, which is the price at which the holder can buy or sell the underlying equity.

The holder then contacts the broker to initiate the exercise. For a call option, the holder pays the strike price and receives the underlying equity. For a put option, the holder receives the strike price after delivering the underlying equity.

Index Options

Index options are financial contracts that give investors the right to buy or sell a stock index at the strike price before the expiration date. They help investors diversify their portfolios and get more exposure in the equity market and execute efficient risk management.

SPX is an index option that tracks the S&P 500 index, which can either be a call option or a put option.

For a call option, the holder has the right to buy the S&P 500 index at the strike price. For a put option, the holder has the right to sell the S&P 500 index at the strike price.

SPX is cash-settled, which means no actual shares are handled when the option is exercised. Instead, the option is settled with cash.

Hedging Long and Short Positions

Hedging is an investment strategy that reduces the exposure to risk in an investment. The most common types of hedging are long and short.

Long Hedging

This is a strategy that involves buying protective instruments, such as options or futures contracts, that are expected to rise in value when the associated underlying securities fall in value. A long hedge aims to protect against potential losses from a decline in the value of owned securities.

For example, an investor with a position in a stock may purchase a put option in the same stock to protect from a decline in its value. If in the future, the value of the stock declines, he or she can exercise the put option by selling the stock at the strike price, potentially higher than the current market price, This strategy allows investors to limit their losses.

Short Hedging

This is a strategy that involves selling securities that are expected to fall in value so that the losses are offset by gains from a short position. Short hedges protect investors during a stock price decline.

For example, an investor with a long position in a stock may initiate a short position in another stock that he believes is overpriced. If the overpriced stock declines in value, the losses from the long position can be balanced out with the gains from the short position.

What Is a Covered Position?

A covered position is an options trading strategy where the investor sells an option contract of an underlying stock or asset that she currently holds. This strategy cuts down the potential gains but also limits the risk of loss.

For example, an investor owns a stock and suspects that its value might decline in the future. To mitigate potential losses, she writes (sells) call options on that stock. If the stock price declines, she will still keep the premium received from selling the call options.

What Is an Uncovered Position?

An uncovered position is an options trading strategy where the investor sells the option contract of a stock that he does not own. This is an extremely risky strategy in case the price of the asset does not go in a favorable direction in the future.

For example, Steve is an investor who sells a put option on a stock he doesn't own. The buyer of the put option will have the right to sell the stock at the strike price if the market value of the asset falls below the strike price.

The seller of the put option is now obligated to buy the shares at the higher strike price, which will incur a significant loss. The investor bets on the future price of the underlying asset, and if it does not follow that direction, it could result in a huge loss.

Due to this reason, investors using the uncovered position strategy should be highly skilled and experienced regarding the market and the underlying asset.

Chapter 12: Investment Returns

Systematic risks, often referred to as “market risks” or “non-diversifiable risks,” are hazards that transcend the confines of a single company or industry and extend their influence over the entire market or specific market segments.

To navigate systematic risks, investors often adopt a strategic approach in which they diversify their investments across multiple asset classes. When investors allocate their resources to fixed income, cash, and real estate, which each possess their own distinct reaction to systematic risks, they diminish the likelihood of substantial losses.

To make judicious investment decisions, it is imperative to understand and manage these risks.

Measuring Systematic Risk

Systematic risk is calculated by a statistical measure called beta, which explains the relationship between the potential return of an investment and the market’s risk.

Beta is the measure of a security or portfolio’s sensitivity to market movements. A beta equal to one indicates that the stock has the same level of risk as the overall market.

A beta greater than one indicates that the stock has greater volatility than the market. This means the stock will be significantly affected by a slight change in market conditions.

A beta of less than one indicates that the stock has less volatility than the market. This means the stock will be negligibly affected by a change in the market.

Investors usually use systematic risk as a tool to diversify their portfolios. They invest in stocks with different values of beta so they will be less subjected to systematic risks.

Impact of Interest-Rate Risk

Changes in interest rates often affect fixed-income securities like bonds. An increase in interest rates causes bond prices to go down, and a decrease in interest rates will cause bond prices to rise. This is a general rule, and there can be exceptions based upon other factors that affect bond prices.

The impact of a change in interest rate depends on the duration of the investment. Long-term investments are more likely to be affected by interest rate risk than short-term investments.

For example, an investor holds a bond with a fixed interest rate of 5%, and the market interest rates rise to 6%. The bond's market value will likely decrease as other investors can now buy new bonds offering a higher interest rate.

However, if the interest rate falls, the investor will receive higher returns as they will now offer higher interest than anyone else in the market.

Investors use many strategies to adjust their returns in response to interest rate fluctuations in the market. For example, they may diversify their fixed-income investments or use bond funds/exchange-traded funds.

What Are Unsystematic Risks?

An unsystematic risk is associated with a specific company or industry. Such risks can be diminished through the diversification of portfolios.

Unsystematic risks are caused by uncertainties within a specific company or industry. Causes of unsystematic risk include regulatory changes, shifts in management, or product recalls. For example, if one of the products of a food company is found to be contaminated, this can affect the company's reputation and cause it to lose its customers' trust.

Sometimes the exact reason for the occurrence of unsystematic risk is difficult to pinpoint. For example, a certain change in health policy may alter the value of investors' health care stocks, but it will be difficult to determine which specific policy change is responsible for it.

Other Types of Risks

Investors face other kinds of risks as well, including capital risk, credit risk, currency risk, legislative risk, opportunity risk, reinvestment risk, and repayment risk. Each of these risks is detailed below.

Capital Risk

Capital risk is the chance that investors will lose part or all of their investments in a company if its share prices fall. This can also be regarded as a market risk where if the market condition goes in an unfavorable direction, the investor might suffer a significant loss.

The most effective method to manage capital risk is regular risk assessment and diversification. A regular risk assessment will examine the underlying assumptions in order to quantify capital risks. No amount of adjustment or diversification can make any investment risk-free, but these strategies can help manage and mitigate potential risks.

Diversification can also help diminish capital risk. Diversification of an investment portfolio cannot guarantee higher gains or less risk of loss, but it can provide the potential to improve returns based on the investor's goals and target level of risk.

Credit Risk

Credit risk is the risk of the borrower not returning the principal amount and interest. It causes a financial loss to the lender, can disrupt cash flow, and increases costs for collection.

The credit risk of a borrower can be measured by the five Cs:

- Credit history.
- Capacity to repay.
- Capital.
- Loan conditions.
- Associated collateral.

If a loan is given to a customer with a high credit risk profile, the individual will be charged higher interest rates to compensate for the higher risk. If the credit history of a customer is too risky, the creditors may decline a loan.

The only way for high-risk borrowers to get lower interest rates is to improve their risk profile.

Currency Risk

Currency risk, also known as exchange-rate risk, is the risk of fluctuations in the price of one currency affecting another. It affects investors with assets or business operations across national borders as it can create unexpected profits or losses.

Currency risks can be effectively reduced by hedging as this balances out currency fluctuations. To avoid losses caused by currency risk, investors usually expand their business operations in countries that have strong rising currencies and interest rates.

Legislative Risk

Legislative risks result from changes in laws or regulations that have a direct impact on the value of investments. This includes laws that directly involve investments and those that change the demand patterns of the company's customers.

Investors usually avoid legislative risk by staying up to date with legislative changes and investing in companies that have successfully adjusted to navigate through government regulatory changes in the past.

Opportunity Risk

Opportunity risk is the risk of not choosing a potential investment opportunity, which happens when investors choose to allocate their resources toward one investment while leaving others.

For example, investors may decide to go with a safe, risk-free option that provides guarantees of a return but not necessarily a high one. By doing that, they might miss out on higher returns on riskier assets like stocks or real estate.

However, opportunity risk is not always negative. Sometimes investors choose the best opportunity out of all the available ones in terms of returns and risk.

Reinvestment Risk

Reinvestment risk refers to the risk that future proceeds may have, to be reinvested at a potentially lower interest rate than the original investment. It is particularly relevant to fixed-income securities such as bonds.

For example, an investor may hold a bond with a fixed interest rate of 5%. The investor initially plans to channel returns back into similar bonds at the same rate. However, when the bond matures and the investor receives the principal, the prevailing interest rates have plunged to a meager 2%. Now the investor can't reinvest the funds at the initially anticipated rate of 5%.

Investors seek to mitigate reinvestment risk through portfolio diversification. By balancing their investments across an array of avenues and assessing prevailing market conditions, they make informed investment decisions that shield them from the whims of the market and optimize their returns.

Repayment Risk

Repayment refers to the process of the borrower returning the borrowed money, including the principal and the interest amount. Repayment risk is the risk that the borrower will be unable to return the borrowed amount on time, which can lead to a decrease in the income of the lender and affect the value of the loan as an investment.

For example, an investor buys a bond from the company. At the time of its maturity, the company is unable to pay back that amount, which includes the full principal and the interest payment. This will cause the investor a loss of income and a decline in the value of the investment.

What Is Passive (Strategic) Asset Allocation?

Passive asset allocation is a strategic way to achieve a balance between potential returns and losses based on the investor's financial goals and risk tolerance. It involves buying and holding a diversified mix of assets without making frequent adjustments to the portfolio.

There are three main components of passive asset allocation: buy-and-hold, indexing, and systematic rebalancing.

Buy-and-hold

Buy-and-hold is when an investor acquires a diversified mix of asset classes and maintains them over an extended period, which allows the investor to prioritize long-term performance over the fluctuations of the market.

Indexing

Indexing is when an investor chooses low-cost index funds or ETFs that mirror the movements of broad market indices. By indexing, investors gain exposure to the expansive market while minimizing fees, which provides a compelling avenue for broad market participation.

Systematic Rebalancing

Systematic rebalancing entails periodic adjustments of the portfolio's assets to maintain the desired asset allocation.

Should certain stocks outperform and begin to dominate the portfolio, rebalancing comes into play. The investor will either sell a portion of these stocks or buy more of other assets to realign the asset allocation based on the investor's objectives.

Chapter 13: Investment Returns

When a dividend of a company is declared, a shareholder must be on the company's books by a set date in order to receive the dividend. These dates are set to ensure the timely payment of dividends to the company shareholders.

Declaration Date

The declaration date is when a statement is released that specifies the details of the next payment. Details include the dividend's size, ex-dividend date, and payment date.

Payment Date

On this date, the stockholders receive the dividend amount. It is usually weeks after the ex-dividend date.

Record Date

This is the date on which the company decides which stakeholders are eligible to receive the dividend. Investors that own shares on this date are eligible. .

Ex-dividend Date

The ex-dividend date is set before the record date. If investors purchase stocks on the ex-dividend date or after, they will not be eligible to receive the next dividend payment.

Example of Dividend Dates and Due Bills

Company XYZ declares a dividend of $5 per share on October 1 with a record date of October 15, an ex-dividend date of October 13, and a payment date of November 1.

The declaration date will be October 1, on which the company has declared that it will pay $5 per share to the shareholders.

Investors who purchase the stock on or after October 13, the ex-dividend date, will not be entitled to receive the dividend.

On October 15, the record date, the company will decide which shareholders will receive the dividend. Only the investors who own the stock on or before the record date will be eligible.

On November 1, the company will distribute the dividend payments to all the eligible shareholders, which includes the investors who own the stock on or before the record date and those who purchased shares during the due bill period.

Note that if investors bought shares of company XYZ on October 4, they would receive their dividend payments on the payment date, i.e., November 1, as they were holders of the stock before the ex-dividend date. However, if an investor sells their shares to another party on or after the ex-dividend date but before the payment date, the seller of the share (not the buyer) will still receive the dividend payment on the payment date.

Stock Dividends

Companies who intend to preserve their cash reserves often pay the dividend amount as additional shares in the company.

Although paying shareholders in stock dividends can be a strategy to conserve cash, it does not necessarily indicate the overall financial condition of the company.

In some scenarios, stock dividends increase the number of outstanding shares, which shows a healthy financial condition.

However, stock dividends can also dilute the value of existing shares and reduce the earnings per share, indicating a decline in financial condition.

The stock dividend provides a tax advantage. This is because stock dividends are not taxed until they are cashed. When they are cashed, investors pay the tax based on the capital gains on the profit they received from a sale.

In the case of cash dividends, the income tax is applied to each cash dividend payment.

For example, Company XYZ has two million shares outstanding and decides to issue a 10% stock dividend. This means for every 10 shares a shareholder holds, the individual will receive one extra share. If a shareholder has 200 shares in the company, now the person will have 220 shares.

Consider the stock price of Company A to be $10 per share; it would adjust to $9.09 per share after the stock dividend. In this way, the number of shares of investors in the company increases, but their value remains the same.

Calculating Current Yield for Equities

The current yield for equities is the income generated by a stock relative to its market price. This is a metric investors use to calculate the amount of income generated on a particular stock based on the current market price of that stock.

The current yield for equity is based on past dividends but does not guarantee future dividend payments.

Return on Bond Investments

The return amount an investor gets from investing in bonds is called return on bond investments. This includes returns from both bond interests and coupon payments. Return on bond investments refers to the total gains an investor receives from a bond, which can include both periodic coupon payments and capital appreciation or depreciation.

A coupon payment refers to the periodic interest payment an investor receives from holding a bond. The bond issuer pays periodic interest, known as the coupon payment, to the bondholder based on the bond's coupon rate.

Price appreciation is the process of receiving higher returns if the face value of the bond rises. Prices of bonds usually fluctuate with the change in market interest rates.

When the market interest rate goes down, the value of existing bonds with higher coupon rates increases and vice versa. This is how bondholders can receive higher returns.

Bond investments depend upon the investor's circumstances, goals, and risk tolerance. Low-yield bonds are a suitable option for investors looking for risk-free mixed portfolio investment. High-yield bonds offer high returns on high-risk grounds.

Nominal and Current Yield on Bonds

Nominal yield, also known as coupon rate, is the interest rate the bond issuer pays to its investor. This is stated on the bond's face value to represent the bond's ultimate return. For example, if a bond has a face value of $5,000 and a coupon rate of 10%, the bond will pay $500 per year in interest ($5,000 x 10%).

The current yield is the amount of return a bond generates based on the market price. As the current yield depends on the current market price, it will fluctuate with changes in the market.

The current yield is the ratio of earned interest to the bond's current price. It depicts the expected rate of return on a bond investment.

Current Yield Calculations

The formula for current yield is:

Annual coupon payment / Bond's current market value.

Current yield is the most effective indication of the profitability of a bond as its calculations involve the purchase price.

For example, if a bond has a face value of $5,000 and a coupon rate of 10%, the bond will pay $500 per year in interest ($5,000 x 10%). If the current market price for the bond is $850, then using the annual interest payment and this market price, the current yield can be calculated.

Other factors such as the bond's credit rating, maturity date, and overall market conditions are not considered while calculating the current yield on bond investment. Investors should carefully consider all factors when making investment decisions.

Price vs. Yield Relationships

Price and yield have an inverse relationship, which means that one will fall while the other rises. If the interest rates rise, the yield of newly issued bonds will also increase to compensate investors for the high risk.

This will make the already existing bonds a less attractive option for investors. To compensate for this, their price will fall.

Price vs. Yield Example

For example, an investor buys a bond of $1000 face value, a coupon rate of 5%, and a maturity date of 10 years. If the interest rate rises to 5.5%, the yield of newly issued bonds will increase. To balance this, the price of the bond will fall to adjust to 5.5%.

The rate of change of the price of the bond will depend upon the original yield of the bond, which is why the relationship between price and yield is not linear; it is convex. The bonds with higher yields will be more sensitive to price change and vice versa.

Yield-to-call (YTC)

Yield-to-call (YTC) applies to callable bonds. Callable bonds allow the issuer to repurchase them on the call date.

YTC is the amount of return bondholders can expect if they hold a bond until the call date, which is somewhere before the maturity date.

YTC is an important factor to be considered for callable bonds. It is especially important for municipal bonds and bonds issued by corporations. A callable bond with a high YTC is much more attractive than a non-callable bond with a lower yield.

However, callable bonds come with certain risks that non-callable bonds do not.

Cost Basis, Capital Events and Capital Losses

Cost basis is the original amount initially invested for an asset plus any fees or commission involved. The cost basis is used to determine the capital gain value. It is also important if the investor is reinvesting the dividends instead of taking earnings in cash.

Reinvesting distributions can adjust the cost basis, and this will potentially affect the amount of capital gain or loss when the asset is later sold. Therefore, calculating the cost basis is essential to calculate gains and losses after a stock is sold.

Capital events refer to all events that affect the ownership or value of an asset. For example, buying or selling an asset, receiving dividends or interest, or participating in a stock split.

A capital loss is the loss an investor suffers when a security is sold at a price less than the purchase price. This loss is used to reduce the income tax burden for future capital gains.

Total Return

The total return is the rate of ROI over an evaluation period. It is a financial term that considers the total return, including interest, capital gains, dividends, and distributions realized over a period to measure the total overall performance of an investment.

The total return is an important factor to consider in the true growth of an investment over time, the company's financial history, and expected future returns.

Measuring Other Investment Returns

Some other returns should be considered by investors.

Risk-Adjusted Return – This refers to the return obtained after subtracting the potential risk that can decrease the return. This return is important to calculate because it can easily differentiate whether an investment with high risk and high loss or an investment with lower return and lower loss is more attractive.

Risk-Free Return – This is the theoretical return obtained from investments with no risk of loss. This is usually used as a benchmark to compare against other investments that have a risk of loss. An investment with the risk of loss should offer higher returns than an investment with no loss at all.

Types of Indexes Investors Use

Narrow-based indexes are tools in finance that allow investors to track the performance of financial markets and specific asset classes. Some of the most commonly used indexes are narrow-based indexes, broad-based indexes, equity indexes, bond indexes, and tracking indexes.

Narrow-based Indexes

These indexes have the role of monitoring a limited segment of the market. For instance, the S&P 500 is an index that follows the performance of 500 leading companies in the U.S. stock market.

Likewise, the Nasdaq 100 Index tracks the performance of the 100 largest companies listed on the Nasdaq exchange.

Broad-based Indexes

These indexes monitor a broader segment of the market. For example, the Dow Jones Composite Average is an equity market index that encompasses 65 companies that are traded on the New York Stock Exchange (NYSE) and the Nasdaq.

Equity Indexes

These indexes track the performance of specific stocks in specific markets.

For example, Wilshire Associates Equity Index tracks the performance of all publicly traded US stocks.

The Russell 2000 Index tracks the performance of small-cap stocks, and the Nasdaq Composite tracks the performance of almost all stocks listed on the Nasdaq stock exchange.

The Nasdaq 100 tracks equity securities issued by 100 of the largest non-financial companies listed on the Nasdaq stock exchange.

Bond Indexes

These indexes track the performance of bonds in specific markets. For example, the Barclays Capital Aggregate Bond Index tracks the performance of investment-grade US bonds.

Tracking Indexes

Investors often need to know how well their investment is performing relative to a benchmark.

Tracking indexes are used by investors to compare their return on investment with the return of the index. This can help investors know where they stand relative to the market.

Chapter 14: Orders and Trading Strategies

Broker-dealers play a key role in ordering and trading. They are financial entities that execute orders and help clients strategize to acquire high returns on their securities. According to FINRA, there are over 3,900 broker-dealers in the financial market today.

What Is a Broker-Dealer?

A broker-dealer is any person or entity that buys and sells securities. This could be a person or a firm that buys or sells securities for their own account or on behalf of another customer.

If someone is trading, i.e., buying or selling, on behalf of another customer, they are referred to as a broker or an agent. If someone trades for themselves or their own account, they act as a dealer or a principal.

Types of Broker-Dealers

There are two types of broker-dealers: wirehouses and independents.

Wirehouse – A wirehouse is a full-service broker-dealer firm, often part of a larger, national corporation, that provides a wide range of services to its customers such as investment advice, research, and financial planning.

Independent – An independent broker-dealer is not affiliated with a particular investment or mutual fund company. This allows them to offer a broader range of investment products to their clients. They may sell or trade products that they acquire from various sources.

Functions of a Broker-Dealer

A broker-dealer facilitates the process of buying and selling securities either on their own behalf or on behalf of a customer. This entails the following functions:

1. Facilitating the free flow of securities in an open market.
2. Ensuring and guaranteeing a market for securities for clients.
3. Buying and selling securities.

Markup and Markdowns

Markups and markdowns are the differences between the purchase or selling price of a security and its original cost or its value at the end of a certain period. They determine the profit or loss a dealer can make on trading securities.

What Is a Markup?

There are two prices to consider when trading securities. One is an offering price that an investment has among the broker-dealers, and the other is the price that a customer is charged for the respective investment.

The offering price is the price that the sellers of the product are willing to sell it for or the price they are willing to accept in exchange for the investment opportunity.

A markup is the difference between the lowest current offering price and the price charged to the customer.

The selling price is usually higher than the cost price if a return or profit is to be earned. The markup between the selling price and the cost price determines the profit.

What Is a Markdown?

Sometimes, a dealer may offer the customer a price lower than the bidding or offering price. The markdown is the difference between the highest bid price of the security at the respective time and the lower price that the customer was charged for it.

There are various reasons for this, such as cutting a loss or trading for a long-term gain.

For whatever reason, the selling price is lower than the cost price, which leads to a markdown.

Fair Prices and Commissions

The financial market operates under specific regulatory mechanisms and factors. These elements guide the setting of market prices for products, ensuring they are priced fairly. To determine a product's price, whether for direct sale to customers or for outsourcing, it is essential to consider the current market conditions and financial situation.

Brokers have to charge a fair fee and a fair commission for their services. This also targets markups. Brokers or dealers are not allowed to charge the customer a price that is too high compared to the bidding price.

Factors That Influence the Charge

Factors that influence the charge include type of security, market availability, price, nature of the member's business, and pattern of markups.

Type of Security

There are multiple kinds of securities. Some demand a higher price than others. For instance, stocks and bonds.

Stocks can carry a different markup than bonds, but it's not universally true that stocks always have a higher markup than bonds. This means it would be fair to charge a higher markup for a stock transaction compared to a bond transaction.

Market Availability

The impact of the availability of security works similarly to the concept of supply and demand. If security is active and guarantees a higher return, it is bound to carry a higher markup.

Price

Lower-priced securities might have a higher percentage markup due to fixed transaction costs. Usually, a higher commission is charged by the broker-dealer. If the transaction involves a small amount of money, the markup is expected to be higher.

Nature of the Member's Business

The services and facilities demanded by each customer are different. This contributes to a difference in service fees and commissions charged. FINRA allows for the adjustment of such discrepancies.

Pattern of Markups

The pattern of markups also influences the fees charged by broker-dealers to the customer. Each markup has to be fair according to the financial circumstances, and the pattern of these markups impacts the financial conditions.

The 5% Policy

The 5% policy was adopted by the National Association of Securities Dealers (NASD) in 1943 to provide guidance on markups, prices, and commissions. It suggests that, in general, broker-dealers' markups or markdowns of 5% or less above or below the prevailing market price would be considered fair. However, it is not a hard-and-fast rule,

The 5% adjustment is deemed a fair markup or markdown, but FINRA emphasizes that the policy should be used as a guide, not a rule. All relevant circumstances should be considered when determining the fairness of a markup or markdown. The cost of the transaction still works as a determining factor for the markup; the 5% policy is merely for reference.

Discretionary Orders

Discretionary orders are those the broker-dealer has authority over. When a broker-dealer has to handle an account or a transaction, certain protocols should be followed. It is up to the client or customer how much latitude the broker is given regarding the financial decision-making during the transaction.

Discretionary Accounts

In the case of discretionary accounts, the broker is given some authority to make decisions regarding certain factors while managing the account. These may include decisions about which securities to buy or sell, the amount of securities to buy or sell, and the timing of transactions.

For instance, decisions such as the timing of the transaction and the price at which to execute a trade can be made by the broker, which allows for a more hands-off approach by the investor.

In this case, the agent or broker does not require complete authorization from the client. However, there are some limitations to the authority of the broker, and each decision made should benefit the client.

Non-discretionary Accounts

With non-discretionary accounts, the broker is given no autonomous authority. Client authorization is required for each step of the transaction. Each financial decision regarding the investment portfolio and transaction is made respecting the demands of the client.

Types of Transactions

There are three types of transactions: purchase, long sale, and short position.

Purchase

Purchase transactions entail the purchase of a security. Investors can purchase a security at a markup from the lower bidding price and invest for a higher return in the future.

Long Sale

The term "long" refers to the expectation that the value of an investment will rise. If someone buys a security and creates a long position, it means the investor owns that security or the respective shares in question, with the expectation that its value will increase.

Short Position

A short position refers to securities sold with the intention of profiting from a decline in the price of that security. If an investor or broker-dealer borrows a security to sell with the intention to repurchase it later at a lower price, this creates a short position.

Types of Orders

In a financial market, different trading strategies call for different order types. Each broker and each exchange may offer a variety of order types. There are two main types of orders: market orders and limit orders.

Market Order

A market order entails buying and selling a financial commodity at the current market price. It is the most basic order, and its execution is fairly simple. However, the selling or buying price is not always exactly equal to the current market price.

Due to the volatility and liquidity of a financial market, there is always a slight discrepancy between the execution price and the expected price. For example, the cryptocurrency market is also highly volatile, which contributes to the inconsistency in market prices.

Limit Order

A limit order does not depend on the market price; it is executed based on the specified price or a better value. There is a difference in how a limit order applies to buying and selling transactions.

Buy Order

A limit buy order is executed at either the limit level price or at a price lower than that level. In the case of buying, a lower price is better than the limit price as it will not cost as much.

For example, if an investor places a buy order for a security at a specified limit price of $50, the next day, the order could be executed at an even better price of $49.75 or at least at what the desired specified limit price was, i.e., $50.

Sell Order

A limit sell order is executed at either the specified limit level price or one that is even higher. If the transaction is made or the order is executed at a price higher than the limit level, a sell order is more profitable as the investor will earn more.

For example, the market rate for the securities you're selling is $50, but you're expecting that you might get a higher return on it, so you will place a sell limit order for $50.20.

If the stock reaches that mark, your order will be executed at the price you wanted.

Stop Orders

The sentiment of trading orders can be influenced by market conditions, such as bullish or bearish trends.

Bullish Markets

Bullish markets are characterized by rising prices. The prices rise when there is an increase in demand for a security.

For instance, the higher the demand for gold, the higher the prices, as investors will go bullish on that commodity. This can happen in the case of shares and stocks as well. So, bullish stocks will have higher demand and higher prices.

Bearish Stocks

Bearish stock markets are characterized by falling prices. The prices fall when the demand for a certain commodity falls and its supply in the market goes up.

Moreover, bearish investors will pour out of the stocks that they lose confidence in, which causes a sharp decline in their prices. Investors may be influenced by bear market cycles that might result from political instability in a country.

Stop and Stop-Limit Orders

Let's look at some of the types of stop and stop-limit orders.

Stop Orders

Stop orders are used primarily to trigger an order when a specific price is reached. They become active and visible to the market once the stop price is reached. Once a stock's market price reaches that value, a stop order is activated.

Stop-Limit Orders

A stop-limit order incorporates features of both limit and stop orders. It has two prices: a stop price and a limit price. In this case, a limit order is activated for the purchase or sale of security once the specific stop price is met.

A stop-limit order works differently in the case of buying and selling a financial commodity.

Sell-Stop Order

A sell-stop order works best in the case of protecting yourself from incurring a huge loss while selling a share.

For example, the trading value for a stock of a company is $75, but an investor wants to protect their funds from potential losses if the price drops significantly. The investor would set a sell-stop order at $71.

If the value for that share actually does drop and sales are made at the value of $71 or below, the order will be automatically activated and the sell order will become a market order.

Buy-Stop Order

A buy-stop order gives traders control over the price and time at which they want to trade. The trade will be triggered at the top level, and the limit price shows the price they are willing to pay to buy that commodity.

Order Qualifiers

There are certain qualifiers for orders.

Day Order

Trading is done over a certain period. A day order is set in a manner carried out during the respective trading day. Once the trading day ends, the day order expires.

Good-Till-Canceled (GTC) or Open Order

A GTC order is quite common with advanced traders. A specified time is set for each respective order, and the open position and the order remain valid until it is canceled by the trader.

Chapter 15: Settlement and Corporate Actions

Navigating the intricate web of trading financial securities requires a deep understanding of the trading process, settlement dates, and the role of the various entities involved.

The Trading Process

The trading process comprises five main steps: order entry, execution, clearing, settlement, and custody.

Order Entry

The first step of trading financial securities is order entry. Chapter 14 explained the types and functions of orders and trade strategies. The orders can be entered as market orders, day orders, GTC orders, stop orders, or limit orders.

Execution

Execution of the order entails the establishment of an agreement between the buyer and the seller. This agreement is legally binding as the securities, shares, or stocks are transferred from the seller to the buyer in exchange for a mutually agreed upon amount of money.

Clearing

The clearing process includes all the protocols that finalize the agreement and lead to the settlement of the trade. The capital or financial accounts of all the parties involved are updated, including any third party, such as a broker.

Members like brokers use clearinghouses to clear the payments and ensure everything is in order for all involved parties. Margin postings, the transfer of net payments, and the recording of all transactions are all part of the process of clearing.

Settlement

Once the books are in order, the trade is settled. This includes the exchange of money for financial commodities between the seller and the buyer. The actual trade is made on the previously agreed-upon settlement date.

Custody

The custody of the shares or securities is handed over to the buyer as the payment is made to the seller. This concludes the process of trading. Note that securities or shares are typically traded electronically, not in physical form.

Settlement Dates

The settlement date is the date on which the trade is finalized. The securities or financial assets are transferred to the buyer, and the money is transferred to the seller in exchange for the asset.

Settlement dates differ for different types of securities.

Corporate and Municipal Securities

Corporate and municipal securities are traded and settled in two business days (T+2) once the order is executed.

US Government Securities and Option

In the case of government securities and options, the trade is settled within one business day (T+1).

Cash Settlement for Any Security

Any cash settlement or net payment to be made to the second party is cleared on the same day of the trade.

Seller's Option

A seller's option grants the decision right to the seller, and the individual can decide upon certain elements of the agreement.

For example, the person can choose the time, mode, and place of the transaction or trade. As it is a negotiated settlement, it cannot be earlier than two business days after the trade.

When Issued

The settlement date can also be set as determined by the terms of the specific security or contract.

Regulation T Payment Date

Sometimes, member firms are required to extend credit to their customers. Because of this, they have to collect margins to prevent credit risk. This allows the clients or customers to purchase securities despite insufficient funds, with delayed or partial payments.

This is where Regulation T comes in.

What Is Regulation T?

Regulation T provides a set of rules governing credit extensions between clients and brokers.

When a client is short on funds, the broker can activate a line of credit so the client can buy the security using that borrowed money. This can also be referred to as buying on margin.

According to Regulation T, an investor or client has to fund 50% of the purchase of an asset with cash. The person can only borrow a maximum of 50% of the funds needed to make that purchase from the broker or firm.

Regulation T Payment Date

Regulation T sets the maximum period for a customer to pay for a securities transaction as two business days from the trade date. If the payment is not made within this period, the brokerage firm may be required to sell out the securities.

What Is a Good Delivery?

A good delivery meets all the essential requirements of the transaction. The result is a smooth transfer of ownership or custody of the financial assets from the seller to the buyer.

The criteria or requirements of a good delivery are unique to each market and product.

General Requirements of a Good Delivery

1. The product must be properly endorsed.

2. Bonds and shares must be delivered respectively to the number previously decided upon.

3. The delivery of the correct denomination of certificates must be made.
4. In cases of specific securities:
    a. Bearer bonds
        i. The bearer bonds are mostly unregistered, so they must be in denominations of $1,000 or $5,000.
        ii. The delivery must include unpaid coupons as they represent interest payments.
    b. Registered bond
        i. Good delivery of registered bonds demands the bond to be in multiples of $1,000 par value, but this doesn't mean that $1,000 is the bond's maximum value.
    c. Stocks
        i. One hundred shares is a common trading unit, often called a 'round lot'. However, with the advent of electronic trading, it is now common for shares to be bought and sold in any number, not necessarily multiples or divisors of 100. These are referred to as 'odd lots.'

Corporate Actions Department

The corporate actions department deals with the following corporate actions: stock splits, rights offerings, proxies, tender offers, mergers and spin-offs, exchange offers, and stock buybacks.

Stock Splits

In a stock split, the company issues more shares to the current shareholders and increases the number of shares. This effectively reduces the price of each individual share, and makes the stock more affordable. As the number of outstanding shares increases, the price of each share drops accordingly. However, it does not necessarily impact the value of the company.

Rights Offerings

A rights offering is made to existing shareholders so they can purchase more shares of stocks proportionate to their previous or initial stock holdings. These additional stock purchases are also known as rights.

The stocks are offered at discounted but specified prices and at a specific time. The rights offering is an invitation to buy more stocks. There is no obligation on the second party to do so.

Proxies

A corporate action department also offers proxies. In case a shareholder cannot be present in person, the management offers the option of voting by proxy.

To formalize the process, the corporate action department will issue proxy statements and ballots. These provide shareholders with relevant information about the issues to be voted upon. They also provide a means for shareholders to give instructions on how to vote.

Tender Offers

The corporate action department provides tender offers. This is primarily a bid to purchase the stocks of a shareholder in a corporation. It is a public declaration of the willingness of a party to buy those stocks and an invitation to shareholders to sell their stocks at a designated time, at a certain price.

The shareholders are further incentivized to sell their stocks by setting a higher buying price for each share. Tender offers are often used in a takeover bid and involve a certain number of shares to be bought or sold for control over a company.

Mergers and Spin-offs

The corporate action department also oversees mergers and acquisitions. A merger is the combination of two or more firms or companies into a single corporation.

This results in the surrender of stocks of one company and its acquisition by another. In a merger, it's not that stocks and shares are physically merged; rather, one company's stocks are exchanged or bought out.

A spin-off involves creating an independent company through the sale or distribution of new shares of an existing firm of a parent company. This new firm is then distinct from the parent company.

In the case of a spin-off, the shares of the new firm are often distributed to the existing shareholders of the parent company. They can also be offered to new investors.

Exchange Offers

Exchange offers entail exchanging one type of security for another. This could involve swapping bonds for stocks, stocks for bonds, or even a bond with a certain maturity and coupon rate for another bond with a different maturity and coupon rate. This process is not limited to fixed-income securities.

Stock Buybacks

Companies tend to buy their stocks back as well. They do so by paying the shareholder the required amount per share in order to buy back the share they had initially distributed or sold to private and public investors.

There are many reasons for stock buybacks, like increasing the value of the equity of the company, consolidating the shares of the company, or as a financial power move.

Cost Basis and Capital Events

Corporate actions such as stock splits, dividends, and distributions play a key role in impacting the cost basis, which is the original value of an asset for tax purposes, usually the purchase price.

What Are Stock Splits or Stock Dividends?

Stock splits and stock dividends are methods by which companies distribute additional shares to their shareholders.

What Are Stock Splits?

Stock splits impact the number of shares that each shareholder owns without changing their overall equity in the company. The primary aim is to increase the liquidity and affordability of the shares.

As the number of stock shares is increased, the price of each share drops accordingly.

What Are Dividends?

A dividend is a portion of the earnings of a company that it distributes to the shareholders. The earnings could be distributed in the form of cash or stock. If the dividend is given in cash, the shareholders get cash for each share they hold.

If the earnings are distributed in the form of stocks, the shareholders get additional shares in the company proportionate to the number of shares they already own. For example, if the shareholders are given a stock dividend of 20%, then for every 5 shares the shareholders own, they get one more share.

Types of Stock Splits

There are two types of stock splits: forward stock splits and reverse stock splits.

Forward Stock Splits

Forward stock splits are the most common form of stock splits. This denotes the splitting of stocks that the shareholders own to increase the affordability of the company's stocks and increase the liquidity of the company, while ensuring the equity remains undisturbed.

These stock splits are commonly in ratios such as 2-for-1, which is 2:1, or 3-for-1, which is 3:1. Other ratios include 10:1 and 3:2. These ratios denote the new number of shares a shareholder receives for each share they previously owned.

For example, if a shareholder initially had ten shares and a two-for-one split occurs, the shareholder will then own 20 shares, but the value of each individual share will be halved. This maintains the overall value of the shares the shareholder owns.

Reverse Stock Splits

Reverse stock splits are the opposite of conventional stock splits. A reverse stock split decreases the number of stocks owned by each shareholder of the company. The outstanding shares of the firm fall, whereas the market price of each share goes up. The equity still remains undisturbed.

For example, if a company has three million outstanding shares, each valued at $6, and the company decides to implement a 3-for-1 reverse stock split, the number of shares will decrease.

Once the policy is executed, the company will end up with one million shares, with each share having a market value of $18. The overall market capitalization of the company and the value of each shareholder's equity remains the same.

Tax Treatment

The cost basis analysis is primarily done for tax purposes. Once the cost basis is determined and adjusted for factors like dividends and stock splits, the resulting gains or losses from the sale of the asset must be reported to the IRS.

The tax treatment dictates that tax rules must be adhered to when computing the gain or loss on the sale of an asset by an individual or company.

Forwarding Official Communications

According to FINRA guidelines and SEC rules, a member is required to process and forward all official information about securities and investments to the beneficial owner. The term "communications" includes communications both at an institutional level and between multiple corporations.

All firms have an annual general meeting for all shareholders to inform them of the financial progress and decisions of the company. If shareholders are unable to attend the meeting in person, they can assign a proxy, which allows them certain authority over the decisions made during the meeting.

Forms 10-K and 10-Q

Form 10-K is an annual report published once a year to disclose company financial information to the SEC and shareholders.

The company is required to disclose the future risks along with the financial standing of the company for public filings. Form 10-K is prepared by the company and must be audited by an independent accountant.

Form 10-Q is a quarterly report. It is less comprehensive than the annual Form 10-K. This quarterly report incorporates the quarter's management discussions, analyses, disclosures, and all relevant financial decisions.

The report helps investors assess the company's performance and decide whether they will make further investments. It is an unaudited document.

Non-objecting Beneficial Owner (NOBO)

A NOBO is an owner whose name is released to companies in which the person owns securities. As the individual's contact information is with the companies, the owner can be contacted for information and communication that is business-related.

Companies, or their agents, may contact NOBOs directly without going through an intermediary.

Objecting Beneficial Owner (OBO)

An OBO opposes the disclosure of personal details, such as name and contact information, to the companies in which the individual holds securities. The owner decides not to release this information and provides instructions to a broker or intermediary to ensure their preferences are respected.

Charging for Services

The firm or person that acts as an intermediary between the buyers and sellers charges the buyers and sellers or the issuers and customers for their services. The fee charged is referred to as a brokerage fee.

Charging Issuers

A broker facilitates the sale of securities to investors. The broker may charge the issuers of those securities a fee for this service.

Charging Customers

According to FINRA guidelines, the brokerage fees charged must be reasonable, and the broker must not unfairly discriminate between customers.

Chapter 16: Customer Accounts

There are three types of accounts available for investors: cash accounts, margin accounts, and options accounts.

Cash Account

A cash account is a basic brokerage account in which customers are obliged to pay full price for the securities purchased at the time of settlement.

Investors are not allowed to borrow funds from their brokers to complete transactions, partake in trading activities, or short-sell securities. A cash account acts like a traditional bank account in which customers are only allowed to use the cash available in their accounts.

Buying securities before paying for them through an investor's cash account violates Regulation T of the Federal Reserve Board. If an investor buys a security in a cash account and sells it before it is fully paid for, this is known as free-riding. Free-riding could force the broker to freeze the account for 90 days.

Margin Account

A margin account is a brokerage account in which investors are permitted to borrow funds from the broker with which to purchase securities. Customers can provide collateral in the form of cash, securities, or investments to cover transaction risks.

Margin accounts allow users to leverage their investment to potentially increase their returns. However, this also magnifies the risk level since borrowed money is invested, and could result in significant losses if the trade does not perform as predicted.

For instance, if Steve buys a stock at $100 per share without using margin and the price rises to $150, he will make a 50% return on his investment. But if he decides to purchase the same stock on margin by paying $50 in cash and borrowing $50 from his broker, he will make a 100% return when the price of the stock rises to $150. This is because he will pay back $50 to the broker, so he will be left with $100. And since he started with $50, he has effectively doubled his money, or had a gain of 100%.

Conversely, if Steve bought the stock by borrowing 50% from a broker and the price plummets to $500 a share, he would lose the entire cash portion of his initial investment. In addition, he would still owe the borrowed amount to his broker, along with interest on the margin loan.

How to Open a Margin Account?

After critical analysis of the benefits and risks of margin, a margin account can be opened with the following steps:

1. Research and select a reputable brokerage firm that offers margin accounts. Meticulously study the account rules to make sure it is suitable for the investor's requirements.

2. A margin agreement will be provided by the broker. The margin agreement outlines the rules and regulations set out by FINRA and the Federal Reserve Board.

3. Provide the investor's name, address, investment experience, financial situation, and source of income.

4. To begin trading on margin, mandatory funds must be deposited as stated by the brokerage firm.

Options Account

Options are financial derivatives that can be used to implement various trade strategies, such as hedging against potential losses, income generation, or future market speculation. They are distinct from stocks, as they provide the right, but not the obligation, to buy or sell the underlying asset.

How to Open an Options Account?

To qualify for an options account, a broker must approve the investor's account eligibility by assessing his knowledge of options contracts, trading strategies, and investment know-how, and his ability to withstand the risks of options trading.

The investor must fill out the options agreement provided by the broker, which generally includes the following:

- Personal financial history, such as annual income, net worth, and employment data.

- Investment goals, such as capital growth, preservation, or speculation.

- Trading experiences, including factors such as the number of years of trading, the number of trades executed per year/month, position sizing, and general investment knowledge.

Broker-dealers will assess the investor's information and determine the level of options trading that he qualifies for. Typically, most brokers offer up to five levels that are designed according to the risk profiles.

Level 1 represents the lowest level of risk, whereas level 5 is considered to be the highest level of risk. Each brokerage firm has variable types of trading levels.

Along with options agreements, FINRA and SEC regulations ensure that brokers will give specific disclosures to investors who are dealing in options. For instance, the broker is advised to provide the investor with a copy of a publication from the Options Clearing Corporation called "Characteristics and Risks of Standardized Options."

Opening an options trading account may require more capital than a simple cash or margin account, depending on the broker and the intended level of trading. It also requires a thorough understanding of the complexities and nuances of options trading. Brokers will put an investor's knowledge and experience to the test. Based on those answers, they will assign an initial trading level based on the level of risk. From that point forward, the investor can begin options trading.

Discretionary Accounts

Some investors may not want to make investment decisions themselves or partake in trading activities due to time constraints or lack of experience or knowledge. They would prefer professionals to manage their accounts on their behalf.

Discretionary accounts are investment accounts that give account holders the ability to authorize financial advisors or trading professionals to make trades or undertake crucial investment decisions. The account holder's approval is not required for each trade. Account holders can approve investment professionals to manage the account based on the holder's risk tolerance and investment goals.

Account managers have a fiduciary responsibility to act in the best interest of the account holders and follow strict guidelines and restrictions set up by the account users.

Discretionary accounts can be beneficial for investors who want to utilize the expertise of professionals to make investment or trading decisions, but it is imperative to review the terms and conditions of the discretionary account agreements before giving financial advisors access to their accounts.

Account holders should regularly monitor their account performance and communicate with the managers to ensure streamlined objectives and goals.

Fee-based Accounts

A fee-based account requires an investor to pay a fee, dependent upon the particular percentage of the assets under management, to an investment professional or financial advisor for investment management services.

In this type of account, the financial advisor or investment professional is incentivized on the overall size of the account instead of commissions on transactions or trades executed.

Fee-based accounts are equipped with several benefits for investors that include:

- A clearly defined fee structure.
- Personalized investment management services set according to investors' financial situation and objectives.
- A healthy relationship between a financial advisor and investor since the interests of both parties are aligned. Advisors who follow the fiduciary standard are obliged to put the interests of their clients before their own.

Not-held Orders

A type of order in which the account holder permits the broker to execute the order at the broker's discretion, without any fixed instructions on how or when to execute the order, is referred to as a "not-held" order.

In this case, the broker has complete flexibility and authority to execute the order when they deem it appropriate by taking liquidity, market conditions, and other relevant factors into account.

Investors prefer placing not-held orders when they are not familiar with the best time of execution of a specific order or the price at which they should buy a specific stock or security.

For instance, an investor could place a not-held order to buy a particular stock but leave the details of execution to the broker. The broker executes the order by analyzing the market condition, investment objective, and the best time for order execution to buy the stock at the best possible value.

Education Savings Plans

Education savings plans are tax-advantaged investment accounts designed to help families save money for their children's future education expenses.

Coverdell Education Savings Account (ESA)

Named after Senator Paul Coverdell, who sponsored the legislation that created the account, Coverdell ESA allows families to save for both primary and secondary as well as higher education expenses.

Contributions made to this account are also invested in mutual funds or other investment vehicles, and earnings grow tax-free, provided they are only used for qualified educational expenses.

In the United States, the total contributions for the beneficiary of a Coverdell ESA cannot be more than $2,000 in any year, no matter how many accounts have been established for that child. It is mandatory to make contributions before the tax-filing deadline for the year in which they are intended to apply.

Moreover, it is restricted to families below a certain income threshold based on their adjusted gross income. The ability to contribute to a Coverdell ESA begins to phase out for individual taxpayers with modified adjusted gross income (AGI) above $95,000 and for joint filers with AGI above $190,000. Taxpayers with higher incomes are not eligible to contribute.

529 Plan

Also referred to as a qualified tuition program, a 529 plan is also a tax-advantaged savings plan originally created to pay for postsecondary education costs. It was later expanded to cover K-12 education in 2017 and apprenticeship programs in 2019. It can be used to pay off student loans up to a lifetime limit of $10,000.

529 plans have significantly higher contribution limits compared to Coverdell Education Savings Accounts (ESAs), often allowing for contributions of hundreds of thousands of dollars. These plans offer flexibility in their usage, as they can be utilized not only to pay off student loans up to $10,000 but also to cover qualified expenses associated with apprenticeship programs that have received approval from the Department of Labor.

No restrictions apply to the income level of contributors; however, fees may apply to 529 accounts and investments have no guaranteed returns.

Traditional IRAs and Roth IRAs

An individual retirement account (IRA) is a type of tax-advantaged savings account available for individuals in the United States to save money for retirement. There are two main types of IRAs: traditional and Roth.

Traditional IRAs

In this type of IRA, individuals are permitted to contribute pretax income up to a certain annual limit and the growth of contributions is tax-deferred until withdrawal during retirement.

At the time of withdrawal, funds are taxed as ordinary income. Furthermore, contributions to a traditional IRA may be tax-deductible, depending upon the individual's income and certain other factors.

Roth IRAs

In Roth IRAs, individuals are permitted to contribute after-tax income. These contributions are not tax-deductible, but the growth of contributions and qualified withdrawals in retirement are tax-free.

For the tax year 2023, the contribution limit for both traditional and Roth IRAs is set as $6,000 for people under age 50 and $7,000 for individuals aged 50 and older.

Traditional vs. Roth IRAs

Withdrawal Penalties

Tax-deferred withdrawals from traditional IRAs are only available without penalty after a person turns 59 1/2. For early withdrawals, a 10% penalty is charged along with the income tax.

In the case of Roth IRAs, contributions can be withdrawn without penalty at any time. Earnings can be withdrawn without penalty and taxes if certain conditions, like the 5-year aging requirement and being over age 59 1/2, are met.

Early withdrawal penalty can be avoided if the investor falls under a short list of IRS-approved purposes that include permanent disability, paying higher educational expenses, or substantially equal periodic payments (SEPPs) under rule 72(t).

Required Minimum Distributions (RMDs)

Unlike traditional IRAs, which mandate the initiation of fund withdrawals at the age of 72, Roth IRAs have no such stipulations for compulsory distributions.

Annual RMD amounts are calculated based on life expectancy and total account balance.

IRA Rollovers

It is generally not advantageous to roll over a Roth IRA into a Traditional IRA due to the potential tax implications.

However, if an investor expects their future tax rate to shoot up compared to the current rate and their earnings are high enough to prevent them from contributing directly to a Roth IRA, a Roth conversion can be used to roll over their traditional IRA to Roth IRA.

401(k) and Profit-Sharing Plans

A 401(k) is a tax-advantaged retirement savings plan offered by various American employers. The name 401(k) is derived from a section of the Internal Revenue Code (IRC).

If an employee signs up for a 401(k), a percentage of the employee's paycheck is sent directly to an investment account. Many employers offer to match part or all of that contribution or even facilitate a profit-sharing plan.

For example, if Sara works at a company and earns $100,000 a year, the company may offer a matching contribution to her 401(k) up to a certain percentage of her salary, or implement a profit-sharing plan which allocates a portion of the company's profits to employees' retirement accounts.

Profit-sharing is usually offered as an incentive to retain employees. A vesting period is declared by the company during which the company's contribution cannot be withdrawn, in order to prevent employees from quitting their job just to access the incentive.

The Setting Every Community Up for Retirement Enhancement (SECURE) Act

The SECURE Act is a federal law that was passed in December 2019. The act was introduced to expand access to retirement savings opportunities and to increase the flexibility of retirement accounts.

Here are some of the prominent provisions of the SECURE Act:

1. The age limit for the required minimum distributions (RMD) was raised for traditional IRAs and 401(k) plans from 70 1/2 to 72.

2. Previously individuals were prohibited from making contributions to a traditional IRA after the age of 70 1/2. The SECURE Act eliminated this age limit.

3. New options were created for part-time workers. The SECURE Act instructed employers to allow long-term and part-time employees to participate in 401(k) plans if they have completed at least 500 hours per year for three consecutive years.

4. The act allowed penalty-free withdrawals of up to $10,000 from retirement accounts for qualifying life events such as the birth or adoption of a child.

5. Annuities in 401(k) plans were introduced through the SECURE Act. Employers can now offer annuities as an investment option in 401(k) plans.

The Employee Retirement Income Security Act of 1974 (ERISA)

ERISA was introduced to avert the mismanagement and misuse of pension plans by establishing standardized rules for the management and operation of these plans. The following are some ERISA rules.

1. **Fiduciary Responsibility** – ERISA requires plan fiduciaries to act solely in the interest of plan participants and beneficiaries rather than for their own personal gain. Fiduciaries must act prudently and make decisions with the exclusive purpose of providing benefits to plan participants.

2. **Reporting and Disclosure Requirements** – ERISA states that employers who offer pension plans must provide transparency by providing participants with specific information, such as summary plan descriptions, annual reports, and plan documents. This ensures that participants are familiar with the terms and conditions of their plan and can easily monitor its management.

3. **Prohibited Transactions** – ERISA forbids certain transactions between pension plans and parties related to it, such as sponsors and fiduciaries. This prevents conflicts of interest that could negatively impact plan participants.

4. **Fiduciary Liability** – Participants are allowed to sue plan fiduciaries for breaches of any fiduciary duty. This acts as a powerful incentive for fiduciaries to act in the best interest of plan participants and beneficiaries.

Chapter 17: Compliance Considerations

FINRA has set forth certain ground rules for brokerage firms to follow.

Brokers can only offer accounts to their customers after they collect the customers' names and residential addresses, their tax identification or Social Security numbers, and source of income/occupation, along with the name and address of employers.

There are also other compliance considerations to keep in mind.

Recordkeeping Requirements for Broker-Dealers

Recordkeeping is imperative in any business, but it is of paramount importance in the financial services sector, which are held to the highest standards of accountability.

Rule 17A-3 of the SEA is a regulation issued by the SEC that lists the rules and requirements of recordkeeping that must be adhered to by broker-dealers.

Rule 17A-3 requires dealers and brokers to meticulously preserve information related to their organization and especially their customers. The following details must be recorded and observed on paper and electronic devices.

- Name and Tax ID numbers of the customers.
- Residential address, contact numbers, and date of birth.
- Employment status of the users and information regarding their association with a different broker.
- Source of income, employment history, and net worth.
- Risk tolerance and financial/investment objectives of the customers.

Updating Client Information

Along with recordkeeping of client information, regular updates and verification are essential for broker-dealers to maintain accuracy and ensure regulatory compliance.

It is compulsory to update the data when:

- The client moves to a new state.
- The client's finances change.

- The client's investment objectives change.

Failure of broker-dealers to regularly update and record relevant information is a violation of the compliance rules. This can result in serious fines amounting to hundreds of thousands of dollars.

What Is Suitability?

The process in which broker dealers match investors with appropriate investment advice and strategies is called suitability. Brokers are advised to analyze their clients' risk tolerance, long-term objectives, financial situation, and other relevant factors in order to provide them with the best possible guidance.

Broker-dealers must create protocols and frameworks to assess customers' investment profiles and make recommendations to ensure compliance with the suitability standard. This can be done by drafting risk tolerance questionnaires and financial information forms and utilizing other tools to define a customer's investment profile.

What Is Institutional Suitability?

Institutional suitability refers to the responsibility of broker-dealers to ensure that their recommendations meet the investment objectives and strategies of institutional investors.

Institutional investors are entirely different from standard retail investors in terms of risk profiles, investment time horizons, capital amounts, and investment instruments. Thus, their investment profiles should be assessed via different protocols.

USA PATRIOT Act

The act was enacted by Congress as a response to the September 11, 2001, terrorist attacks. It was introduced to enhance law enforcement investigatory tools and punish terrorist acts.

Customer Identification Program (CIP)

The Customer Identification Program (CIP) was introduced as part of the USA PATRIOT Act. This is a set of procedures that businesses, financial institutions, and broker-dealers must establish and follow to verify the identity of users and customers.

CIPs have several key requirements, some of which are outlined below:

- Set up a documented CIP program.
- Collect four important pieces of customer identification information: the customer's name, address, date of birth, and government-issued identification number or SSN.
- Establish crucial identity verification procedures.
- Compare the individuals against official government lists.
- Meet recordkeeping requirements established by the law.
- Establish a key process for providing customers with a notice that you require their information for identity verification.

Money Laundering

Money laundering is the process of using large sums of "dirty" or illegal money and making it "clean" so that it can be used as a medium of exchange for investments, trading, or other activities. It involves disguising the original source of illegally obtained money.

The laundering process generally involves three stages: placement, layering and integration.

In the initial stages of placement, the launderer places the illegal proceeds into a legitimate investment instrument or institution to hide the original source of funds. During the layering stage, funds are moved in a series of transactions to further mix and hide the origin.

Integration is the final stage, where the launderer uses the "cleaned" funds for legitimate purposes, such as purchasing luxury goods, investment purposes, buying properties, etc.

What Is the AML Compliance Program, and Why Must Firms Establish It?

Anti-money laundering (AML) refers to a set of procedures, laws, or regulations that are designed to stop the practice of generating income through illegal actions. An AML compliance program specifically refers to the policies and procedures that firms establish to adhere to these regulations, including measures to prevent terrorist financing and fraud-related risks. It is imperative to create a robust AML compliance program for the following reasons.

Heavy Penalties

Regulatory authorities like FATF, FINCEN, and FCA impose heavy monetary fines on organizations that do not adopt an effective AML program. The penalties are not limited to monetary fines. They can also lead to loss of credit ratings and even temporary or permanent closure of the business.

Fraudulent Activities

As the world progresses due to technological shifts, financial institutions and online payment systems are at a high risk of fraud.

Fraudsters can easily exploit every loophole in the AML compliance of banks and other organizations. An attack could result in the loss of customers and millions of dollars.

Customer Value

Businesses that implement effective AML compliance programs can attract thousands of customers. Safety measures allow customers to feel secure about their interaction with a business and encourage them to conduct business with peace of mind.

A bad reputation regarding AML can drop an organization's customer retention and plummet its market value.

FinCEN's Reports

The Financial Crimes Enforcement Network (FinCEN) is a bureau of the Department of the Treasury. FinCEN is responsible for the collection and analysis of financial transactions to combat issues like money laundering and terrorist financing.

Financial institutions and businesses are obligated to file FinCEN reports under the reporting requirements of the Bank Secrecy Act (BSA) and other laws related to AML and counter-terror financing (CTF).

FinCEN reports provide critical information regarding potentially suspicious activity, large transactions, wire transfers from high-risk countries, and other relevant information.

Protecting Client Information

Financial institutions, broker-dealers, and investment companies are strongly advised to keep their clients' information confidential under compliance rules and regulations.

Sensitive client information must not be shared with any non-affiliated third party. Firms can only disclose customer information when:

- It is ordered by a court or government entity.
- The client provides written permission to disclose specific data.

Regulation S-P

The Privacy of Consumer Financial Information Rule, also known as Regulation S-P, is a federal regulation enacted by the SEC in response to the privacy provisions of the Gramm-Leach-Bliley Act.

Under Regulation S-P, all SEC-regulated entities are required to:

- Provide their clients with a privacy notice at the time of establishing the relationship and annually thereafter. The privacy notice must outline and explain how the client's data will be collected, used, and shared with other bodies.
- Ensure that clients are given the provision to opt out of sharing their non-public personal information with third parties.
- Establish a contractual relationship with third-party service providers to ensure that the service providers also maintain strict rules for safeguarding the clients' sensitive information.

Identity Theft Prevention

Identity theft is the crime of obtaining sensitive or personal information, such as the credit card numbers, social security numbers, and bank account details, of another person for the purpose of using their identity to commit fraudulent activities, make unauthorized purchases, or damage the victim's image.

Federal Trade Commission's Red Flags Rule

The Red Flag Rule requires organizations to draft a written identity theft program to identify red flags that signal identity thefts in daily operations. Red flags are specific suspicious activities or practices that suggest the possibility of identity theft.

The FTC outlines five categories of red flags that financial institutions and businesses must be aware of:

1. Notifications, alerts, or warnings from a consumer reporting agency.
2. Unusual or suspicious activity related to an account.
3. Suspicious documents.
4. Dubious personal identification information, such as suspicious inconsistency with a last name or address.
5. Notifications from law enforcement, customers, or victims regarding possible identity theft linked to a specified account.

Use of Stakeholder Information as a Solicitation

The practice of soliciting business through the misuse of stakeholders' sensitive, personal information is very common in the modern world. Fake promotional emails, sales calls, and phishing links are readily used to scam customers.

Businesses should pay attention to the way they communicate with their stakeholders and establish a unique channel to share relevant information with their customers for solicitation purposes. Avoiding misleading and deceptive tactics for business solicitation can be very useful in preventing identity theft.

Account Statements

Broker-dealers are responsible for sending customers their account statements under regulations set out by FINRA. The customer account statement is a periodic summary of customers' investment holdings, assets and overall account activity.

Account statements contain specific customers' basic details, such as account number, name and address, as well as details about held securities, including gains/losses, transactions, and any dividends or interest earned.

Customer account statements help customers monitor their investments and detect any potential discrepancies or issues within their accounts.

Holding Customer Mail

Holding customer mail can be a potential risk for fraud and unauthorized access. Because of this, regulators have stringent rules on the subject to safeguard the privacy and security of customer information.

FINRA Rule 3150 specifies the limited conditions in which FINRA members can hold mail (i.e., customer statements and conformations) for customers. Members can only hold mail if members receive written instructions from the customer requesting that mail be held for a specific time period.

If the time period for holding a request is over three months, there must be an acceptable reason stated. FINRA has strictly stated that "convenience" cannot be used as a reason for holding mail beyond three months.

FINRA members must contact customers and outline the alternate methods of receiving statements, such as email or online portals. Furthermore, FINRA members must obtain the customer's confirmation of receiving this notice and then verify if the mail hold instruction is still valid under "reasonable intervals."

Trade Confirmations

A trade confirmation is a financial document that contains all the relevant details of the trades completed through a brokerage account. It is separate from account statement documents.

Generally, trade confirmations include the date and time of a transaction, the price at which a security was bought or sold, the total quantity of shares traded, the net value of a transaction, the type of order, and fees or commissions on a particular transaction.

Customers should review trade confirmations and point out any discrepancies to their brokers as soon as possible.

Customer Protection Rule

The Customer Protection Rule, otherwise known as Exchange Act Rule 15C3-3, is a regulation established by the SEC for safeguarding customer assets held by broker-dealers, especially under unfortunate circumstances such as the broker-dealers' insolvency or bankruptcy.

Firms are obligated to segregate customer funds and securities from the broker-dealer's assets and promptly deliver them to their owners upon request. Broker-dealers must also store accurate records of customer transactions and provide them with regular statements that accurately reflect account balances and holdings.

In the event of a broker-dealer's bankruptcy or insolvency, customer funds are protected under SIPA. SIPA ensures the protection of customer funds and includes the ability to recover securities and cash up to a certain limit if the broker-dealer goes out of business.

Fidelity Bond

A fidelity bond is an insurance product designed to provide employers with protection against losses resulting from fraudulent or dishonest acts committed by their employees. This coverage extends to both financial and physical losses incurred by the employer.

There are two types of fidelity insurance available on the marketplace.

1. Financial institution bonds (offered to financial institutions).
2. Commercial crime insurance policies (offered to non-financial commercial entities).

Retention of Books and Records

FINRA rule 4511 requires broker-dealers to keep certain books and records on file. It is important to have proper documentation of customer interactions or general business problems in case of an unfortunate event.

The record retention period ranges from three years up to the entire lifetime of the firm, depending on the record type.

Chapter 18: Prohibited Activities

The Securities Exchange Act (SEA) regulates securities (stocks, debentures, bonds) that trade on secondary financial markets.

The act was enacted by the SEC to ensure transparency and a fair environment for investors, prohibit fraudulent activities, and provide important information to existing and future shareholders.

Prohibited Trading Practices

Market Rumors

A market rumor is speculative or misleading information that is spread across market participants regarding a particular security or market event.

Rule 10b-5 of the SEA strictly prohibits the manipulation of a security's price using false information.

Front-Running

This is the illegal practice of purchasing securities based on undisclosed, nonpublic knowledge of a particularly large transaction or market event that could affect the price of the security.

Front-running is a manipulative practice and a form of insider trading because the person who participates in front-running activity can anticipate the security's price movement based on nonpublic information.

Trading Ahead of Customer Orders

If a market maker prioritizes the interest of their own firm rather than that of their clients or investors, this phenomenon is referred to as trading ahead.

Trading ahead takes place when a broker-dealer uses their firm's account to make a trade rather than matching available bids and asks from other participants in the market. This gives market makers an unfair advantage to the detriment of other traders and retail investors.

For instance, a broker receives two simultaneous orders of 1,000 shares of TSLA stock, one to buy 1,000 shares and another to sell 1,000 shares. Instead of matching those orders, the market maker decides to use their firm's account to sell 1,000 shares of TSLA.

This puts the buyer at an unfair disadvantage because the next order in line will be the sell order of 1,000 shares from the previous participant in line. This will likely put downward pressure on the price.

Trading ahead is illegal and strongly condemned by FINRA. It is important to note that trading ahead is part of what is known as *negative obligation*, not to be confused with *front-running*.

What Is Regulation M?

Regulation M is a rule designed to prevent manipulation by any entity or individual with interest in the outcome of an offering during securities offerings, including secondary offerings, private placements, and initial public offerings.

Moreover, Regulation M is formulated to prevent people who participate in the market, such as issuers, underwriters, and selling shareholders, from manipulating the price of a particular security from the leading phase to an offering's completion.

What Is Regulation T?

As discussed earlier, Regulation T states that investors may borrow up to 50% of the purchase price of securities as a loan and cover the remaining 50% of the amount using cash.

For example, an investor wants to obtain a loan from a broker to purchase 100 shares of a stock, with a total purchase amounting to $1,000. According to Regulation T, investors can borrow no more than 50% of the purchase price, which, in this case, is $500, from the broker and must cover the remaining $500 using cash within their account.

When investors purchase securities by borrowing loans up to 50% of the purchase price, the remaining amount must be paid within two business days of the purchase.

If the investor fails to pay the remaining amount, which is referred to as the "Reg T call," the broker-dealer can force sell the securities to meet the call. This is known as "Reg T liquidation."

Along with the liquidation of the securities, investors might be subject to other penalties and restricted from accessing further credit extensions.

Anti-Intimidation/Coordination Interpretation

The anti-intimidation/coordination interpretation is part of section (f) of the Securities Exchange Act of 1934.

This regulation is designed to prohibit brokers and dealers from engaging in activities that may be subject to intimidation or coercion or could instigate the coordination of a grouped trading activity among brokers and dealers.

Trading Rules

The MSRB and FINRA regulate securities trading rules in the US.

MSRB Trading Rules

Rule G-30 – Municipal securities dealers are required to charge fair and reasonable prices in securities transactions.

Rule G-18 – Municipal securities dealers are required to use sound diligence to get the best possible prices for their customers' orders.

Rule G-26 – Municipal securities dealers must establish relevant procedures for the purpose of transferring customer accounts between firms.

Rule G-27 – Municipal securities dealers must establish and maintain a foolproof system to supervise the activities of their employees and ensure compliance with MSRB rules along with federal securities laws.

FINRA Trading Rules

Rule 5320 – Trading ahead of customers is strictly prohibited.

Rule 5270 – Front-running is condemned. Broker-dealers are strongly advised to refrain from taking advantage of nonpublic information related to block transactions.

Rule 5210 – Broker-dealers are required to refrain from influencing the closing price of securities.

Rule 6370 – Broker-dealers are required to report transactions in TRACE-eligible securities to FINRA's TRACE system.

Rule 2020 – Broker-dealers are strongly advised to refrain from engaging in deceptive, manipulative or fraudulent practices linked with the buying or selling of a security.

Insider Trading

Insider trading is an illicit form of trading that involves buying and selling securities based on private or nonpublic information, material, or data.

The SEC actively investigates and prosecutes insider trading cases by charging the perpetrators with severe sanctions.

The New Issue Rule

FINRA introduced the New Issue Rule as a regulation that sets a framework for how the allocation and distribution of new issues of securities, such as IPOs or secondary offerings, will take place.

The New Issue Rule is designed for the sole purpose of promoting transparency, fairness, equal rights, and access to new issues for all eligible investors.

Some important provisions of the regulation include:

1. Broker-dealers are prohibited from selling new issues to accounts in which "restricted persons" have a benefit of interest. According to FINRA Rule 5130, restricted persons include a broader range of individuals and entities, not just the direct or indirect owners of a broker-dealer. They can be broker-dealer personnel, their immediate family members, and other people.
2. Member firms participating in the distribution of new issues are obligated to make a bona fide public offering of the securities at the offering price. Firms cannot withhold or allocate shares to their preferred customers.
3. Allocation of new shares is to be made fairly and impartially, with consideration for important factors such as investors' objectives, trading history, and financial situation. Member firms are required to establish written procedures to ensure compliance and maintain records of their allocation decisions.

What Is Financial Exploitation?

A type of abuse in which a particular person or entity takes advantage of another person's financial resources for the purpose of personal gain is called financial exploitation.

Seniors and people with disabilities or cognitive impairments are typically the victims of financial exploitation. It can take place in the form of theft, fraud, scam, or coercion.

Financial exploitation is illegal, and perpetrators can face serious consequences in the form of criminal charges, monetary fines, and in some cases, life imprisonment.

Financial Exploitation Rules

Senior Safe Act

The Senior Safe Act is a federal law enacted in 2018 that encourages institutions to report financial exploitation of vulnerable adults and elderly people by providing immunity when they report in good faith and under eligible circumstances.

Bank Secrecy Act

Financial institutions are obligated to establish anti-money laundering (AML) programs and report suspicious activities related to the financial exploitation of vulnerable adults.

Temporary Holds

FINRA Rule 2165 was recently amended to permit firms to take the following steps as of March 17, 2022:

- Temporary holds can be placed on securities transactions or disbursement of funds or securities from the accounts of seniors or specified adults if the member believes that financial exploitation of the account holder has occurred.
- Temporary holds on disbursements and transactions can be extended for an additional thirty days if the victim files a request to a state regulator or agency.

Chapter 19: SRO Requirements for Associated Persons

SROs like FINRA and exchanges enforce certain rules and regulations to ensure their members (associated persons) meet the ethical standards of society. The SEC oversees these SROs.

In this chapter, we'll talk about SRO requirements for associated persons.

What Are Associated Persons?

Associated persons are people under the FINRA member firms. Many professionals come under the term "associated persons," such as officers, directors, partners, branch members, employees, and persons engaged in investment banking or securities business.

Associated persons may also include brokers, sales representatives, investment advisors, compliance officers, operation and support staff, and investment bankers. These people are bound by regulatory bodies like FINRA.

Unregistered Persons

Unregistered persons work for FINRA member firms but are not registered with FINRA. These individuals are involved in unregulated services like administrative tasks, operations, and technical support, or they provide support to registered persons at firms and indirectly work on their tasks.

Unregistered persons are not required to qualify for the extensive series of examinations to be eligible to work at firms. They are also not expected to abide by specific ethical and professional standards.

However, being employees of a firm, they are expected to follow the basic rules and regulations and internal policies of the company.

Registered Representatives

Registered representatives are individuals who work for broker-dealer firms that are members of FINRA and are responsible for engaging in securities sales or trading activities. These representatives are either brokers or financial advisors who are authorized to buy and sell securities on behalf of clients.

Registered representatives are generally responsible for dealing with clients, understanding their financial goals and risk tolerance, and recommending investment products that align with those objectives.

Usually, registered representatives work with certain broker-dealers or financial institutions and are specialized in certain securities such as stocks, bonds, mutual funds, or options.

To qualify as a registered representative, an individual must pass the Securities Industry Essentials (SIE) exam and a specific representative-level qualification exam like the Series 6 or Series 7, based on the type of business they will engage in.

Series 6

This exam is conducted to test a person's skill as an investment company and variable contracts products representative. This exam assesses a person's ability to deal with mutual funds, variable annuities, and other packaged investment products.

Series 7

The Series 7 is the general securities representative qualification exam.

The exam is designed to equip individuals with the necessary skills to carry out essential responsibilities as a general securities representative. These responsibilities include conducting the sales of corporate securities, variable annuities, and government securities.

Series 22

The Series 22 is the direct participation program representative exam. It prepares an individual to carry out the essential duties of a representative of a direct participation program, including soliciting, buying, and selling limited partnerships, among other items.

Series 52

The Series 52 is the municipal securities representative qualification exam. It tests an individual's ability to engage in the underwriting, trading, and sale of municipal securities, such as bonds issued by state or local governments.

Individuals take this test to work for firms that specialize in the municipal bond market.

Series 57

The Series 57 is the securities trader representative exam. It tests an individual's ability to perform a job as a securities trader representative and prepares them for important securities trading operations, such as executing transactions in equity, preferred, or convertible debt securities.

NASAA Exams: Series 63, 65, 66

The North American Securities Administrators Association (NASAA) is an organization of securities regulators in the US, Canada, and Mexico. They develop a series of exams for state securities regulations that are administered by FINRA.

- The Series 63 exam, which is also known as the uniform securities agent state law examination, tests an individual's knowledge of state securities laws.
- The Series 65 exam, which is also known as the uniform investment advisor law examination, tests an individual's knowledge of state securities laws related to investment advisors.
- The Series 66 exam, which is also known as the uniform combined state law examination, tests an individual's knowledge of state securities laws and federal securities laws.

Series 79

The Series 79 is the investment banking representative exam.

This exam prepares individuals for the important duties of an investment banking representative, including merger and acquisition facilitation, advice on or facilitation of debt, or equity securities offerings through a private placement or a public offering.

Series 86/87

The Series 86/87 is the research analyst exam. It tests a person's ability to engage in the production and distribution of research reports for broker-dealers. This exam covers the topics of regulatory requirements and ethical standards related to research reports and the analysis and valuation of individual securities.

Series 99

The Series 99 is the professional operations exam. This exam prepares individuals to carry out the essential duties of an operations professional, such as customer onboarding, financial control, receiving and delivering securities and money, transferring accounts, and maintaining and investing collected money.

Who Are Principals?

Principals are individuals responsible for supervising the securities-related activities of a member firm, such as sales, trading, compliance, or operations. They are registered with FINRA and hold certain security licenses that give them the authority to perform their supervisory roles.

Some of the principal roles and respective license securities include:

- General Securities Sales Supervisor: Series 9/10.
- General Securities Principal: Series 24.
- Investment Companies and Variable Contracts Products Principal: Series 26.

Principals are specific to a certain area of a firm and are responsible for maintaining FINRA and SEC regulations for that specific area.

Examinations

The SIE exam is the gateway to the security industry. Qualifying for this test is crucial to become registered with FINRA. Preparation should be taken seriously.

Resources are available for preparation for the test, such as textbooks, online courses, and practice exams. FINRA also provides detailed content on its website to help an individual understand the details of an SIE exam.

Failing the SIE Exam

The passing score of the SIE exam is 70%. If individuals fail the exam once, they can take it again after a thirty-day waiting period. If they fail a second time, they can again retake it after another thirty-day waiting period.

However, the waiting period after a third failed attempt is 180 days. It should be noted that one must pay the exam fees each time they take the test.

Exam Confidentiality

FINRA takes strict measures to ensure the integrity of its qualification exams and prevent cheating. Under FINRA's rules, the contents of the exam are considered confidential and are only disclosed to a few authorized personnel.

Registration Requirements

There are certain requirements for registration with FINRA, such as:

- **Sponsorship by a Broker-Dealer** – A person looking for registration with FINRA must be associated with a broker-dealer or a firm that is registered with FINRA. The broker-dealer or firm that sponsors the individual is responsible for ensuring that they meet all the qualifications, including passing required exams.

- **File Form U4 and a Fingerprint Card with the CRD** – The applicant for registration must submit a Uniform Application for Securities Industry Registration or Transfer (Form U4) to FINRA's Central Registration Depository (CRD).

  Form U4 contains a person's personal and professional history, including criminal records, if any. The applicant is also required to submit a fingerprint card to FINRA, which is used to run a background check on the applicant.

What Is Statutory Disqualification (SD)?

Statutory disqualification is a situation where an individual or a firm is disqualified or prohibited from engaging in certain activities, such as trading securities or providing investment advice.

It is a critical situation that can also result in losing one's license and being barred from the securities industry.

Grounds for Statutory Disqualification

There are a few grounds for statutory disqualification, such as conviction of certain crimes like securities fraud, mail fraud, or wire fraud.

Firms or individuals that have violated securities laws and regulations, such as insider trading, market manipulation, or failure to supervise, may be subject to statutory disqualification.

Association with an individual or firm that has been statutorily disqualified can also lead to statutory disqualification.

Eligibility Proceeding

Once a firm or individual is subject to statutory disqualification, they or a sponsoring firm may initiate an eligibility proceeding. This is a legal process that is carried out under FINRA in which the facts and figures surrounding the circumstances of statutory disqualification are carefully reviewed again.

During this process, the individual or firm must prove to the panel that they are fit to work in the security industry and won't harm the clients or market integrity.

The FINRA Department of Member Regulation may investigate, and a FINRA hearing panel will hold a hearing and make a decision in the eligibility proceeding.

Background Checks and Fingerprinting

FINRA's rules state that any individual seeking registration with a broker-dealer must undergo a background check and fingerprinting. This process is critical to ensure only qualified and trustworthy individuals are allowed to participate in the securities industry.

The background check procedure requires a review of a person's employment history, criminal history, and any additional relevant information. This information is gathered and double-checked by sources such as government agencies, public records, and previous employers.

The broker-dealer who sponsors the applicant is responsible for conducting a thorough background check, and FINRA ensures that the information gathered is accurate.

FINRA also requires applicants to provide a set of fingerprints. The fingerprints are taken at an authorized location and electronically sent to FINRA's Central Registration Depository (CRD) system.

State Registration

Let's look at aspects of state registration.

Blue-Sky Rule

State registration, also known as the Blue-Sky Rule, refers to each state having its own set of rules and regulations regarding the sale of securities. It requires the issuers of securities to register their offering with the state in which they plan on selling them.

This is in addition to compliance with the federal laws and regulations of securities established by the SEC and FINRA.

State registration is responsible for overseeing the registration process, including all the details like reviewing the registration statements, prospectuses, and other relevant documents filed by issuers. State registration also conducts investigations and takes action against entities that violate the laws.

Continuing Education

Continuing education mainly consists of two components.

Regulatory Elements

Regulatory Element training is a computer-based education program that keeps registered persons updated on regulatory and industry topics. Registered persons are required to complete Regulatory Element training on the second anniversary of their initial securities registration and every three years thereafter.

Firm Elements

Firm Element training is the continuing education program that broker-dealers are required to administer to their registered representatives each year. It is designed to keep employees updated on job- and product-related topics. The topics can include regulatory requirements and the firm's internal policies and procedures.

Chapter 20: Employee Conduct and Reportable Events

If an individual aspires to pursue a career within the security sector and establish an affiliation with either a broker-dealer or a financial institution operating under the purview of FINRA, the person must submit a comprehensive Form U4.

The form contains a multitude of specific regulations and obligatory disclosures that necessitate fulfillment in order to facilitate the registration of the individual with FINRA.

Form U4 Disclosures

The disclosure within Form U4 is a crucial evaluative tool used to ascertain the suitability of a participant within the security industry.

The application features information specific to the individual, such as details concerning their personal and professional background, educational qualifications, comprehensive employment data, and any prior instances of legal or regulatory repercussions.

Disclosure Reporting Page (DRP)

The Disclosure Reporting Page (DRP) is designed to uncover specific employee details to prospective employers well in advance of any potential engagement.

It usually provides information about reportable occurrences throughout the professional life of the applicant, including (but not limited to) criminal charges or convictions, civil judgments, regulatory interventions, and customer grievances.

Predispute Arbitration Agreement

The predispute arbitration agreement (PAA) is signed between the employee and the employer, who is a broker-dealer or a financial institution.

The purpose of this agreement is to resolve any disputes between the employee and the employer through arbitration rather than a court system. It not only streamlines the dispute-resolving process but also saves the cost of visiting the court.

The objective underlying the agreement is to resolve any potential conflicts between the employee and the employer and to opt for arbitration as opposed to resorting to court.

By embracing this alternative dispute resolution mechanism, the process of conflict resolution is not only streamlined but also offers substantial financial benefits by reducing the need for court appearances.

Arbitration Disclosures

Arbitration disclosures pertain to the disclosure of any prior involvement the applicant has had in arbitration proceedings within the past decade. These disclosures comprise the entirety of said proceedings and feature details regarding the nature of the dispute at hand and the ultimate outcome of the arbitration process.

Moreover, the purpose of arbitration disclosures is to provide FINRA and potential employers with an overview of the applicant's legal and regulatory history. For example, an applicant with a clean legal history will have a higher chance of being chosen for a project rather than a person with legal and regulatory violations on their record.

Form U5 and Form U6

The Uniform Disciplinary Action Reporting Form is often referred to as 'Form U6', and is used by securities regulators to disclose disciplinary actions. It serves to report actions against those entities that are registered with FINRA. It includes the report of the individual's employment, which covers the reason for termination, the individual's registration and employment history, and any customer complaints or regulatory actions involving the individual. This information is used by FINRA to monitor the activities of registered individuals and to identify potential regulatory violations.

In contrast, Form U6, also known as the Uniform Disciplinary Action Reporting Form, is used by securities regulators to disclose disciplinary actions against individuals or firms registered with FINRA. It must be filed within thirty days of the disciplinary action being taken. This form is used by FINRA to keep track of regulatory violations and take steps against them.

Broker Check

FINRA offers a free online tool called Broker Check, which can be used by anyone to research and verify the background history and registration of brokers and brokerage firms with FINRA.

Broker Check enables investors to assess the professional backgrounds of brokers and brokerage firms and assist them in making informed decisions about with whom to work in conducting their financial transactions. They can verify whether any legal actions have been taken against the firm and whether the information they provided regarding their education and qualifications is true.

FINRA Investor Education Rule and Expungement

There isn't a rule specifically called the "Investor Education Rule" within FINRA's regulations. It is more accurate to say that FINRA requires member firms to ensure investors are adequately informed about the risks, benefits, and costs of various investment products and strategies. This rule helps investors make an informed decision once all the risks, benefits, and costs of various investment products and strategies are out in the open.

In contrast, expungement is the process of removing certain details from a broker's record. Usually, brokers remove customer complaints or regulatory actions from their records. This practice makes it difficult for investors to make an informed decision about whether to do business with them, as certain brokers have negative information wiped off their records.

FINRA has now implemented several rules and regulations in response to concerns regarding expungement. For example, FINRA Rule 2080 states that any broker seeking expungement of any record is required to provide a written notice to all parties associated with the underlying dispute, which includes customers, other brokers, and the firm itself.

FINRA Rule 2080 allows for expungement of customer dispute information under specific circumstances, which include an arbitration award recommending expungement, a court order, or a finding that the claim was false or that the representative was not involved in the alleged misconduct.

What Are Customer Complaints and How Should They Be Dealt With?

The perspectives and experiences shared by clients or customers regarding the services they were provided or the products they acquired from a business or individual are known as customer complaints. These expressions of concern might encompass a wide range of issues, such as allegations of misconduct, fraudulent practices, and deceptive behaviors.

When confronted with such circumstances, a securities firm or broker is advised to diligently adhere to the following protocol to ensure issues are resolved quickly.

Acknowledge the Complaint – Swiftly recognize the grievance, which will demonstrate a genuine commitment to its significance and assure the client of your attention.

Conduct a Thorough Investigation – Research the complaint and scrutinize the facts and circumstances. This may mean collecting evidence, engaging in witness interviews, and analyzing financial documentation.

Provide a Customer Response – Once the investigation reaches its culmination, provide the client with a comprehensive response to the findings, accompanied by a detailed outline of measures to effectively address the underlying issue.

Document the Complaint – Document the complaint and the corresponding remedial actions undertaken by the company or broker. Record-keeping serves as a safeguard in potential future conflicts or regulatory inquiries.

Engage in Follow-up – Maintain ongoing communication with the client. Proactively inquire about their satisfaction with the resolution of the complaint and address any lingering concerns or unresolved matters.

Securities companies and brokers can contribute to making sure that their clients are treated fairly and that their interests are safeguarded by taking complaints seriously, properly examining them, and responding to them promptly and professionally.

Reporting Requirements

To uphold investor protection and the integrity of the securities industry, FINRA has formulated a series of reporting requirements. These are binding for all firms and brokers affiliated with FINRA and leave no room for exemption.

A fundamental reporting obligation is the mandatory submission of precise reports to the organization. These include forms U4 and U5, which serve as essential tools for registrations and termination notifications. Form U6, known as the Uniform Disciplinary Action Reporting Form, is used by securities regulators to report disciplinary actions.

Furthermore, FINRA requires its members to disclose certain information to potential investors. This includes various aspects related to the investment at hand, such as fees, costs, commissions, inherent risks, and potential conflicts of interest that arise during or after the completion of the investment transaction.

These measures ensure comprehensive investor awareness and foster trust and informed decision-making before the finalization of any investment. Failure to comply with these rules can result in disciplinary actions like fines, suspensions, or revocation of a firm or broker's registration, depending upon the severity of the violation.

Additionally, failure to disclose the entire relevant information to the potential investors can lead to legal action and damage to the firm or broker's reputation.

What Are Red Flags?

Red flags are indicators of illegal activities, such as potential fraud or misconduct that could directly affect the investors. All unusual or suspicious behavior, transactions, or activities are considered red flags.

What to Do When Red Flags Are Discovered

Firms and brokers must identify and address potential red flags. This not only safeguards investors from fraudulent transactions but also protects a firm's reputation.

Initiating this process requires sudden actions like halting suspicious activities, implementing account freezes, suspending transactions, or engaging law enforcement agencies when needed. This must be followed by an investigation.

An investigation usually consists of interviews with clients and review of transactional data. After an investigation ends, firms must inform SEC or FINRA of the results and ensure that the clients who fell victim to the fraudulent activity are apprised of the impact it had on their accounts.

Firms should prioritize preemptive measures that reduce the likelihood of potential red flags. This could include implementing systems and procedures for keeping track of account activity, doing routine audits and reviews, and training staff members on how to spot and address red flags.

MSRB Rule G-20

MSRB Rule G-20 was established to govern the permissible value of gifts that brokers, dealers, and municipal securities dealers were authorized to offer to prospective customers or existing customers as part of their engagements within municipal securities transactions.

The main purpose of the gift limit is to ensure that dealers do not use gifts or any other form of compensation to influence customers to purchase a security or be part of a deal that may be harmful or violates any of the rules of fair trading or ethical conduct.

Political Contribution Rule (MSRB Rule G-37)

The Political Contribution Rule, also known as Rule G-37, prohibits broker-dealers from engaging in pay-to-play practices regarding the business of municipal securities. Some of the provisions of Rule G-37 include:

- Prohibition on political contributions to officials of municipal securities.
- Recordkeeping of all the political distributions made by the dealer.

Failure to abide by these rules can lead to severe legal and financial losses, such as fines, suspension, or revocation of licenses, and legal liability for any damages suffered by clients.

Test 1: Questions

(1) What is the core responsibility of the FRB?
(A) To monitor money laundering practices.
(B) To prevent insider trading.
(C) To maintain price stability.
(D) To regulate brokerage firms.

(2) Brad's Investments is a real estate investment company established in 1999 in Chicago, Illinois. It will go public in early 2024 to enable investors to purchase company shares.
According to the Securities Act of 1933 compliance protocol, what information does Brad's Investments have to disclose to its investors before the initial public offering?
(A) Dividend policy, investment projections, and compliance.
(B) Financial statements and information about the offered securities.
(C) The mission statement, corporate history, and long-term goals.
(D) None of the above

(3) Why was the FDIC created?
(A) To provide insurance for savings accounts.
(B) To protect annuities, bonds, and stocks.
(C) To regulate banks and other financial institutions.
(D) To prevent bank runs and ensure the safety of customers' funds.

(4) Which associations protect investors against fraudulent activities and are responsible for providing licenses to investment professionals and securities firms?
(A) SEC.
(B) FINRA.
(C) FDIC.
(D) NASAA.

(5) The Investment Advisers Act was enacted in 1940 to regulate investment advisers. It required advisers to register with the SEC if they matched the definition of an investment adviser.
Which of the following individuals is NOT exempt from the act?
(A) Lawyers.
(B) Teachers.
(C) Publishers.
(D) None of the above.

(6) Alex is a professional day trader who trades securities on the Nasdaq stock exchange. One of his friends, John, works for Apple Inc. as a senior product manager.
One day, John shares confidential information about an upcoming product launch with Alex. Alex buys Apple stock for $10,000 to earn a financial incentive before he announces the same news to the public.
What type of trading is this?
(A) Front-running.
(B) Churning.
(C) Interpositioning.
(D) Insider trading.

(7) What was the primary reason for the introduction of the Telephone Consumer Protection Act of 1991?
(A) To regulate and restrict business telemarketing practices.
(B) To ban business solicitation over the telephone.
(C) To prohibit prerecorded messages.
(D) To eliminate autodialing systems.

(8) After the disastrous events of September 11, 2001, the USA PATRIOT Act was introduced to combat money laundering and terrorist financing.
Which statement is incorrect about this act?
(A) Required the financial services industry to report money laundering.
(B) Strengthened measures to prevent corrupt officials from using the US financial system for personal gain.
(C) Prohibited the repatriation of stolen assets to the citizens of the countries to whom the assets belonged.
(D) All of the above.

(9) What is the primary function of the Municipal Securities Rulemaking Board (MSRB)?
(A) To oversee the sale of corporate stocks and bonds.
(B) To regulate securities firms and professionals selling municipal securities.
(C) To administer licenses to securities professionals.
(D) To ensure transparency in the commodities market.

(10) What is the primary focus of FINRA Rule 5250?
(A) To prohibit payments from a security's promoters or issuers to the firm that acts as a market maker for that security.
(B) To ensure broker-dealers set reasonable prices and commissions for security transactions.
(C) To mandate that broker-dealers have a documentation system for all written customer complaints.
(D) To require SIPC member firms to inform customers in writing about SIPC protections.

(11) William has recently been promoted in his corporate job and wants to diversify his investment portfolio. While living in Europe, he became interested in options and futures trading, especially volatility indexes. Which exchange is best known for these trading opportunities?
(A) NASDAQ.
(B) NYSE.
(C) CBOE.
(D) AMEX.

(12) Why was the Penny Stock Reform Act of 1990 introduced?
(A) To protect investors from fraudulent practices and offer transparency in the trade of penny stocks.
(B) To allow small companies to list their stocks on national exchanges.
(C) To offer retail investors the ability to trade penny stocks.
(D) To grow the OTC market's transaction volume.

(13) "Firms are obligated to disclose any participation or interest in a primary or secondary distribution of securities to their customers," per FINRA rule _______.
(A) 4513.
(B) 4530.
(C) 2266.
(D) 2241.

(14) Which banking system moderates long-term interest rates?
(A) The Federal Reserve Board.
(B) Bank of America.
(C) JPMorgan Chase.
(D) Wells Fargo.

(15) What are equity securities?
(A) A type of financial instrument that represents a stock ownership interest in a company.
(B) They represent stock ownership in a company without stockholder voting rights.
(C) Any trade in the stock exchange market.
(D) An allowance for stockholders to easily sell their shares without permission from a corporation.

(16) Investors who have bought company shares have voting rights. What does this mean?
(A) They share the gains if the company produces a profit.
(B) The investors can decide which managers should stay in their positions if there are more than 100 shares.
(C) The investor has the right to fifty votes if they own fifty shares.
(D) Only investors who have invested in preferred stocks can vote.

(17) What is the difference between restricted and controlled stock?
(A) Restricted stock is comprised of the registered shares of a company, whereas controlled stock is only sold to directors.
(B) Unlike restricted stock, controlled stock is a grant of company stock that controls the recipient's rights until shares are vested.
(C) There is a difference in the holding period for both types of stocks.
(D) Restricted stock includes company shares sold to employees as part of their pay, whereas major shareholders own controlled stock.

(18) Which of the following statements about the MSRB is correct?
(A) It is a federal government entity.
(B) It protects investors through the regulation of equity securities.
(C) It sets rules for professionals who deal with municipal securities but does not enforce them.
(D) It operates under the direct guidance of the SEC.

(19) What is an American Depositary Receipt (ADR)?
(A) An ownership certificate for a foreign firm.
(B) Ownership rights in a company's restricted securities.
(C) A voting right in a corporation's stock.
(D) A dividend that a business gives to its stockholders.

(20) What are warrants?
(A) Derivatives that allow the right to buy or sell a company's stock.
(B) Share buybacks to reduce the number of outstanding shares.
(C) Trade restrictions on acquired restricted securities.
(D) Fixed payments required for debt financing.

(21) Which of the following is not the reason behind bond price fluctuation from par?
(A) A decrease in the credit rating of the issuer.
(B) An increase in interest rates.
(C) An increase or decrease in potential investors.
(D) The supply of the bond exceeds its demand.

(22) Which credit rating agency provides forward-looking credit opinions and rates the viability of investments relative to the likelihood of default?
(A) Standard and Poor's.
(B) Fitch Investors Service.
(C) Moody's Investor Service.
(D) All of the above.

(23) What will be the coupon payment if a bond's coupon rate is seven percent and the par value is 1000?
(A) 0.7.
(B) 7000.
(C) 70.
(D) 700.

(24) The yield-to-maturity of a bond takes into account __________.
(A) Coupon rate and bond price.
(B) Market price and the bond's face value.
(C) Current yield and coupon rate.
(D) Coupon rate, market price, face value, and time to maturity.

(25) What is the conversion price for each common share if a business raises $1 million in convertible debt with the right to convert 20,000 shares of common stock for fifty dollars each within two years?
(A) Twenty dollars per share.
(B) Forty dollars per share.
(C) Sixty dollars per share.
(D) Fifty dollars per share.

(26) What is the mandatory call provision?
(A) The issuer can redeem the bonds if certain conditions are met.
(B) The issuer specifies certain circumstances when they might call the bond.
(C) The bond can be called whenever the issuer wants.
(D) The issuer must redeem a certain number of bonds on a set schedule.

(27) Which provision allows the issuer to repurchase and retire the debt security before maturity?
(A) Call provision.
(B) Put provision.
(C) Conversion provision.
(D) Redemption provision.

(28) What are convertible debentures?
(A) Short-term debt instruments.
(B) Government-issued bonds.
(C) Bonds that can be converted into equity shares.
(D) Bonds with high credit ratings.

(29) Which type of debt instrument offers the greatest flexibility in terms of maturity, interest rate, security, and repayment?
(A) Stock options.
(B) Debentures.
(C) Bonds.
(D) Mortgages.

(30) Which of the following statements best describes callable preferred shares?
(A) They can be redeemed by the issuer at any time without notice.
(B) They guarantee a fixed dividend rate for the lifetime of the security.
(C) They give the issuer the right to buy back the shares at a predetermined price after a specified date.
(D) They allow the shareholder the option to convert the shares into common stock.

(31) Which type of corporate bond promises only the repayment of the principal and does not guarantee interest or coupon payments?
(A) Eurodollar bonds.
(B) Income bonds.
(C) Yankee bonds.
(D) Euro bonds.

(32) How might an investor's returns be impacted if their callable preferred shares are called?
(A) They could decrease if the shares are called and reissued at a higher dividend rate.
(B) They would increase due to the investor benefits from the premium paid by the issuer.
(C) They could decrease if the shares are called when market interest rates have dropped.
(D) They are not impacted by the call feature as the dividends are guaranteed.

(33) Which of the following is not a disadvantage of a municipal bond?
(A) They do not involve federal taxes.
(B) They provide minimal protection against inflation.
(C) Their prices may fluctuate.
(D) They have a limited supply.

(34) What distinguishes closed-end investment firms from open-end firms?
(A) Closed-end companies only sell shares to investors directly, while open-end corporations issue shares that can be purchased and sold on a stock exchange.
(B) Closed-end businesses only issue a maximum of fifty shares compared to open-end businesses.
(C) Closed-end enterprises can be bought and sold on a stock exchange, unlike open-end firms.
(D) Closed-end businesses manage a fixed securities portfolio, whereas open-end businesses handle publicly traded shares.

(35) A face-amount certificate company is ____________.
(A) An investment company that issues fixed-income securities and offers investment certificates.
(B) Insurance that commits to pay out a specified sum at a later time.
(C) A financial intermediary that invests money for individual investors in a range of assets.
(D) A mutual fund that invests in securities in each category as well as a range of varied assets.

(36) What is a prospectus?
(A) A document that gives information about a public investment offering.
(B) A document that outlines a mutual fund's investment goals.
(C) A paper that outlines the dangers associated with trade contracts.
(D) A document that gives general background information about operating expenses.

(37) How are qualified annuities different from non-qualified annuities?
(A) Qualified annuities offer better returns than non-qualified annuities.
(B) Payments to qualified annuities are tax-free. Non-qualified annuity payments are taxed.
(C) Qualified annuities have a shorter accumulation phase than non-qualified annuities.
(D) Qualified annuities have more flexible payment possibilities than non-qualified annuities.

(38) What is the difference between fixed and variable annuities?
(A) A fixed annuity has a fixed payment amount that must be made daily.
(B) A fixed annuity is high-risk, and a variable annuity is low-risk.
(C) A fixed annuity has a fixed payment at the time of investment.
(D) None of the above.

(39) Which of the following is not an annuity pay-out option for payment withdrawal in the distribution phase of the contract?
(A) Life annuity with a specific period.
(B) Non-qualified annuity.
(C) Unit refund life annuity.
(D) A and C.

(40) Which of the following statements is true about annuities?
(A) They are suitable for all individuals regardless of their financial condition.
(B) They have low fees.
(C) They offer immediate access to funds without any charges.
(D) They are designed for long-term investment and may incur charges for early withdrawals.

(41) What type of real estate program involves investment in underdeveloped land?
(A) New construction.
(B) Existing.
(C) Low income (government-assisted).
(D) Raw land.

(42) How are the interest payments from TIPS (Treasury Inflation-Protected Securities) bonds taxed at the federal level?
(A) They are tax-free.
(B) Annually, even if the investor has not received the payment.
(C) When the bond matures or is sold.
(D) At a rate lower than other federal bonds.

(43) Which of the following is true about a hedge fund?
(A) It is an investment vehicle with low risk.
(B) It is heavily regulated by government agencies.
(C) It welcomes all types of investors.
(D) It is predicted to provide higher positive returns.

(44) What is the disadvantage of a limited liability company?
(A) The risks are not distributed.
(B) The owner has to take care of everything.
(C) It risks conflict between partners.
(D) It provides management flexibility.

(45) Which type of yield refers to the promised compound rate of return received from a bond held until maturity?
(A) Normal yield.
(B) Current yield.
(C) Yield-to-maturity.
(D) Yield spread.

(46) What is the second step of exercising equity?
(A) The strike price is determined.
(B) The bond is issued.
(C) The expiration date is determined.
(D) The holder directs the broker to initiate the exercise.

(47) Which of the following is a strategy in which investors sell a call option on a stock they own?
(A) Hedging.
(B) Covered call.
(C) Speculation.
(D) Breakeven.

(48) Which of the following is an unsystematic risk?
(A) Credit risk.
(B) Opportunity risk.
(C) Legislative risk.
(D) None of the above.

(49) How does tactical asset allocation help a company?
(A) It adjusts the portfolio's asset allocation to maximize assets and minimize loss.
(B) It involves making spontaneous decisions on the best way to allocate money as a single asset.
(C) Despite having higher risk, it provides higher returns.
(D) It has a lower fee than other methods.

(50) An investor thinks a potential market downturn may decrease a product's value, so he purchases a put option to sell the product at a strike price. What type of strategy is this?
(A) Tactical asset allocation.
(B) Passive asset allocation.
(C) Hedging risk.
(D) Buy-and-hold.

(51) Which of the following is the risk of loss due to unforeseen events?
(A) Inflation risk.
(B) Event risk.
(C) Sudden risk.
(D) Market risk.

(52) Alex is a software engineer. He invests his disposable income in the stock market and purchases NVIDIA stocks. His investment goal is to generate passive income and preserve the long-term value of his initial investment.
What will help generate passive income if he holds his NVIDIA stocks and does not trade them?
(A) Stocks loaned to a friend.
(B) Stocks loaned to a bank.
(C) Dividends.
(D) All of the above.

(53) The date shareholders receive their dividends is the ______.
(A) Declaration date.
(B) Payment date.
(C) Distribution date.
(D) None of the above.

(54) To be eligible to receive stock dividends from a company, it is essential to buy the shares before the ____________.

(A) Start of a new fiscal year.

(B) End of a fiscal year.

(C) Record date.

(D) Ex-dividend date.

(55) What are the two main methods companies use to pay dividends to their shareholders?

(A) Stock and cash dividends.

(B) Stock dividends and bonus shares.

(C) Cash dividends and bonus shares.

(D) None of the above.

(56) What is a declaration date?

(A) The date companies decide which stakeholders can receive dividends.

(B) The date a statement about the following payment details is released.

(C) The date companies announce their earnings report.

(D) The date companies announce their plans and objectives to their stakeholders.

(57) If an investor holds a stock with an annual dividend of $130 per share and the current market price per share is $2,057, what is the current equity yield?

(A) 5.50%.

(B) 6.32%.

(C) 2.32%.

(D) 7.89%.

(58) Periodic interest payments made by the bond issuer to the investor who buys and holds the bonds are known as _______.

(A) Bondholder returns.

(B) Bond yields.

(C) Return on bond investments.

(D) Coupon payments.

(59) Zara is a retail investor who actively invests in stocks, bonds, and commodities. She recently purchased some municipal bonds from her brokerage firm to diversify her investment portfolio and earn periodic interest payments.
Her bonds have a face value of $1,300, and the bond issuer is offering her a coupon rate of seven percent.
What is Zara's annual coupon payment?
(A) Ninety-one dollars.
(B) Ninety dollars.
(C) Eight-six dollars.
(D) Eighty-eight dollars.

(60) The amount of yield generated by a bond by taking into account the bond's market price is called ________.
(A) Annual yield.
(B) Current yield.
(C) Quarterly yield.
(D) Net yield.

(61) What is the maturity date of a bond?
(A) The date the bond issuer is obligated to repay the principal value to the bondholder.
(B) The date the bond investment expires.
(C) The date new bonds are issued to the current bondholders.
(D) None of the above.

(62) Jenny owns a bond with a face value of $5,000 and a coupon rate of nine percent. If the government announces an interest rate hike, what will happen to the bond price owned by Jenny?
(A) It will decrease.
(B) It will increase.
(C) It will remain the same.
(D) None of the above.

(63) Which of the following statements is correct about callable bonds?
(A) Issuers can only retire the bonds after the maturity date.
(B) Issuers can change the maturity date without prior notice or call.
(C) Issuers can repay the bondholders and retire the bonds before the original maturity date.
(D) Both A and B.

(64) Which statement is correct about the cost basis?
(A) It excludes the initial investment amount.
(B) It is the initial investment for a particular asset and includes fees and commissions.
(C) Both A and B.
(D) None of the above.

(65) Why are narrow-based indexes used?
(A) To analyze specific asset classes within a broader market.
(B) To understand the overall financial market.
(C) To hedge against sector-specific risks.
(D) Both A and C.

(66) What type of index is the Nasdaq Composite Index?
(A) A bond index.
(B) An equity index.
(C) A broad-based index.
(D) None of the above.

(67) Which of the following is an example of a bond index?
(A) The Russell 2000 Index.
(B) S&P 500.
(C) ICE BofA US Corporate Index.
(D) Dow Jones Industrial Average (DJIA).

(68) Which type of dividends can dilute the ownership of current shareholders?
(A) Property dividends.
(B) Special dividends.
(C) Cash dividends.
(D) Stock dividends.

(69) A loss that occurs when investors sell securities at a lower price than the original purchase is known as a/an ________.
(A) Unrealized loss.
(B) Loss on investment.
(C) Both A and B.
(D) Capital loss.

(70) Which of the following are examples of risk-adjusted returns?
(A) Sharpe ratio.
(B) Treynor ratio.
(C) Sortino ratio.
(D) All of the above.

(71) What methods do companies use to increase their outstanding shares?
(A) Stock issuance.
(B) Stock splits.
(C) Both A and B.
(D) None of the above.

(72) How is yield-to-maturity measured?
(A) YTM = [C + (FV – PV)/n]/[(FV + PV)/2].
(B) YTM = [FV + (C – PV)/n]/[(C + PV)/2].
(C) YTM = [PV + (FV – C)/n]/[(FV + C)/2].
(D) YTM = [C + (FV – PV)]/[(FV + PV)].

(73) A corporate action in which companies divide existing shares into multiple shares to increase total outstanding shares is called a stock split.
Why do companies perform stock splits?
(A) To adjust the price of the shares.
(B) To make shares more affordable.
(C) To reduce liquidity in the market.
(D) Both A and B.

(74) A technique that consolidates multiple shares into one share to reduce the number of outstanding stock shares is called a __________.
(A) Forward stock split.
(B) Reverse stock split.
(C) Stock merger.
(D) Stock compression.

(75) What is a tender offer?
(A) A private bid to sell stocks to investors.
(B) A private bid to purchase stocks from corporations.
(C) A public bid to purchase shareholder's stocks.
(D) A private bid to purchase shareholder's stocks.

(76) A corporate action in which companies buy their own outstanding shares from stakeholders is referred to as a ________.
(A) Stock redemption.
(B) Stock withdrawal.
(C) Stock acquisition.
(D) Buyback.

(77) What is the impact of a stock split on a cost basis?
(A) It increases.
(B) It remains unchanged.
(C) It decreases.
(D) It is irrelevant to the stock split.

(78) ________ are associated with self-regulatory organizations.
(A) Broker-dealers.
(B) Investors.
(C) Individuals who work for broker-dealers.
(D) Creditors.

(79) Self-regulating organizations like FINRA are not required to________?
(A) File yearly reports at their annual conference.
(B) Adhere to the standards on trade practices.
(C) Ensure all employees hold a Ph.D. in finance.
(D) Establish procedures compliant with the dispute resolution process.

(80) Which individuals can engage in financial activities like trading securities?
(A) All individuals associated with FINRA.
(B) Non-registered individuals associated with FINRA.
(C) Registered personnel associated with FINRA.
(D) Non-registered, FINRA-associated personnel with specific training and education.

(81) Registered representatives do which of the following?
(A) Sell securities, manage operations, and recommend investment products.
(B) Trade securities, buy stocks, and recommend investment opportunities.
(C) Trade securities, manage administrative tasks, and buy stocks for clients.
(D) Sell securities, offer technical support, and recommend investment products.

(82) Which test assesses information about representing general securities?
(A) Series 6.
(B) Series 7.
(C) Series 22.
(D) Series 52.

(83) A municipal securities representative does which of the following?
(A) Buys and sells limited partnerships.
(B) Sells corporate and government securities.
(C) Has command over trading operations.
(D) Underwrites, sells, and trades municipal securities.

(84) The Series twenty-two exam prepares a candidate to do which of the following?
(A) Sell corporate and government securities.
(B) Solicit and deal with limited partnerships.
(C) Trade and handle mutual funds and other packaged investment products.
(D) Trade municipal bonds issued by the state or local authorities.

(85) Which exam prepares a candidate to deal with packaged investment products, mutual funds, and variable annuities?
(A) Series 6.
(B) Series 7.
(C) Series 22.
(D) Series 52.

Test 1: Answers and Explanations

(1) (C) To maintain price stability.
The FRB utilizes monetary policy to manage the country's money supply. The goal is to achieve maximum employment, stabilize prices, and moderate long-term interest rates. Price stability is crucial to prevent inflation or deflation.

(2) (B) Financial statements and information about the offered securities.
The Securities Act of 1933 requires companies to disclose information that is easily accessible to potential investors before the IPO. This ensures compliance with the act. Required information includes a description of the security and the company's business, properties, and financial statements verified by independent accountants.

(3) (D) To prevent bank runs and ensure the safety of customers' funds.
In the era of the Great Depression, groups of people withdrew their money because of fear that banks were on the verge of collapse. The FDIC was created to insure customer funds against such events.

(4) (B) FINRA.
The Financial Industry Regulatory Authority (FINRA) is a self-regulatory organization. They provide licenses to investment professionals and securities firms, write rules for these entities, and ensure compliance to protect investors against fraudulent activities.

(5) (D) None of the above.
The Investment Advisers Act of 1940 requires eligible financial advisers to register with the SEC and prioritize their clients' interests over their own. Some people are excluded and not subject to the provisions of this act. These include lawyers, teachers, publishers, accountants, and engineers.

(6) (D) Insider trading.
Insider trading is the illicit practice of buying or selling securities based on confidential information. In this case, John gave private information to Alex. Alex used the tip to form a basis for making a trade, which is insider trading.

(7) (A) To regulate and restrict business telemarketing practices.
The Telephone Consumer Protection Act of 1991 was not introduced to ban business solicitation, autodialing systems, or prerecorded messages but to limit and restrict

telemarketing practices. Through this act, unwanted telemarketing calls were significantly reduced.

(8) (C) Prohibited the repatriation of stolen assets to the citizens of the countries to whom the assets belonged.
The USA PATRIOT Act of 2001 did not prohibit the repatriation of stolen assets to the citizens of specific countries but promoted it. The act was created to combat money laundering and terrorism financing. One of its key objectives was to return stolen assets to their country of origin.

(9) (B) To regulate securities firms and professionals selling municipal securities
The Municipal Securities Rulemaking Board (MSRB) creates rules and regulations for securities firms and professionals who underwrite, trade, and sell municipal securities. These securities are bonds issued by cities, states, and other local entities. The MSRB does not oversee corporate stocks or bonds, does not administer licenses, and is not involved in the commodities market.

(10) (A) To prohibit payments from a security's promoters or issuers to the firm that acts as a market maker for that security.
FINRA Rule 5250 primarily addresses potential conflicts of interest. It stipulates that firms cannot receive payments from the promoters or issuers of a security if they are a market maker for that same security. This rule helps maintain the integrity and transparency of the financial markets and prevents possible manipulations or biases in securities trading.

(11) (C) CBOE.
The Chicago Board Options Exchange (CBOE) is renowned for its options trading, especially products related to volatility indexes, such as the VIX.

(12) (A) To protect investors from fraudulent practices and offer transparency in the trade of penny stocks.
The Penny Stock Reform Act of 1990 was introduced as a federal law to prevent fraud in non-exchange listed stocks, known as penny stocks.

(13) (D) 2241.
Per FINRA Rule 2241, firms must disclose any participation or interest in a primary or secondary distribution of securities to their customers. This is important to ensure transparency and manage potential conflicts of interest. This rule primarily addresses

research analysts' need for disclosures to ensure the integrity and reliability of their analyses and recommendations.

(14) (A) The Federal Reserve Board.
The FRB is the central banking system in the US that creates and manages the country's monetary policy. One of its key objectives is to use monetary policy to keep long-term interest rates at a moderate level.

(15) (A) A type of financial instrument that represents a stock ownership interest in a company.
An equity security is a share of capital stock. It includes common and preferred stock and symbolizes shareholders' ownership stake in a legal company.

(16) (C) The investor has the right to fifty votes if they own fifty shares.
The right to vote is granted to stockholders who hold common stock shares in a corporation. Typically, these investors are given one vote per share. A shareholder who owns 100 shares is entitled to 100 votes.

(17) (D) Restricted stock includes company shares sold to employees as part of their pay, whereas major shareholders own controlled stock.
Restricted stock often refers to shares given or sold to employees as part of their pay. These shares are subject to a few limitations or requirements. A controlled stock describes significant investors' equity shares in a publicly traded corporation. Instead of an employee, a business affiliate owns these shares.

(18) (C) It sets rules for professionals who deal with municipal securities but does not enforce them.
The MSRB creates rules for the municipal securities market. However, these rules are enforced by the Financial Industry Regulatory Authority (FINRA) and the Securities and Exchange Commission (SEC). The MSRB is not a federal entity. It coordinates with the SEC but does not directly regulate equity securities or operate under its guidance.

(19) (A) An ownership certificate for a foreign firm.
ADRs are financial instruments that represent ownership in shares of foreign companies. They are issued by a depositary bank and traded on US stock exchanges. They enable investment in foreign enterprises, and the investors do not need to trade on foreign exchanges or deal with currency conversions physically.

(20) (A) Derivatives that allow the right to buy or sell a company's stock.
Warrants are financial derivatives. They provide the holder with the option to purchase (call) or sell (put) a specified number of shares at a predetermined price (exercise price) within a predetermined period. Businesses commonly issue them to generate funds or as part of debt or equity transactions. It is worth noting that warrants do not give the holder the right to vote, unlike stocks.

(21) (C) An increase or decrease in potential investors.
Due to their reliance on the revenue generated by interest rate-related coupon payments, bonds are subject to price fluctuations. If the bond's price is currently lower than its face value, it is considered below par. This can occur for the following reasons:

- An increase in interest rates.
- A decrease in the credit rating of the issuer.
- The supply of the bond exceeds its demand.

(22) (D) All of the above.
Standard and Poor's, Fitch Investors Service, and Moody's Investor Service are renowned credit rating agencies that provide forward-looking credit opinions. They analyze the creditworthiness of entities like corporations and governments and securities like bonds. They rate them based on their analysis. This rating significantly influences the perceived risk associated with the investment and can impact the interest rates of these investments.

(23) (C) 70.
The formula for finding the coupon payment is as follows:
Par value multiplied by coupon rate, e.g., 1000 x 0.07 = 70.

(24) (D) Coupon rate, market price, face value, and time to maturity.
Yield-to-maturity is calculated with regard to the coupon rate, market price, face value, and time to maturity of a bond. It represents the promised compound rate of return received from a bond purchased at the current market price and held until maturity.

(25) (D) Fifty dollars per share.
In the example, the company raises $1 million in convertible debt with the conversion privilege of 20,000 common shares for fifty dollars each. Therefore, the conversion price per share is given as fifty dollars.

(26) (D) The issuer must redeem a certain number of bonds on a set schedule.
A mandatory call provision is a term in the bond indenture that requires the issuer to redeem a particular portion or the entirety of a bond issue at a predetermined price after a certain period.

(27) (A) Call provision.
Corporate bonds commonly use this provision to repurchase and retire debt before maturity.

(28) (C) Bonds that can be converted into equity shares.
Convertible debentures are long-term financial instruments that a corporation issues and, after a predetermined time, may be converted into equity shares. Investors have the option to convert their bonds into business stock shares.

(29) (B) Debentures.
Debentures offer greater flexibility compared to other debt instruments. They provide choices in terms of maturity, interest rate, security, and repayment options. Governments, companies, and organizations use debentures to raise debt finance. They include a contract for the return of the principal sum and the interest payment at a set rate. Debentures, as opposed to loans or bonds, allow for greater customization and can be modified to meet specific financial demands.

(30) (C) They give the issuer the right to buy back the shares at a predetermined price after a specified date.
Callable preferred shares allow the issuing company the right, but not the obligation, to buy back or "call" these shares at a predetermined price after a specified date. The issuer would typically call back the shares when interest rates fall. This allows them to issue new shares at a lower dividend rate. The first option is incorrect because there is typically a specified call date and often a notice period. The second option is misleading because while they might offer fixed dividends, the lifetime of the security can be shortened if the shares are called. The last option describes convertible shares, not callable shares.

(31) (B) Income bonds.
Income bonds are corporate bonds in which the repayment of the principal amount is promised, and the interest or coupon payments are paid only if the issuer has sufficient earnings. Interest or coupon payments are contingent on the earnings of the issuer. If

the company has sufficient earnings, interest may be paid to bondholders. These bonds are usually issued when corporate debt is restructured. Income bonds are advantageous for companies seeking to raise capital as they provide flexibility in interest payments, and failure to pay interest does not result in default.

(32) (C) They could decrease if the shares are called when market interest rates have dropped.
When market interest rates fall, issuers might call their current callable preferred shares. They can then reissue new shares at a lower dividend rate, which saves them money. An investor might have to reinvest the capital they receive from the called shares at this new lower interest rate, which could reduce their returns. The first option is incorrect because the issuer would call shares to reissue at a lower rate, not higher. The second option is misleading because while there might be a slight premium, the potential reinvestment at a lower rate could negate that advantage. The last option is incorrect because the dividends might be fixed, but the potential to call shares can impact overall returns.

(33) (A) They do not involve federal taxes.
The main benefit of these bonds is that they have no federal taxes imposed upon the earned interest. However, some of the disadvantages of municipal bonds are as follows:

- There is little protection against inflation.
- The fixed income cannot keep up with the rise in living expenses.
- Bond prices may fluctuate with changes in market interest rates, i.e., when interest rates rise, the bond value typically declines.
- There is a limited market.
- Bid-ask spreads are large, which affects the investors' total return.

(34) (C) Closed-end enterprises can be bought and sold on a stock exchange, unlike open-end firms.
Shares of open-end companies can be sold directly to investors, and the shares of closed-ended companies can be bought and sold via a stock exchange.

(35) (A) An investment company that issues fixed-income securities and offers investment certificates.
A face-amount certificate company is a specific type of investment company that issues debt securities, known as face-amount certificates, which commit the issuer to pay the holder a stated amount (the face amount) at a specified maturity date. In return, the holder agrees to pay the issuer a set amount in a lump sum or installments.

(36) (A) A document that gives information about a public investment offering.
A prospectus is a legal document the SEC requires that details a public investment offering.

(37) (B) Payments to qualified annuities are tax-free. Non-qualified annuity payments are taxed.
Pretax funds are used to fund qualified annuities, so contributions to the annuity are made before taxes are deducted. On the other hand, non-qualified annuities are paid with after-tax money as the contributions have already been taxed.

(38) (C) A fixed annuity has a fixed payment at the time of investment.
For the duration of the contract, a fixed annuity ensures payments of a fixed sum. It cannot decrease or increase. The returns on the mutual funds in which a variable annuity is invested change over time. Its value may increase or decrease.

(39) (B) Non-qualified annuity.
A non-qualified annuity refers to the tax status of an annuity. This indicates it is purchased with after-tax dollars. It does not describe a specific payout option in the distribution phase of the contract. A life annuity with a certain period and a unit refund life annuity are specific types of annuity payout options.

(40) (D) They are designed for long-term investment and may incur charges for early withdrawals
Annuities are designed explicitly for long-term investment and retirement plans. They should be chosen based on individual financial situations, risk tolerance, and long-term goals. Annuities have a number of fees that make early withdrawals costly.

(41) (D) Raw land.
Raw land real estate investment involves the purchase of underdeveloped land.

(42) (B) Annually, even if the investor has not received the payment.
The interest payments from TIPS are subject to federal tax annually, even if the interest has not been paid out and is reinvested. This is known as phantom income. The interest is exempt from state and local taxes. TIPS interest is not tax-free at the federal level. TIPS are taxed at regular federal income tax rates.

(43) (D) It is predicted to provide higher positive returns.
The active management techniques used by hedge funds to produce large returns frequently use a variety of investment strategies. These include short sales, leverage, and derivatives to pursue profits while minimizing risks. In contrast to other investment vehicles, hedge funds are typically only available to accredited or institutional investors and are not as closely regulated.

(44) (C) It risks conflict between partners.
The limited partners are not involved in the management and operations of the business, but their investment is. This means they have little or no control over the business. This could lead to conflicts between the general and limited partners.

(45) (C) Yield-to-maturity.
Yield-to-maturity is the promised compound rate of return received from a bond purchased at the current market price and held until maturity.

(46) (D) The holder directs the broker to initiate the exercise.
Several steps are involved in the exercise of a stock option. The holder would initiate the exercise by contacting their broker to determine the strike price and expiration date. The second step is for the holder to direct their broker to initiate the exercise of the option.

(47) (B) Covered call.
A covered call is an options trading strategy where investors sell an option contract of an underlying stock or asset that they currently hold. This strategy cuts down the potential gains and limits the risk of loss.

(48) (A) Credit risk.
Credit risk is an example of unsystematic risk, as it is associated with specific companies or sectors. Legislative risk and opportunity risk are not typically classified as unsystematic risks.

(49) (A) It adjusts the portfolio's asset allocation to maximize assets and minimize loss.
Tactical asset allocation reallocates a portfolio's assets to take advantage of the changing market conditions. This strategy helps adjust the portfolio's asset allocation to maximize assets and minimize loss.

(50) (C) Hedging risk.

Investors who purchase market-linked securities frequently utilize hedging. This entails investment in two unrelated assets with a negative correlation.

(51) (B) Event risk.
Any unforeseen or unexpected circumstance that could result in losses for investors or other stakeholders in a business or investment is referred to as an event risk—for example, a hurricane or an earthquake.

(52) (C) Dividends.
When a publicly traded company makes profits, it usually distributes a portion of those profits among its shareholders. Dividends are the payments made by a corporation to its shareholders as part of its profit distribution plans. Eligible shareholders can automatically receive dividends in cash or stocks just by holding their shares. This can be a good source of passive income.

(53) (B) Payment date.
The date stockholders receive their dividend amount is known as the payment date. This date is usually set after the ex-dividend date.

(54) (D) Ex-dividend date.
Investors who purchase stocks on the ex-dividend date or after are not eligible to receive the next dividend payment from the corporations.

(55) (A) Stock and cash dividends.
Companies use two methods of paying dividend amounts to their shareholders: stock and cash dividends.

(56) (B) The date a statement about the following payment details is released.
The declaration date, or announcement date, is when the company's board of directors meets and declares that a dividend will be distributed to the shareholders. It is an important date on which details such as the dividend's size, payment date, and ex-dividend date are announced.

(57) (B) 6.32%.
The current equity yield is calculated by dividing the annual dividend payment by the market price per share and multiplying the result by 100. In this case, (130/2057) x 100 = 6.32.

(58) (D) Coupon payments.
A bond issuer, like a company or a government entity, agrees to make regular interest payments to the bondholders until the bond expires. These interest payments are referred to as coupon payments.

(59) (A) Ninety-one dollars.
An annual bond coupon payment is calculated by multiplying the face value with the coupon rate. In this case, $1,300 x 0.07 = $91.

(60) (B) Current yield.
Current yield is a measure of the annual income return of a bond relative to its market price. The current yield is expressed as a percentage and calculated by dividing annual interest by the bond's market price.

(61) (A) The date the bond issuer is obligated to repay the principal value to the bondholder.
The maturity date refers to the date a bond issuer, like a government or company, must repay the principal amount (face value) to the bondholder. Maturity marks the end of the bond's term and duration.

(62) (A) It will decrease.
The coupon rate and price of the bond exhibit an inverse relationship. This indicates that any increase in one will result in a decrease in the other. When interest rates are raised, the coupon rates experience an upward adjustment. This action causes a decline in the bond's price.

(63) (C) Issuers can repay the bondholders and retire the bonds before the original maturity date.
Callable bonds grant the issuers the capacity to recall or redeem the bonds ahead of their predetermined maturity dates. They have designated call dates, prearranged and specified periods, that signify the issuer's ability to exercise their option to redeem the bonds.

(64) (B) It is the initial investment for a particular asset and includes fees and commissions.
The cost basis is mostly used for tax purposes and refers to the original value of an asset. It is usually the purchase price that is adjusted for stock splits and dividends. This value determines the capital gain, equal to the difference between the asset's cost basis and

the current market value. The cost basis includes not just the price of the asset but also any additional costs, such as broker fees and commissions related to the purchase.

(65) (D) Both A and C.
Narrow-based indexes are stock market indexes used to analyze, benchmark, and research specific industries, sectors, or individual securities within a broader market.

(66) (C) A broad-based index.
The Nasdaq Composite Index is an example of a broad-based index. It tracks and represents the performance of the entire Nasdaq stock market.
(67) (C) ICE BofA US Corporate Index.
The ICE BofA US Corporate Index is a bond index that tracks the performance of investment-grade corporate bonds issued in the United States.

(68) (D) Stock dividends.
Stock dividends are a type of dividend distribution that increases the number of outstanding shares of the company. When a company issues stock dividends, additional shares of stocks are distributed to existing shareholders based on their current holdings. This increases the total outstanding shares and dilutes the ownership of stockholders.

(69) (D) Capital loss.
When securities are sold at a price lower than the original price, this loss is referred to as a capital loss.

(70) (D) All of the above.
A risk-adjusted return evaluates the investment return and estimates its potential return and associated risk level. The Sharpe ratio, Treynor ratio, and Sortino ratio are all examples of risk-adjusted returns.

(71) (C) Both A and B.
Stock issuance through a secondary offering process can increase total outstanding shares. In stock splits, existing shares are divided into multiple shares, which can also contribute to an increase in outstanding shares.

(72) (A) $YTM = [C + (FV - PV)/n]/[(FV + PV)/2]$

Yield-to-maturity is calculated using the formula YTM= [C + (FV – PV)/n]/[(FV + PV)/2], where C is the coupon price, FV is the face value, PV is the current market price, and n is the number of compounding periods.

(73) (D) Both A and B.
Stock splits help lower the share price, which makes stocks more affordable for individual investors. It also increases the trading volume and liquidity of the stocks, which makes it easier for investors to trade shares without a significant impact on the stock's price.

(74) (B) Reverse stock split.
Reverse stock splits are a corporate action to decrease the number of outstanding shares while the price per share proportionally increases.

(75) (C) A public bid to purchase shareholders' stocks.
A tender offer is a public bid made by a company to purchase the shares of a different company directly from its shareholders.

(76) (D) Buyback.
A stock buyback is a repurchasing action in which companies purchase their stocks from the open market.

(77) (B) It remains unchanged.
When a stock split occurs, the number of shares increases while the price per share decreases proportionally. So, the total cost basis remains unchanged.

(78) (C) Individuals who work for broker-dealers.
SROs are associated with trained individuals who work with broker-dealers in financial markets.

(79) (C) Ensure all employees hold a Ph.D. in finance.
FINRA, the Financial Industry Regulatory Authority, does not require all member firm employees to hold a Ph.D. in finance. FINRA has educational and examination requirements, but they do not stipulate specific advanced degrees.

(80) (C) Registered personnel associated with FINRA.
Only registered representatives of FINRA can trade securities and participate in other financial activities.

(81) (B) Trade securities, buy stocks, and recommend investment opportunities.
A registered representative has many responsibilities. They interact with clients, provide investment advice, and execute trades on behalf of clients. They also trade securities, buy stocks on behalf of clients, and recommend investment opportunities.

(82) (B) Series 7.
The Series Seven exam, also known as the General Securities Representative Qualification Exam, qualifies a candidate to deal with cases related to general securities. A general securities representative deals with corporate securities, variable annuities, and government securities.

(83) (D) Underwrites, sells, and trades municipal securities.
A municipal securities representative specializes in the municipal bond market. Option (D) is the only one that mentions trading and dealing with municipal securities.

(84) (B) Solicit and deal with limited partnerships.
The Series 22 exam is taken to become a direct participation program's limited representative.

(85) (A) Series 6.
The Series 6 exam covers investment company issues and variable contract products. It enables candidates to officially deal with packaged investment products like mutual funds and variable annuities.

Test 2: Questions

(1) Aaron Cohan is an entrepreneur who wants to establish a new company that sells high-quality smartphone accessories worldwide but lacks the capital to kickstart his business.

He wants a potential investor to help him with capital, especially in the start-up phase, when the risk will increase exponentially.

What is the most suitable type of investor Aaron can use to raise capital?

(A) A venture capitalist.

(B) A peer-to-peer lender.

(C) An angel capitalist.

(D) A bank.

(2) Smith is a novice personal investor who wants to actively invest in stocks and trade them as a new hobby. He finds it difficult to determine the most suitable way to buy and sell securities.

He seeks out a professional to help him buy stocks. Which financial intermediary can make the process easier for Smith?

(A) A dealer.

(B) A broker.

(C) A bank.

(D) A lender.

(3) What are the key roles of municipal advisors?

(A) To assess project feasibility, after-selling, and risk evaluation.

(B) To regulate municipal securities, market-making, and interposition.

(C) Both A and B.

(D) None of the above.

(4) What is underwriting?

(A) A documentation process financial institutions use to maintain the records of their customers and clients.

(B) A process investors use to borrow loans by providing collateral.

(C) A risk evaluation system financial advisors use to advise personal investors.

(D) A process financial institutions use to take on financial risk at a premium and help companies or other agencies raise funds by issuing securities.

(5) Which institution helps manage investors' financial records and maintain account balances?
(A) Transfer agents.
(B) State or local governments.
(C) Depositories and clearing corporations.
(D) None of the above.

(6) Which of the following is a kind of debt security?
(A) Corporate bonds.
(B) CDs.
(C) Government bonds.
(D) All of the above.

(7) What is the role of market makers in financial markets?
(A) To provide liquidity.
(B) To ensure a smooth market.
(C) To make markets transparent for traders.
(D) All of the above.

(8) What is the difference between investment advisors and municipal advisors?
(A) Municipal advisors advise individual and institutional investors, whereas investment advisors assist government entities.
(B) Municipal advisors work with government entities on municipal finance, whereas investment advisors manage and advise individual investors, institutional investors, and families.
(C) All of the above.
(D) None of the above.

(9) Which investors are eligible to become qualified institutional buyers?
(A) They manage at least $50 million in securities not affiliated with buyers.
(B) They manage at least $100 million in securities not affiliated with buyers.
(C) They manage at least $150 million in securities not affiliated with buyers.
(D) They manage at least $200 million in securities not affiliated with buyers.

(10) Why are penny stocks commonly traded on OTC dealer networks instead of major stock exchanges?
(A) They meet the stringent listing requirements of major stock exchanges.
(B) They have a high transaction volume.
(C) Their market capitalization is very low.
(D) They do not meet the listing requirements of major stock exchanges and have low transaction volume.

(11) When a large transaction is transmitted via a wire transfer, it undergoes a clearing procedure where the sender's bank submits payment instructions to an interbank clearing network for processing.
What is the primary clearinghouse in the US for large bank transactions?
(A) The SEC.
(B) CHIPS.
(C) The Fed.
(D) FINRA.

(12) Which of the following is a department in a securities firm?
(A) Research.
(B) Anti-money laundering.
(C) Investment management.
(D) Both A and C.

(13) What is the difference between institutional and retail investors?
(A) Retail investors primarily invest in hedge funds, but institutional investors prefer retirement accounts.
(B) Institutional investors handle large pools of governmental funds, whereas retail investors buy and sell securities.
(C) Institutional investors can participate in insider trading, but retail investors cannot.
(D) Retail investors are personal investors who make investment decisions based on their beliefs. Institutional investors manage large funds, such as hedge funds, on behalf of others.

(14) How is the principal adjustment of TIPS bonds, which accounts for inflation, treated for tax purposes?
(A) It is tax-exempt at the federal and state levels.
(B) It is taxed annually, even if the bond has not been sold.
(C) It is only taxed at maturity or when the bond is sold.
(D) It is taxed as capital gains.

(15) Which type of stock offers fixed dividends but no voting rights?
(A) Common stock.
(B) Preferred stock.
(C) Blue-chip stock.
(D) Growth stock.

(16) A lock-up agreement used to ________.
(A) Regulate the resale of restricted securities.
(B) Allow shareholders to maintain percentage ownership.
(C) Provide discounts on stock for shareholders.
(D) Prevent insiders from immediately selling shares.

(17) What is the main difference between cumulative and non-cumulative preferred stock?
(A) Cumulative preferred stock offers higher dividends.
(B) Non-cumulative preferred stock provides voting rights.
(C) Cumulative preferred stock allows conversion into common stock.
(D) Non-cumulative preferred stock does not accumulate dividends.

(18) Which voting method multiplies shares by the number of director seats?
(A) Cumulative.
(B) Statutory.
(C) Restricted.
(D) Preferred.

(19) Which stock is characterized by stable earnings in economic crises?
(A) Blue chip stock.
(B) Growth stock.
(C) Income stock.
(D) Defensive stock.

(20) Which bond requires payments in installments over time?
(A) Term bonds.
(B) Serial bonds.
(C) Zero-coupon bonds.
(D) Callable bonds.

(21) __________ is associated with bonds that arise from interest rate fluctuations in the market.
(A) Credit risk.
(B) Reinvestment risk.
(C) Interest rate risk.
(D) Concentration risk.

(22) What primary risk is associated with Direct Participation Programs (DPP) investments?
(A) Interest rate risk.
(B) Liquidity risk.
(C) Default risk.
(D) Systematic risk.

(23) What is the equation to determine a bond's current yield?
(A) Current yield = annual coupon/bond price.
(B) Current yield = bond price/annual coupon.
(C) Current yield = bond price – annual coupon.
(D) Current yield = bond price + annual coupon.

(24) Which type of debt instrument is a T-note?
(A) A short-term loan.
(B) A long-term bond.
(C) A mortgage.
(D) A treasury bill.

(25) Which debt instrument has a maturity of one year or less and is supported by the Treasury?
(A) T-bonds.
(B) Treasury notes.
(C) T-bills.
(D) Mortgage-backed securities.

(26) What type of investment is a treasury inflation-protected security (TIPS)?
(A) A high-risk bond.
(B) A municipal bond.
(C) A mortgage-backed security.
(D) A bond that protects against inflation.

(27) What is the purpose of a revenue bond?
(A) To finance public projects with tax-exempt funds.
(B) To provide short-term liquidity to the government.
(C) To fund agricultural loans.
(D) To support transportation services.

(28) What function does a transfer agent serve in the investment sector?
(A) To offer clients investing advice.
(B) To manage and invest funds on behalf of clients.
(C) To maintain records of ownership and distribute dividends.
(D) To oversee the operations of a mutual fund company.

(29) Which type of investment company manages publicly issued fund shares bought and sold on a stock exchange?
(A) A closed-end company.
(B) An open-end company.
(C) A unit investment trust.
(D) A face amount certificate company.

(30) What function does a prospectus serve in the financial sector?
(A) To be transparent about the investing risks.
(B) To provide details about an investment offering to the public.
(C) To compare different investment classes.
(D) To disclose the operating expenses of an investment company.

(31) What kind of product is often sold by insurance companies, combines the benefits of insurance and investment, and potentially includes elements such as mutual funds, stocks, or bonds?
(A) An insurance policy.
(B) An investment company.
(C) A bond.
(D) A mutual fund.

(32) Variable contracts are also known as______.
(A) Mutual funds.
(B) Fixed annuities.
(C) Municipal fund securities.
(D) Variable annuities.

(33) Which phase of an annuity converts the investment into regular income payments?
(A) The accumulation phase.
(B) The distribution phase.
(C) The annuity phase.
(D) The payout phase.

(34) What is the primary difference between a straight-life annuity and a life annuity with a certain period?
(A) A straight-life annuity provides death benefits, while a life annuity with a certain period does not.
(B) A straight-life annuity guarantees a fixed payment, while a life annuity with a certain period offers variable payments.
(C) A straight-life annuity pays benefits only until the owner's death, while a life annuity with a certain period continues payments to beneficiaries.
(D) A straight-life annuity offers a lump-sum payment, while a life annuity with a certain period provides a series of payments.

(35) What are surrender charges associated with annuities?
(A) Charges incurred for early withdrawals that exceed the permitted amount.
(B) Charges paid to compensate the insurance company for the risk of death benefits.
(C) Charges for administration and management of the annuity contract.
(D) Charges imposed on the owner's beneficiaries after death.

(36) What are exchange-traded funds?
(A) Stock market investments that are exchanged in groups.
(B) Investments that are only priced at the end of the day.
(C) Loans taken from financial institutions.
(D) Securities that track the performance of an index.

(37) How do exchange-traded notes generate money for investors?
(A) Through interest payments on investments.
(B) Through the difference between purchase and sale prices.
(C) Through dividends from underlying assets.
(D) Through capital gains from the stock market.

(38) What is the primary distinction between ETFs and index funds?
(A) ETFs can be purchased and sold anytime, whereas index funds can only be traded at the end of the day.
(B) ETFs outperform index funds in terms of returns.
(C) ETFs are more tightly regulated than index funds.
(D) ETFs track an index's performance, whereas index funds invest directly in the index.

(39) In the context of DPP investments, which risk pertains to the potential revenue decline due to economic downturns that impact the DPP industry?
(A) Business risk.
(B) Financial risk.
(C) Operational risk.
(D) Regulatory risk.

(40) What benefits can limited partnerships offer?
(A) Flow-through of income and limited liability.
(B) Illiquidity and lack of control.
(C) Increased tax complexity and calls to contribute additional funds.
(D) Tax law changes and reduced returns.

(41) What does a real estate option contract seek to accomplish?
(A) Enables the buyer to sell the asset to other buyers.
(B) Provides the buyer the right to acquire the asset.
(C) Safeguards the seller from other potential bidders.
(D) Specify the conditions of the deal.

(42) What distinguishes a call option from a put option?
(A) A put option enables a buyer to purchase, while a call option enables a seller to sell.
(B) Buyers exercise a call option when they believe the price will increase and a put option when they believe the price will decrease.
(C) Unlike a put option, a contract between two sellers, a call option is a contract between two buyers.
(D) Buyers exercise a call option when they anticipate a price decline and a put option when they anticipate a price increase.

(43) What is the long call option breakeven point?
(A) The sum of the option's strike price and premium.
(B) The difference between the strike price and the option premium paid.
(C) The underlying asset's current market value.
(D) The expiration date of the option contract.

(44) What is the risk of a short-put option?
(A) A decline in the price of the underlying asset.
(B) An increase in the price of the underlying asset.
(C) The option loses its value.
(D) None of the above.

(45) What role does the Options Clearing Corporation (OCC) fulfill in options trading?
(A) To act as an intermediary for the buyer and seller's interests.
(B) To offer clearing and settlement services for options transactions.
(C) To oversee and regulate the options market.
(D) To ascertain the strike price for options contracts.

(46) What is systematic risk?
(A) Risk that impacts a particular company or industry.
(B) Risk that influences the entire market or a specific segment.
(C) Risk associated with fluctuations in interest rates.
(D) Risk from unexpected events.

(47) Which risk category pertains to the potential losses from shifts in market factors, such as interest rates or economic downturns?
(A) Market risk.
(B) Interest-rate risk.
(C) Inflation risk.
(D) Event risk.

(48) How is systematic risk measured?
(A) Statistical measures like beta.
(B) Analysis of market trends and indicators.
(C) Assessment of the borrower's credit risk.
(D) Regular assessments and diversification.

(49) Which risk pertains to the potential changes in the value of one currency relative to another?
(A) Market risk.
(B) Interest-rate risk.
(C) Inflation risk.
(D) Currency risk.

(50) What is the purpose of asset allocation?
(A) To maximize returns and minimize risk.
(B) To diversify the investment portfolio.
(C) To gain profits at maximum risk.
(D) To adjust the portfolio's asset allocation based on market conditions.

(51) Which strategy spreads out purchases by investing in stocks or funds at regular periods?
(A) Systematic rebalancing.
(B) Dollar-cost averaging.
(C) Hedging risk.
(D) Strategic asset allocation.

(52) What is the difference between a broker and a dealer?
(A) Brokers facilitate transactions between buyers and sellers. Dealers, or market makers, buy and sell securities and match orders between buyers and sellers.
(B) Brokers have an inventory of securities, whereas dealers do not maintain inventories.
(C) Brokers impact the markets, but dealers do not impact market prices.
(D) None of the above.

(53) A financial institution that provides a comprehensive range of investment services such as market research, portfolio management, and trading analysis is called a ________.
(A) Dealership.
(B) Full-service brokerage firm.
(C) Credit union.
(D) Investment bank.

(54) The difference between the lowest offering price and the price charged to the end customer is known as the ___________.
(A) Equity difference.
(B) Final distribution.
(C) Best offering.
(D) Markup.

(55) What is a potential reason for a dealer to offer a markdown on a securities purchase?
(A) To sell distressed securities.
(B) To market the securities offering.
(C) To reduce the outstanding shares.
(D) All of the above.

(56) What factors contribute to the fee a broker charges customers?
(A) Supply and demand of the product.
(B) Price of the security.
(C) Transaction costs.
(D) All of the above.

(57) Which statement is correct about the five percent policy rule?
(A) It is a stipulation of the MSRB.
(B) It advises brokers not to charge a commission of more than five percent on standard trades.
(C) It does not apply to markups.
(D) None of the above.

(58) What account is most suitable for an investor who wants the broker to decide the security price and the purchase time?
(A) A discretionary account.
(B) A margin account.
(C) A cash account.
(D) A non-discretionary account.

(59) What customers should opt for non-discretionary accounts?
(A) Customers with no investment preferences.
(B) Customers who do not demand a high level of transparency.
(C) Customers who do not want to oversee their accounts.
(D) Customers with experience and knowledge in investing.

(60) Identify the types of transactions usually executed by investors.
(A) Long sale.
(B) Short sale.
(C) Both A and B.
(D) None of the above.

(61) What is the difference between a long and a short position?
(A) A long position becomes profitable when the asset price falls, whereas a short position becomes profitable when the asset price rises.
(B) Both long and short positions become profitable when the trading asset price increases.
(C) A short position becomes profitable when prices fall, whereas a long position becomes profitable when prices rise.
(D) None of the above.

(62) If the market is in a sustained downtrend, what is the best way to make money?
(A) Long sale.
(B) Short sale.
(C) Both A and B.
(D) None of the above.

(63) Which statement is accurate about market orders?
(A) Orders filled at the exact market price at the specified time.
(B) Orders executed after a slight delay.
(C) Orders are immediately filled, but the average price of the order might be slightly different from the security's current market price.
(D) None of the above.

(64) What is the primary purpose of an inverse ETF?
(A) To replicate the performance of a specific index.
(B) To provide returns opposite to a specific index.
(C) To hedge against currency fluctuations.
(D) To double or triple the returns of a specific index.

(65) What is the key difference between bullish and bearish stocks?
(A) Bullish stocks indicate a downtrend in growth and demand, while bearish stocks indicate an uptrend in growth and demand.
(B) Bearish stocks are more volatile than bullish stocks.
(C) Bullish stocks experience upward price movement, while bearish stocks experience downward price movement.
(D) Investor and market sentiment are positive for bearish stocks and negative for bullish stocks.

(66) A person who invests in inverse ETFs over extended periods should be aware of what risk?
(A) Dividends could be inconsistent.
(B) The compounding effect may cause deviations from the expected performance.
(C) The ETF could outperform its benchmark index.
(D) Excessive portfolio turnover could end in higher broker fees.

(67) What is the best way to mitigate risk in trading?
(A) Use technical indicators for trading decisions.
(B) Use market orders to quickly get in and out of positions.
(C) Use a stop-loss.
(D) None of the above.

(68) What is a good-till-canceled (GTC) order?
(A) A buy or sell order that is canceled after forty-eight hours.
(B) A buy or sell order that remains active for seven days.
(C) A buy or sell order that remains active until filled or canceled.
(D) A buy or sell order that is canceled after three days.

(69) How can you determine if a stock is bearish?
(A) The price of the stock stays in a certain range.
(B) The price of the stock keeps plummeting.
(C) Market demand for the stock rises.
(D) Both A and C.

(70) Why is it important to use market orders to set up a stop-loss?
(A) To close the positions at the specified price.
(B) The stop-losses are less complicated.
(C) To incur fewer fees.
(D) To instantly open or close positions.

(71) Scarlet wants to purchase a stock at $100 a share but wants to get out of the market if the share price falls below $80.
How should she place a buy-stop order to protect herself?
(A) Place a limit order at $100 and put a stop at $80.
(B) Place a limit order at $105 and put a stop at $100.
(C) Place a limit order at $80 and put a stop at $100.
(D) Place a limit order at $100 and put a stop at $99.

(72) A type of order that expires after the end of the respective trading day is referred to as a ____________.
(A) Good-till-canceled order.
(B) Day order.
(C) Open order.
(D) Both B and C.

(73) An options strategy in which an investor sells options contracts without owning the underlying asset is referred to as a __________.
(A) Covered option.
(B) Naked option.
(C) Futures option.
(D) Interest rate option.

(74) What are the most suitable options contracts for an investor who owns an underlying asset and intends to generate income with the premiums from selling the options?
(A) Futures options.
(B) Call options.
(C) Covered options.
(D) Naked options.

(75) The ability and resources of an entity to conduct commercial activities and trade goods or services are called _________.
(A) Trading leverage.
(B) Trading ability.
(C) Trading activity.
(D) Trading capacity.

(76) What is a long trade?
(A) The purchase of assets to profit from the price appreciation.
(B) To buy and sell assets to profit from the price depreciation
(C) To buy and sell assets to earn a premium.
(D) None of the above.

(77) Which of the following represents legitimate trading capacities?
(A) Agency trading.
(B) Retail trading.
(C) Principal trading.
(D) All of the above.

(78) Which duties are not the responsibilities of an investment banking representative?
(A) To facilitate a merger or an acquisition.
(B) To offer advice related to equity securities offerings.
(C) To facilitate debt security offerings.
(D) To execute equity transactions.

(79) Adam is a registered employee at an SRO like FINRA. He produces and distributes research reports.
Which of the following exams did he have to take to be qualified for his job?
(A) Series 86.
(B) Series 79.
(C) Series 87.
(D) Both A and C.

(80) Which option correctly lists the responsibilities of an operations professional?
(A) Onboard customers, transfer accounts, and manage finances.
(B) Conduct research and make and distribute research reports to broker-dealers.
(C) Facilitate debt offering securities, manage mergers, and advise on acquisitions.
(D) Execute equity transactions, perform other trading operations, and deal with equities, which include preferred and convertible debt securities.

(81) Which role is not directly tied to principal responsibilities or specific securities licensing?
(A) Securities sales supervisor.
(B) General securities principal.
(C) Operations professional.
(D) Investor.

(82) How do you become a registered FINRA professional?
(A) Take the SIE exam.
(B) Pass the SIE exam.
(C) Successfully trade securities for a client.
(D) Work for FINRA.

(83) What could disqualify a candidate's exam or revoke their registration?
(A) They did not attempt the entire SIE exam.
(B) They failed the SIE exam.
(C) They disclosed exam questions or answers.
(D) Both A and B.

(84) __________ ensure a firm operates under the laws and regulations of the financial authorities.
(A) Written supervisory procedures.
(B) FINRA guidelines.
(C) SRO requirements.
(D) None of the above.

(85) How does FINRA ensure its written supervisory procedures (WSPs) remain relevant and effective as the financial landscape evolves?
(A) Review the guidelines and regularly update them.
(B) Ensure firms keep a record of their implementation.
(C) Invest and trade securities.
(D) Both B and C.

Test 2: Answers and Explanations

(1) (C) An angel capitalist.

Angel capitalists are investors who provide funds to entrepreneurs or start-ups as a one-time investment or on an ongoing basis. Angel investors are known to provide funds when a business is high-risk.

(2) (B) A broker.

Brokers are financial firms or individuals who act as middlemen between buyers and sellers of securities like bonds and stocks. Their fiduciary duty is to encourage and facilitate trades between sellers and buyers. These companies, funds, or people also provide investors with marketing data so they can invest at the right time.

(3) (A) To assess project feasibility, after-selling, and risk evaluation.

Municipal advisors guide municipal entities or individuals who require information about municipal financial products. They recommend the structure, timing, and terms of these products or transactions, which include project feasibility, after-selling, and risk evaluation.

(4) (D) A process financial institutions use to take on financial risk at a premium and help companies or other agencies raise funds by issuing securities.

Underwriting is how individuals or institutions take financial risks on financial instruments such as security issuance, loans, and insurance. For a fee, they share the risk and issue securities to help companies raise funds.

(5) (A) Transfer agents.

Transfer agents are financial institutions, such as banks or trust companies, that manage investors' financial records and monitor account balances. They maintain transaction records, manage investor correspondence, issue and cancel certificates, and resolve issues related to stolen or lost funds.

(6) (D) All of the above.

Debt securities are financial instruments that represent borrowed funds. They outline specific loan terms, repayment dates, and interest rates. Corporate bonds, government bonds, and certificates of deposits are all debt securities.

(7) (D) All of the above.

Market makers are financial institutions such as brokerage firms or banks. They buy and sell securities at quoted prices to ensure there is always a willing buyer and a seller for a particular security. They create transparency and liquidity to help the markets run efficiently.

(8) (B) Municipal advisors work with government entities on municipal finance, whereas investment advisors manage and advise individual investors, institutional investors, and families.
Investment advisors assist and manage investment portfolios for individual investors, families, and institutional investors. Municipal advisors financially assist state and local governments and entities such as nonprofits.

(9) (B) They manage at least $100 million in securities not affiliated with buyers.
According to Rule 144A of the U.S. Securities Act of 1933, a Qualified Institutional Buyer (QIB) is a company that manages at least $100 million in securities from issuers not affiliated with the buyer. This rule allows for the trade of privately placed securities not registered with the Securities and Exchange Commission (SEC) to these QIBs without the need to meet the public registration requirements.

(10) (D) They do not meet the listing requirements of major stock exchanges and have low transaction volume.
Penny stocks are often issued by small companies that do not meet the listing requirements of the majority of reputable exchanges. This is because penny stocks are highly speculative and usually have a low transaction volume.

(11) (B) CHIPS.
The Clearing House Interbank Payments Systems (CHIPS) is the primary clearinghouse that carries out the clearing process of large transactions in wire transfers. CHIPS settles over 250,000 daily trades, valued at more than $1.5 trillion in local and cross-border transactions.

(12) (D) Both A and C.
Millions of individual investors entrust their money to investment dealers and large security firms. To maintain investors' trust, securities firms have various departments that handle different tasks. Investment management and research departments are two of the many departments in most security firms.

(13) (D) Retail investors are personal investors who make investment decisions based on their beliefs. Institutional investors manage large funds, such as hedge funds, on behalf of others.
Institutional investors manage large pools of funds for other entities, such as insurance companies, pension funds, endowments, and hedge funds. Retail investors invest on their own behalf to maximize profits.

(14) (B) It is taxed annually, even if the bond has not been sold.
For TIPS, the principal adjustment, which accounts for inflation, is taxable annually at the federal level, even though the investor does not receive the inflation-adjusted principal until maturity or upon sale. This leads to a scenario where an investor may owe taxes on income they have not yet received, another instance of phantom income. It is taxed as ordinary income, not capital gains.

(15) (B) Preferred stock.
Fixed dividends, often greater than those given to regular stockholders, are a common feature of preferred stock. Preferred stockholders typically lack voting privileges within the corporation.

(16) (D) Prevent insiders from immediately selling shares.
A lock-up agreement is a legal structure that prohibits the sale of insider's shares directly after an IPO or other significant event. Insiders include firm executives, workers, and large shareholders. A lock-up agreement stops the decline in stock price due to an oversupply in the market from insiders' sales.

(17) (D) Non-cumulative preferred stock does not accumulate dividends.
Cumulative preferred stock accumulates unpaid dividends, which must be settled before any compensation is distributed to common stockholders. In contrast, non-cumulative preferred stock does not accumulate unpaid dividends. If dividends are not paid in a specific period, they are not carried over or owed to the stockholders.

(18) (A) Cumulative.
To strengthen their voting power in corporate elections, shareholders might use the cumulative voting technique, which multiplies their shares by the number of director seats. This can be advantageous if minority shareholders seek representation on the board of directors because it enables them to focus their votes on fewer candidates.

(19) (D) Defensive stock.
Defensive stocks are company stocks considered to have stable earnings and are less affected by economic downturns or crises. These companies typically operate in industries that provide essential goods or services, such as utilities, health care, or consumer staples. Investors often turn to defensive stocks in economic uncertainty as they are resilient.

(20) (B) Serial bonds.
Serial bonds require installment payments, which makes it easier for the borrower to meet bond obligations as they become due.

(21) (C) Interest rate risk.
Interest rate risk, or interest rate sensitivity, affects bond owners. Any change in the general interest rate could result in a fall in a bond's value.

(22) (B) Liquidity risk.
Direct Participation Programs (DPPs) are typically less liquid investments. This means that investors might find it difficult to quickly convert their investment into cash without losing value. Interest rate risk is not primarily associated with DPPs, though interest rates can indirectly affect them. Default risk is more relevant for bonds. Systematic risk is a market-wide risk that affects all securities.

(23) (A) Current yield = annual coupon/bond price.
The current yield of a bond can be determined by dividing the annual coupon payment by the bond price.

(24) (B) A long-term bond.
T-notes are marketable government debt securities with a fixed interest rate and a maturity between two and ten years. They are considered long-term debt instruments.

(25) (C) T-bills.
T-bills are short-term government debt obligations with maturities of one year or less and are backed by the treasury.

(26) (D) A bond that protects against inflation.
TIPS are marketable treasury securities that match their principal value and interest payments to protect against inflation. They offer a guaranteed return and help protect purchasing power.

(27) (A) To finance public projects with tax-exempt funds.
Revenue bonds offer tax-exempt financing for public infrastructure projects, which include water and sewage systems.

(28) (C) To maintain records of ownership and distribute dividends.
Transfer agents record any changes in ownership, maintain the issuer's securities, and distribute dividends to investors.

(29) (A) A closed-end company.
Closed-end businesses issue a predetermined number of shares that can be traded on a stock exchange by investors.
(30) (B) To provide details about an investment offering to the public.
A prospectus is an official document mandated by the SEC that offers details about an investment. These include goals, dangers, and management's assessment of the offering.

(31) (A) An insurance policy.
A packaged product often refers to an investment strategy pre-arranged and available to investors through a financial institution. An insurance policy can sometimes include elements of investments, like mutual funds, stocks, or bonds. Insurance companies often sell these policies, designed to provide policyholders with the dual benefit of insurance and investment. They can include whole life, universal life, and variable life policies.

(32) (D) Variable annuities.
Variable contracts are also known as variable annuities or variable life assurance policies. These contracts allow investors to invest in assets like bonds and funds.

(33) (B) The distribution phase.
The distribution phase is the second phase of an annuity, often known as the annuitization phase. In this phase, the investment is converted into consistent income distributions.

(34) (C) A straight-life annuity pays benefits only until the owner's death, while a life annuity with a certain period continues payments to beneficiaries.
A straight-life annuity provides a stable income stream throughout the owner's life, but the payments end upon the owner's death. In contrast, a life annuity with a certain

period guarantees payments for the owner's lifetime but also ensures that beneficiaries receive payments if the owner dies before a specified period.

(35) (A) Charges incurred for early withdrawals that exceed the permitted amount.
Owners incur surrender charges if they withdraw an amount greater than the scheduled payment amount in the surrender fee period. These charges discourage early withdrawals from annuity contracts.

(36) (D) Securities that track the performance of an index.
Exchange-traded funds (ETFs) are investment funds traded on stock exchanges, similar to stocks. An ETF holds assets such as stocks, commodities, or bonds and generally operates to replicate an index's returns. Therefore, ETFs track the performance of a specific index, sector, commodity, or asset class.

(37) (B) Through the difference between purchase and sale prices.
ETNs make money for investors through the difference between the purchase and sale prices minus fees.

(38) (A) ETFs can be purchased and sold anytime, whereas index funds can only be traded at the end of the day.
Unlike index funds, which may only be exchanged after the market closes, ETFs can be bought and sold anytime throughout the day.

(39) (A) Business risk.
Business risk relates to the inherent risk in the industry or sector in which the DPP operates. For instance, an oil and gas DPP might suffer from a decline in oil prices, while a downturn in the property market could impact real estate DPP. Financial risk pertains to the method of financing and debt servicing. Operational risk is about the risks from internal processes, systems, and people. Regulatory risk deals with potential legal and regulatory changes that affect the DPP's operations.

(40) (A) Flow-through of income and limited liability.
Limited partnerships provide the benefits of income flow-through, where taxes are only applied to the partners' share of the partnership, and limited liability, where partners are not individually liable for the company's financial commitments.

(41) (B) Provides the buyer the right to acquire the asset.
An option contract in real estate gives the prospective buyer the right, but not the obligation, to purchase the property within a specific time frame.

(42) (B) Buyers exercise a call option when they believe the price will increase and a put option when they believe the price will decrease.
The right to purchase an asset at a specific price is granted to the buyer of a call option. This indicates an optimistic estimate of the asset's future worth. A put option, which expresses a downbeat prediction of the asset's future value, gives the buyer the right to sell an asset at a specific price.

(43) (A) The sum of the option's strike price and premium.
The breakeven point for a long call option is the price at which the underlying asset equals the total of the strike price and the option premium paid. There is no immediate gain or loss for the option holder.

(44) (A) A decline in the price of the underlying asset.
In a short put option, the seller gives up the right to sell the underlying asset at the strike price and risks a decrease in the underlying asset's value. This could oblige the seller to provide a bigger payment than initially anticipated.

(45) (B) To offer clearing and settlement services for options transactions.
The OCC is the largest clearing organization in the world. It works for the SEC and offers clearing and settlement services for options. It is a go-between for the buyer and the seller to lower the risk of counterparty default and promotes swift trade settlement.

(46) (B) Risk that influences the entire market or a specific segment.
Systematic risks affect the entire market or market segment, not just a specific company or industry. They are also known as market or non-diversifiable risks.

(47) (A) Market risk.
Market risk is the potential for losses brought on by market variables such as interest rates, currency exchange rates, geopolitical events, or recessions. Diversification cannot diminish the severity of their effects because these risks are market-wide.

(48) (A) Statistical measures like beta.
Systematic risk is calculated by a statistical measure called beta, which explains the relationship between the potential return of an investment and the market's risk.

(49) (D) Currency risk.

The danger of changes in the value of one currency to another is referred to as currency risk or exchange-rate risk. This impacts investors who have assets or conduct business internationally.

(50) (A) To maximize returns and minimize risk.
Asset allocation is an investment strategy that balances risk and reward. It divides a portfolio's assets into categories that include an individual's goals, risk tolerance, and investment horizon.

(51) (B) Dollar-cost averaging.
The dollar-cost-averaging technique uses a predetermined sum of money to invest at regular periods. This approach helps investors deal with uncertain market situations while saving investors' efforts to make regular investments.

(52) (A) Brokers facilitate transactions between buyers and sellers. Dealers, or market makers, buy and sell securities and match orders between buyers and sellers.
Brokers execute trades on behalf of others, but they do not buy or sell securities for their own accounts. Dealers buy and sell financial instruments for their own accounts. They purchase securities at lower prices and sell at higher rates to make a profit and create liquidity in the market.

(53) (B) Full-service brokerage firm.
A full-service brokerage firm is a financial institution that provides its clients with various financial services like wealth and portfolio management, market analysis, and account services.

(54) (D) Markup.
Generally, a markup is the difference between a product or service's cost and the selling price. In terms of investments, a markup refers to the difference between the offering price of a security and the final price at which it is sold to the customer.

(55) (A) To sell distressed securities.
Distressed securities are financial instruments that are in financial difficulty. To sell distressed securities, dealers usually offer markdowns to attract buyers.

(56) (D) All of the above.
Brokers charge higher fees and commissions on securities that are in high demand. Furthermore, brokers usually charge higher markups if the security price or the total transaction amount is low.

(57) (B) It advises brokers not to charge a commission of more than five percent on standard trades.
The five percent policy rule is the FINRA stipulation that requires broker-dealers to charge fair commissions and fees on standard trades.

(58) (A) A discretionary account.
Discretionary accounts empower brokers with the authority to determine the price and timing of security purchases on behalf of their clients. This grants less experienced investors the opportunity to engage in securities transactions at affordable rates with the financial expertise of their brokers.

(59) (D) Customers with experience and knowledge in investing.
Seasoned investors or traders can opt for non-discretionary accounts, wherein they must grant their brokers explicit permission before they make any investment decision. This allows users to maintain control over their accounts and closely monitor all activities executed by their brokers.

(60) (C) Both A and B.
Long and short sales of securities are two of the most common types of transactions in the financial world. Millions of investors utilize them.

(61) (C) A short position becomes profitable when prices fall, whereas a long position becomes profitable when prices rise.
A long trade position is a trade that has financial incentives when the asset price rises. Short trade positions are the opposite because they become profitable when the asset price declines.

(62) (B) Short sale.
If there is a bearish market and the price of an asset is in a steady decline, short selling is the best option to make money.

(63) (C) Orders are immediately filled, but the average price of the order might be slightly different from the security's current market price
Market orders execute trades instantaneously at the market price without delay. However, due to volatility, the final price at which the order gets filled might differ from the advertised market price.

(64) (B) To provide returns opposite to a specific index.
Inverse ETFs produce daily returns opposite to a particular index. So, if the index decreases by one percent on a given day, the inverse ETF should ideally increase by one percent. A traditional ETF's purpose is to replicate a specific index's performance. Currency-hedged ETFs are a precaution against currency fluctuations. A leveraged ETF, which might also exist in inverse forms, doubles or triples the returns of a specific index.

(65) (C) Bullish stocks experience upward price movement, while bearish stocks experience downward price movement.
The term bullish refers to the expectation that the asset's price will rise, whereas the term bearish is used for an asset whose price is expected to decline. The same concepts apply to bullish and bearish stocks.

(66) (B) The compounding effect may cause deviations from the expected performance.
Inverse ETFs are typically designed to achieve their stated objectives daily. Over extended periods, due to the effects of compounding, their performance can deviate significantly from the benchmark index's performance. Active fund management, not ETFs, could have excessive portfolio turnover.

(67) (C) Use a stop loss.
A stop loss order executes if the security price falls to or below the specified stop price. Investors and traders can get out of the position if the price goes in the opposite direction and minimize losses.

(68) (C) A buy or sell order that remains active until filled or canceled.
A good-till-canceled order remains active until it executes at the set price or if the user decides to cancel it.

(69) (B) The price of the stock keeps plummeting.
When the stock price falls rapidly, it creates lower highs and lows on the chart. This indicates that the stock is in a bearish trend.

(70) (D) To instantly open or close positions.
Stop-loss orders protect investors and minimize losses. Since the price of the assets is volatile, other orders, like limit orders, are often not executed when the price accelerates in any direction. Market orders trigger immediately after the stop price is reached, without any delay.

(71) (A) Place a limit order at $100 and put a stop at $80.

When Scarlet places her limit order at $100 and a stop order at $80, the stock will be bought at $100 a share, but if the price hits $80, the stock will be automatically sold to prevent further downside risk.

(72) (B) Day order.
A day order is used to buy or sell securities within the same trading day it is placed. The order is automatically canceled if not executed before the trading day's end.

(73) (B) Naked option.
Naked options, or uncovered options, refer to an option sold in which the seller (contract writer) does not possess the underlying security or asset to hedge the potential risk of the position.

(74) (C) Covered options.
In a covered call strategy, an investor who owns the underlying asset sells call options to generate income from the option premiums. The term covered refers to the investor's risk, which is mitigated because they already own the underlying asset.

(75) (D) Trading capacity.
Trading capacity refers to the authorized level of trading activity allowed to an entity or individual within the regulatory framework of a given market.

(76) (A) The purchase of assets to profit from the price appreciation.
A long trade is a trading position in which the buyer of a security profits from the security's price appreciation.

(77) (D) All of the above.
Principal trading, agency trading, and retail trading are all types of trading capacities.

(78) (D) To execute equity transactions.
Securities traders execute equity transactions. They advise clients on mergers and acquisitions and help them with debt and equity security offerings via private and public placements.

(79) (D) Both A and C.
Adam took Series 86 and Series 87 to qualify for his job. The exam covers the ethical standards and regulations that must be followed to conduct research.

(80) (A) Onboard customers, transfer accounts, and manage finances.
Operations professionals help new customers onboard. They also maintain financial control over accounts, keep track of money, and invest it for further capital generation.

(81) (D) Investor.
Principals are personnel registered with FINRA. They manage sales, trading, and compliance, help broker-dealers and firms work with clients, and manage company accounts.

(82) (B) Pass the SIE exam.
An unregistered individual can work with FINRA. However, they must pass the SIE exam to become a registered professional.

(83) (C) They disclosed exam questions or answers.
A candidate who disclosed questions or answers to questions on the SIE exam could have their exam disqualified or registration revoked.

(84) (A) Written supervisory procedures.
Written supervisory procedures are codified policies that guide firms, corporations, and other financial entities. Financial regulatory authorities like FINRA define these laws.

(85) (A) Review the guidelines and regularly update them.
FINRA reviews the guidelines and regularly updates them. It continuously monitors new market developments, regulation changes, and emerging financial trends to ensure the relevance and effectiveness of WSPs. This dynamic approach allows it to regularly update the guidelines to reflect the changes in the financial landscape.

Test 3: Questions

(1) What is a recession?

(A) A period of robust economic growth in which businesses thrive, employment rates are high, and consumer spending soars.

(B) A sustained duration of economic decline that results in reduced business activity, lower consumer spending, and diminished employment rates.

(C) An economic phase in which GDP starts to decline while interest rates experience a substantial rise.

(D) A business cycle marked by a significant increase in consumer spending and worker layoffs.

(2) What occurs in the trough phase of a business cycle?

(A) Economic growth rates plummet to their lowest levels.

(B) The demand for goods and services rises.

(C) Industrial production reaches its peak.

(D) Worker layoffs decrease.

(3) What is the S&P 500?

(A) A crypto index that tracks the performance of the top 500 cryptocurrencies by largest market capitalization.

(B) An ETF that represents a basket of the top 500 assets by transaction volume.

(C) A stock market index that tracks the performance of the top 500 companies with the best P/E ratio.

(D) A stock market index that tracks the performance of the top 500 publicly traded companies listed on American stock exchanges.

(4) Which of the following is a collection of provisions designed for investors that detail how cash accounts should be governed and how broker-dealers should extend credit to their clients to purchase securities on margin?

(A) Regulation S-P.

(B) Regulation T.

(C) Regulation M.

(D) None of the above.

(5) Which committee makes crucial decisions about interest rates and the money supply?
(A) FINRA.
(B) MSRB.
(C) FOMC.
(D) Both A and B.

(6) What is the difference between GDP and GNP?
(A) GDP evaluates a specific country or region's economic performance, whereas GNP tracks a particular country's political stability.
(B) GNP measures the net employment rate, whereas GDP tracks the economic activity of businesses and citizens regardless of geographical location.
(C) GDP and GNP are the same.
(D) GNP measures the value of all services and goods produced by the residents of a country, while GDP represents the monetary value of services and goods produced in a country.

(7) A financial statement that presents a summary of the company's shareholders' equity, assets, and liabilities is called a/an _________.
(A) Business continuity plan.
(B) Balance sheet.
(C) Retention of books and records.
(D) Account statement.

(8) Which financial statement should be used to evaluate the revenue and expenses of a particular company over a specific period?
(A) An account statement.
(B) A balance sheet.
(C) An income statement.
(D) All of the above.

(9) What does the Consumer Price Index (CPI) primarily measure?
(A) The average change in the prices of goods and services paid by consumers.
(B) The average change in the prices of goods and services produced by businesses.
(C) A measure of deflation.
(D) The average change in the wages of workers.

(10) Which of the following can result from economic deflation?
(A) Stimulated economic growth.
(B) A surge in consumer spending.
(C) An increase in the employment rate.
(D) A cycle of reduced consumer spending that causes decreased business output and layoffs.

(11) Which global economic factors affect how businesses conduct their operations?
(A) Exchange rates.
(B) US balance of payments, foreign exchange, and balance sheets.
(C) GDP and GNP.
(D) All of the above.

(12) The Federal Reserve Board uses which tools to create and implement monetary policy?
(A) Regulation T and discount rates.
(B) Regulation M.
(C) Regulation S-P.
(D) All of the above.

(13) What is the market capitalization range of mid-cap stocks?
(A) $300 million to $2 billion.
(B) Less than $10 billion.
(C) $2 billion to $10 billion.
(D) $50 million to $300 million.

(14) Which list represents accurate classifications of stocks?
(A) Commodities, technology, and IoT.
(B) Technology, supply chain, and finance.
(C) Growth, cyclical, and defensive.
(D) Defensive, growth, and commerce.

(15) Which of the following is a requirement for equity securities to be traded?
(A) Issued on a certain date.
(B) Issued with a specific price.
(C) Listed on the stock exchange.
(D) Carry voting rights.

(16) What document is crucial for creating a corporation?
(A) Appointment of a board of directors to oversee all operations.
(B) A certificate of business to determine the commencement of a corporation.
(C) An official document filed with the state per its rules and regulations.
(D) A detailed business plan that outlines the corporation's strategies.

(17) What is a potential effect on the stock market when companies buy back their shares?
(A) The value of the remaining shares falls.
(B) The market capitalization of the company falls.
(C) An increase in dividend payments.
(D) The value of the outstanding shares increases.

(18) Why do companies repurchase their shares from shareholders?
(A) To maintain and protect the stock prices.
(B) To improve their financial ratios.
(C) To reduce the capital cost.
(D) All of the above.

(19) Which rights are common shareholders granted?
(A) To review the company's financial documents.
(B) To request proof of share ownership with purchase details.
(C) To transfer their shares to another stockholder once the company has approved the request.
(D) All of the above.

(20) What does an ADR represent?
(A) The value of shares that belong to a national company.
(B) The number of shares in the stock of a foreign company.
(C) All national shares.
(D) A foreign company's shares listed on multiple foreign stock exchanges.

(21) What does a convertible preferred stock do?
(A) It enables shareholders to convert their stock into the desired number of common stock shares.
(B) It limits the income flow of investors.
(C) It decreases the cost of capital.
(D) Both A and C.

(22) Which of the following is a type of warrant?
(A) Fixed warrant.
(B) Call warrant.
(C) Asset warrant.
(D) None of the above.

(23) Which of the following mandates that members release their balance sheets to customers and FINRA upon request?
(A) FINRA 2261.
(B) Rule 130.
(C) SEC Rule 18b-10.
(D) All of the above.

(24) A corporation can ________ to raise money.
(A) Offer securities to investors in the form of stocks.
(B) Sell products that have a fixed income.
(C) Sell financial commodities, which include bills, bonds, and notes.
(D) All of the above.

(25) What does an investor do to convert company bonds into shares?
(A) Grant a convertible debenture.
(B) Purchase debt instruments.
(C) Pay the conversion parity price.
(D) Both A and B.

(26) What factors can impact government bond prices?
(A) The credit rating of the financial assets.
(B) The supply and demand in the financial market.
(C) The interest rate.
(D) All of the above.

(27) If Max has a ten-year $4,000 bond with a forty percent coupon rate, what will he make annually for ten years?
(A) $160,000.
(B) $1,600.
(C) $10,000.
(D) $16,000.

(28) What kind of bonds are treasury bills?
(A) Zero-coupon bonds.
(B) Serial bonds.
(C) Term bonds.
(D) Treasury bonds.

(29) Which of the following is not a characteristic of a zero-coupon bond?
(A) Guarantees a fixed return.
(B) Pays interest on the principal amount over its life.
(C) Not taxed.
(D) Gives the holder the face value and the accrued interest.

(30) How are bonds traded in financial markets?
(A) Invested in the financial markets.
(B) Listed with the state to regulate all transactions.
(C) Traded among major broker-dealers over the counter.
(D) Only traded among bond dealers.

(31) What is the difference between the sale price and purchase price of bonds?
(A) Spread.
(B) Markup.
(C) Markdown.
(D) All of the above.

(32) Which of the following is not a debt instrument?
(A) Loans.
(B) Stocks.
(C) Leases.
(D) Bonds.

(33) What kind of bonds demand payment of the total initial bond amount at the designated maturity date?
(A) Serial bonds.
(B) Term bonds.
(C) Long-term bonds.
(D) Medium bonds.

(34) Which bonds have a higher reinvestment risk than others?
(A) Callable bonds.
(B) Perpetual bonds.
(C) Municipal bonds.
(D) Corporate bonds.

(35) Which of the following is not a type of credit risk?
(A) Credit default risk.
(B) Concentration risk.
(C) Country risk.
(D) Collateral risk.

(36) Long-term insurance contracts, units, and shares are referred to as _________.
(A) Packaged products.
(B) Unit products.
(C) Open-end products.
(D) Trust products.

(37) Why do companies choose to diversify?
(A) To grow financially.
(B) To maximize the effective utilization of resources.
(C) To avoid an unsuitable industrial environment.
(D) All of the above.

(38) A/An __________ is a document filed with the SEC that offers investment details to the public.
(A) Prospectus.
(B) Mutual fund statement.
(C) Investment report.
(D) None of the above.

(39) In a typical mutual funds structure, who has the fiduciary duty to protect the interests of the shareholders?
(A) Fund sponsors.
(B) Trustees.
(C) Asset management companies.
(D) Boards of directors.

(40) Which US Federal law prevents corporate directors and officers from the trade of securities based on material non-public information?
(A) The Securities Act of 1933.
(B) The Investment Company Act of 1940.
(C) The Securities Exchange Act of 1934.
(D) The Sarbanes-Oxley Act of 2002.

(41) What is a face-amount certificate company?
(A) A company that deals with securities.
(B) A company that issues varying-value debt securities to investors to preserve capital.
(C) A company that issues specified value debt securities to investors to raise capital.
(D) A company that receives tax advantages for trading securities.

(42) Which securities protect against inflation?
(A) Separate trading of registered interest and principal securities.
(B) Treasury inflation-protected securities.
(C) Bidding securities.
(D) State securities.

(43) What is one potential disadvantage of Treasury Inflation-Protected Securities (TIPS)?
(A) They carry interest rate risk.
(B) They guarantee a return even during deflation.
(C) The interest earned is not taxable.
(D) They protect the principal amount from depreciation.

(44) Which of the following is considered an unlawful debt instrument?
(A) Payday loans with interest rates that exceed local usury laws.
(B) Treasury bonds issued by the government.
(C) Corporate bonds issued by a well-established company.
(D) Mortgage loans provided by a registered bank.

(45) Which authority can issue federal agency securities?
(A) The Government National Mortgage Association.
(B) The Small Business Administration.
(C) The Federal Housing Administration.
(D) All of the above.

(46) Herman wants to buy a house valued at $675,000. He calls his bank and gets a twenty-year mortgage to fund the purchase of the house at an interest rate of 2.33%. What will he pay for the next twenty years as a homeowner?
(A) The principal amount in twenty-year installments.
(B) 2.33% of the principal amount over the next twenty years in annual installments.
(C) The principal and interest payments.
(D) None of the above.

(47) Transportation revenue, special tax, special assessment, and double-barreled are all types of ________.
(A) Revenue bonds.
(B) Industrial development bonds.
(C) Agency bonds.
(D) Both A and B.

(48) In municipal bond underwriting, how do competitive and negotiated bonds differ in their pricing process?

(A) A competitive bond is submitted to an issuer for bids, whereas a negotiated bond is submitted directly to an investor.

(B) A competitive bond incorporates competitive prices, whereas a negotiated bond incorporates non-negotiated prices.

(C) The negotiations between the seller and the buyer determine a negotiated bond's price. However, the buyer determines the price of a competitive bond due to the availability of many sellers in the market.

(D) A competitive bond's price is determined by the highest bid from multiple underwriters. However, a negotiated bond's price is determined through negotiation between the issuer and a single, pre-selected underwriter.

(49) Which statement best defines a debenture?

(A) A debt that is used exclusively for residential mortgages.

(B) A debt that is issued by the government for municipal purposes.

(C) A debt that one bank owes to another bank.

(D) A type of long-term business debt that is not secured by any collateral.

(50) Which of the following is a probable cause of a company's decision to liquidate?

(A) The inability to clear all debts.

(B) To reduce the discrepancy in assets and liabilities when assets exceed the total liabilities.

(C) The pressure of the trading market is too great for the directors to handle.

(D) Both A and C.

(51) Which of the following is not a money market instrument?

(A) Equity share.

(B) Interbank loan.

(C) Municipal note.

(D) Repurchase agreement.

(52) What are the key components of the trading process?

(A) Settlement.

(B) Execution.

(C) Order entry.

(D) All of the above.

(53) How is the clearing stage typically facilitated in the securities trading process?
(A) The buyer pays the seller to transfer securities.
(B) Brokers use clearinghouses to reconcile trades and facilitate payments.
(C) Buyer and seller place orders.
(D) None of the above.

(54) In the securities trading process, at what stage is the ownership of securities transferred from seller to buyer, and the buyer transfers funds to the seller?
(A) Custody.
(B) Settlement.
(C) Execution.
(D) None of the above.

(55) How quickly does the settlement of government securities trades typically occur after the trade date?
(A) Within two business days.
(B) Within three business days.
(C) Within four business days.
(D) Within five business days.

(56) Regulation T allows investors to borrow money to purchase securities. Under this regulation, what is the minimum amount to be paid with cash to access the loan?
(A) Seventy percent of the purchase amount.
(B) Sixty percent of the purchase amount.
(C) Fifty percent of the purchase amount.
(D) Forty percent of the purchase amount.

(57) According to Regulation T, what is the maximum duration for investors to meet the initial margin requirement and pay for securities purchased in a margin account?
(A) Ten business days.
(B) Twenty-one business days.
(C) Five business days.
(D) Two business days.

(58) Which company facilitates the trading processes of clearing and settlement and manages securities transactions?
(A) The Financial Industry Regulatory Authority.
(B) The Depository Trust and Clearing Corporation.
(C) The Securities and Exchange Commission.
(D) The Federal Deposit Insurance Corporation.

(59) Which clearinghouse offers settlement instructions to DTCC and shares trading information with buyers and sellers of securities?
(A) The Depository Trust Company.
(B) The New York Stock Exchange.
(C) Nasdaq.
(D) The National Securities Clearing Corporation.

(60) In securities trading, what term refers to a requirement that securities must be in the proper form to transfer ownership from the seller to the buyer legally?
(A) Securities settlement.
(B) Good delivery.
(C) Securities execution.
(D) Order entry.

(61) What are the requirements for good delivery?
(A) Compliance with all market regulations.
(B) Appropriate documentation for the transfer of securities.
(C) High standards for the transfer of physical or electronic securities.
(D) All of the above.

(62) What is the most suitable offering for a publicly traded company to sell more shares to its current shareholders?
(A) Rights offering.
(B) Private placement.
(C) Public placement.
(D) Initial public offering.

(63) A person who can vote on a shareholder's behalf is a ______.
(A) Proxy holder.
(B) Subordinate.
(C) Partner.
(D) Deputy.

(64) A company wants to purchase the stocks of another company from its shareholders through a tender offer.
How will this benefit shareholders?
(A) They can avoid capital gains tax when they sell their securities back to the company.
(B) They can make higher returns when they sell for the premium prices offered by the company.
(C) They can rebalance their portfolios or exit a position in sound shape.
(D) Both B and C.

(65) When two companies or firms merge into a single corporation, which of the following is usually true about the stocks of the individual companies?
(A) Both companies' stocks are often retired, and new stocks are issued for the merged entity.
(B) One company surrenders the stocks to the other.
(C) Both companies keep their stocks.
(D) None of the above.

(66) What is a spin-off?
(A) The sale of a company to a third party.
(B) The process in which a company creates a new, independent entity.
(C) The process in which a company expands its operations with the purchase of another company.
(D) The process in which a company sells a non-performing business unit.

(67) Which of the following is a type of legal tender?
(A) Partial tender offer.
(B) Reverse tender offer.
(C) Share exchange offer.
(D) None of the above.

(68) Why do companies repurchase their stocks?
(A) To support their share prices.
(B) To reduce the number of outstanding shares.
(C) To save capital gains tax.
(D) Both A and B.

(69) What is the difference between forward and reverse stock splits?
(A) Reverse stock splits decrease the number of outstanding shares, whereas forward stock splits increase the number of outstanding shares.
(B) Total outstanding shares remain the same in reverse stock splits but increase in forward stock splits.
(C) In forward stock splits, the company divides its existing shares into multiple shares. However, the company consolidates multiple shares into one in reverse stock splits.
(D) None of the above.

(70) US government securities and options trades are settled in ________.
(A) One business day.
(B) Three business days
(C) Five business days.
(D) None of the above.

(71) Which of the following statements about FINRA's guidelines on forwarding official communications is correct?
(A) Proxies cannot be assigned to attend annual general meetings.
(B) Regulatory notices from FINRA cannot be shared with member firms.
(C) Firm members must send official information about securities to beneficial owners.
(D) None of the above.

(72) What is Form 10-K?
(A) An annual report filed by publicly traded companies with the FDIC.
(B) A quarterly report filed by publicly traded companies with FINRA.
(C) A biannual report filed by publicly traded companies with FINRA.
(D) An annual report filed by publicly traded companies with the SEC.

(73) What is an objecting beneficial owner?
(A) A financial institution that objects to owning securities in their company's name.
(B) A shareholder who refuses to disclose personal information to the company.
(C) A stockbroker who shares contact information with clients.
(D) None of the above.

(74) Why might an investor choose to purchase unregistered bearer bonds?
(A) They provide a higher interest rate than registered bonds.
(B) Interest payments are made directly to the bondholder.
(C) They offer voting rights in the company's annual general meeting.
(D) Ownership details of the bond are publicly available for transparency.

(75) What is a put option?
(A) A financial contract that allows the buyer to buy the underlying asset at a predetermined price.
(B) A financial contract that allows the option holder to sell the underlying asset at a predetermined price.
(C) A financial contract that allows the seller to sell the underlying asset at the market price.
(D) All of the above.

(76) What is a primary concern about unregistered bearer bonds from a regulatory perspective?
(A) They may facilitate money laundering or other illicit activities.
(B) They have a higher default risk compared to registered bonds.
(C) They provide tax benefits to corporate entities.
(D) They are usually associated with lower credit ratings.

(77) What is an exchange offer?
(A) To swap securities from one company with another
(B) To list securities on a stock exchange
(C) To offer a company's existing securities to holders in exchange for a different class of securities.
(D) None of the above.

(78) Which of the following is a crucial requirement to register with FINRA?
(A) List of clients.
(B) Background in finance.
(C) Sponsorship by a broker-dealer.
(D) Security trading.

(79) A broker-dealer who acts as a sponsor for an individual associated with FINRA has what responsibilities?
(A) To ensure the individual is qualified to be associated with FINRA.
(B) To ensure the individual has taken and passed all the required exams to be associated with FINRA.
(C) To ensure the individual is financially capable of taking on the job.
(D) Both A and B.

(80) Eva intends to register with FINRA. She is affiliated with a broker-dealer and must submit a form.
Which of the following documents should she submit?
(A) U2.
(B) U3.
(C) U4.
(D) U5.

(81) The U4 must be submitted to __________.
(A) FINRA's Securities Industry Registrar's Office.
(B) FINRA's Central Registration Depository.
(C) FINRA's Registration Office.
(D) FINRA's Application Office.

(82) Which of the following best defines a statutory disqualification?
(A) A statutory disqualification advises an individual to pause all financial activities and continue them later.
(B) A statutory disqualification facilitates client-broker relationships.
(C) A statutory disqualification barres a firm or financial entity from trading activities as they face disqualification.
(D) A statutory disqualification stops an investor or creditor from trading activities.

(83) Which of the following does not ensure statutory disqualification?
(A) Securities fraud.
(B) Market manipulation.
(C) Insider trading.
(D) Loan default.

(84) A FINRA-registered individual must comply with which of the following?
(A) Federal laws established by the SEC.
(B) Securities regulations defined by FINRA.
(C) The Blue-Sky Rule.
(D) All of the above.

(85) What is another name for Series 65?
(A) Uniform Securities Agent State Law Examination.
(B) Uniform Investment Adviser Law Examination.
(C) Uniform Securities Investment Advisor Law Examination.
(D) Uniform Combined State Law Examination.

Test 3: Answers and Explanations

(1) (B) A sustained duration of economic decline that results in reduced business activity, lower consumer spending, and diminished employment rates.
A recession is a prolonged economic downturn characterized by a contraction in economic activity. Historically, it has been identified by two consecutive quarters of negative GDP growth. In a recession, there is a substantial reduction in consumer spending, which causes elevated unemployment rates and layoffs.

(2) (A) Economic growth rates plummet to their lowest levels.
In a business cycle, the trough phase has a negative economic growth rate, which falls to its lowest point. Supply and demand of goods and services, expenditure, and national incomes also hit rock bottom. The trough marks the beginning of the next expansion phase when businesses gradually recover and start new investment endeavors.

(3) (D) A stock market index that tracks the performance of the top 500 publicly traded companies listed on American stock exchanges.
The S&P 500 is a stock market index that tracks and measures the performance of the top 500 publicly traded companies listed on American stock exchanges weighted by their market capitalization. It is a prominent economic indicator investors and financial experts use to determine the health of the US stock market and economy.

(4) (B) Regulation T.
Regulation T is a regulatory framework that establishes the permissible amount of credit broker-dealers can extend to their customers to purchase securities. It provides guidelines for the management of cash and margin accounts. Regulation T details information on maintenance margin, minimum equity requirements, and loan terms.

(5) (C) FOMC.
The Federal Open Market Committee (FOMC) is an oversight board established by the Federal Reserve System that monitors open market operations. The FOMC makes decisions about interest rates and the money supply within America. FINRA and the MSRB are governing bodies.

(6) (D) GNP measures the value of all services and goods produced by the residents of a country, while GDP represents the monetary value of services and goods produced in a country.
Gross domestic product (GDP) and gross national product (GNP) measure a country’s economic activity. The GDP quantifies the total monetary value of all goods and services

produced within the country over a specific period, typically a year. The GNP measures the total value of all goods and services a country's citizens produce, irrespective of their geographical boundaries.

(7) (B) Balance sheet.
A balance sheet is a financial statement with vital information about a company at a given time. It overviews the company's assets, liabilities, and shareholders' equity. Balance sheets are used to calculate investor return rates and establish a company's capital structure.

(8) (C) An income statement.
An income statement is a financial statement that offers a comprehensive view of a company's revenue and expenses. It enables the measurement of a company's profit or loss over a specific period. An income statement details revenue, gross profit, operating income, taxable income, and net profit or loss.

(9) (A) The average change in the prices of goods and services paid by consumers.
The Consumer Price Index (CPI) measures the average change in the price paid for goods and services over time. It is primarily used to assess changes in consumer cost of living.

(10) (D) A cycle of reduced consumer spending that causes decreased business output and layoffs.
Deflation is the general decline in prices for goods and services. It can result in a cycle of reduced consumer spending as individuals hold off on purchases in anticipation of further price drops. This can reduce business output and cause layoffs as businesses adjust to decreased demand.

(11) (D) All of the above.
Many global factors beyond any specific organization's control influence how businesses operate. Foreign exchange rates, balance sheets, GDP, and GNP impact businesses.

(12) (A) Regulation T and discount rates.
Discount rates, Regulation T, FOMC, and reserve requirements are some of the Fed's tools to create monetary policy.

(13) (C) $2 billion to $10 billion.

The range for mid-cap stocks is $2 billion to $10 billion.

(14) (C) Growth, cyclical, and defensive.
Investors use the classification of stocks to determine companies' financial condition and investment potential. Some stock classifications include cyclical, defensive, growth, and value.

(15) (C) Listed on the stock exchange
Equity securities, such as stocks, must be listed on a stock exchange to be publicly traded. They must meet and maintain specific regulatory requirements to be listed.

(16) (C) An official document filed with the state per its rules and regulations.
To legally establish a corporation, an official document known as an article of incorporation (also called a charter or certificate of incorporation) must be filed with the state. This document provides essential details about the corporation, such as its name, purpose, duration, and the type and number of authorized shares.

(17) (D) The value of the outstanding shares increases.
When a company repurchases its shares, it reduces the number of shares available in the market. This can increase the price of the outstanding shares. A reduction in the supply of shares may increase the demand, which drives up the price.

(18) (D) All of the above.
If a company wants to secure the prices of its stocks and ensure their protection, one solution is to repurchase its shares. This also positively impacts capital cost issues and makes the company seem financially strong.

(19) (D) All of the above.
Common shareholders are granted several rights. They may look into the past and current records of the firm. Moreover, they must be provided proof of share ownership with purchase details. They have the right to transfer ownership of their shares to another party.

(20) (B) The number of shares in the stock of a foreign company.
An ADR is a document that shows the shares of a foreign company listed only on the American Stock Exchange. A depositary bank in the United States grants ADRs.

(21) (A) It enables shareholders to convert their stock into the desired number of common stock shares.

There are several types of preferred stocks. A convertible preferred stock gives stockholders or shareholders the option to convert stocks into a certain number of common stock shares, given a predetermined date. It positively impacts the inflow of the investor's capital.

(22) (B) Call warrant.
The company issues warrants for a shareholder. It can be a put or a call warrant. A shareholder can trade a security for a fixed price with a put warrant. A call warrant enables an investor to buy a financial asset at a fixed price.

(23) (A) FINRA 2261.
FINRA Rule 2261 mandates that members must make available their balance sheets to customers and the Financial Industry Regulatory Authority (FINRA) upon request. This rule is designed to increase transparency and provide customers with financial information about the firm.

(24) (D) All of the above.
A company can employ several strategies to raise capital. It can finance its debt with the sale of products that have a fixed income. It can also sell products such as bills, bonds, and notes.

(25) (A) By granting a convertible debenture.
An investor can convert company bonds into shares by using convertible debentures. These types of long-term debt instruments can be converted into shares of the issuing company. The conversion parity price is the effective price paid for the common stock when a security is converted and does not directly cause the conversion of bonds into shares.

(26) (D) All of the above.
Credit rating, inflation, interest rates, maturity time, and supply and demand all impact government bond prices. The higher the demand for bonds, the higher the prices will go. If the government increases the supply of bonds, the price will decrease. Similarly, a high credit rating will positively impact the prices of government bonds.

(27) (B) $1,600.
Max's earnings over the ten years are the coupon value. The formula for calculating that is as follows:

Coupon = coupon rate x par value
Coupon = (40/100) x 4000
Coupon = 1600
Max will earn $1,600 annually for the next ten years.

(28) (A) Zero-coupon bond.
A zero-coupon bond can be purchased at a value lesser than its face value. When this debt instrument matures, it can be traded at its actual value, which earns a return at maturity. Treasury bills operate similarly. The government issues these bonds, and they earn the individual no interest.

(29) (B) Pays interest on the principal amount over its life.
A zero-coupon bond does not pay interest during its life. Interest on the bond is only earned once the bond has matured.

(30) (C) Traded among major broker-dealers over the counter.
Bonds can be traded in financial markets in several ways. One such way is the OTC method, which allows traders or bond dealers to trade bonds among themselves. Moreover, bond dealers and investors can trade bonds in the financial market.

(31) (A) Spread.
The spread is the only way bond dealers profit or incur a loss while trading bonds. The spread is the difference between the bond's purchase and sale prices. A profit will be earned if the sale price exceeds the purchase price. Conversely, the dealer will incur a loss if the sale price is lower than the purchase price.

(32) (B) Stocks.
Stocks are not debt instruments. A debt instrument is a financial commodity that promises the holder a fixed return per the contractual terms. Debt instruments include mortgages, loans, bonds, and leases.

(33) (B) Term bonds.
Term bonds require full payment of the face value of the bond at the stated maturity date. Serial bonds do not have a single maturity date, and their payments can be made in installments over long periods.

(34) (A) Callable bonds.

The risk incurred on an investment that expects a lesser return on the cash when reinvested is called reinvestment risk. Callable bonds are redeemable bonds and exchanged at a lower interest rate. This makes the reinvestment risk much higher.

(35) (D) Collateral risk.
A credit risk is the risk of a loss if a person or firm defaults on a loan. For instance, if a lender issued a loan to Adam and he failed to pay it back on the stated date, the lender incurs a loss. This can be called a credit default risk, a concentration risk, or a country risk.

(36) (A) Packaged products.
Products that banks offer customers or investors are called packaged products. All insurance contracts, debt instruments, securities, and stocks are packaged products.

(37) (D) All of the above.
Diversification causes an upward growth trend in the market, maximizes the use of resources, and creates an industry that supports and favors growth. All three could be reasons for a firm to diversify.

(38) (A) Prospectus.
A prospectus is an official document that briefs the public about any offer open for investment. It lists the objectives of the investment, discloses the risk factors, reports the past performance, and details other financial elements the public or interested stockholders would need to make an offer.

(39) (B) Trustees.
The trustees, or the board of trustees, have a fiduciary duty to protect the interests of the shareholders of a mutual fund. The trustees ensure that the fund is managed in the best interests of the fund's shareholders. They approve contracts, select the investment adviser, and review the fund's investment activities.

(40) (C) The Securities Exchange Act of 1934.
The Securities Exchange Act of 1934 specifically addresses insider trading. This law makes it illegal for corporate directors, officers, or anyone with material non-public information about a company (insiders) to trade its securities. This law promotes fairness in the market and ensures that all investors have equal access to the same information.

(41) (C) A company that issues specified value debt securities to investors to raise capital.
A face-amount certificate company issues debt securities to generate capital. The issuer must pay a stated amount of money at the maturity date. This debt instrument has a specified, not a varying, value.

(42) (B) Treasury inflation-protected securities.
Treasury inflation-protected securities are the only securities in the market indexed to inflation. They hold a low risk of inflation and maintain and preserve the purchasing power of the commodity.

(43) (A) They carry interest rate risk.
While Treasury Inflation-Protected Securities (TIPS) protect against inflation, they also carry interest rate risk. This means that if interest rates rise, the value of the TIPS can decrease. This can potentially cause capital losses if the securities are sold before maturity.

(44) (A) Payday loans with interest rates that exceed local usury laws.
Usury laws regulate the amount of interest that can be charged on a loan. If a payday or other type of loan has an interest rate that exceeds the maximum rate set by local usury laws, it can be considered unlawful or predatory.

(45) (D) All of the above.
The US government backs federal agency securities that issue regular interest payments to investors. All the listed authorities deal with federal agency securities.

(46) (C) The principal and interest payments.
A mortgage for a house is also referred to as a mortgage-backed security. The house's value, which is $375,000, will be financed by the mortgage the bank gave Herman to cover the purchase expenses. He must repay the principal amount of the loan and the interest on that amount each year.

(47) (A) Revenue bonds.
The operating revenues of an instrument repay revenue bonds. Transportation, taxes, and others depend on operating revenues to repay the obligation.

(48) (D) A competitive bond's price is determined by the highest bid from multiple underwriters. However, a negotiated bond's price is determined through negotiation between the issuer and a single, pre-selected underwriter.

In competitive underwriting, multiple underwriters submit bids. The highest bidder gets the issuance, which determines the bond's price. The issuer and a pre-selected underwriter negotiate in negotiated underwriting to determine the price.

(49) (D) A type of long-term business debt that is not secured by any collateral.
A debenture is a type of debt instrument that is not secured by physical assets or collateral. Instead, debentures are backed only by the general creditworthiness and reputation of the issuer. Companies and governments typically issue debentures to raise capital.

(50) (D) Both A and C.
An inability to clear debt payments and an increase in trading market pressure can force a company into a corner. This can end in liquidation. A company will never be forced to liquidate if its assets are much higher than its liabilities.

(51) (A) Equity share.
Money market instruments have high liquidity and low maturity. The maturity of these instruments is typically under one year. Equity shares are long-term instruments with greater maturity time.

(52) (D) All of the above.
In the purchase and sale of securities, the trading process includes settlement, order entry, and execution.

(53) (B) Brokers use clearinghouses to reconcile trades and facilitate payments.
Clearinghouses play a crucial role in the securities trading process in the clearing stage. They reconcile the trade details, ensure all parties have met their contractual obligations, and facilitate the transfer of funds and securities.

(54) (B) Settlement.
The settlement stage is when the securities' ownership transfers from the seller to the buyer, and the buyer transfers funds to the seller. The transaction is finalized at this stage.

(55) (A) Within two business days.

Per the Securities and Exchange Commission (SEC) rules, the settlement of government securities trades typically occurs within two business days after the trade date. This is a convention known as T+2 (Trade date plus two days).

(56) (C) Fifty percent of the purchase amount.
Under the rules of Regulation T, if an investor wants to purchase a security by paying fifty percent of the purchase amount with a loan, it is required that they pay the rest of the amount with cash.

(57) (D) Two business days.
According to Regulation T, investors have up to two business days to meet the initial margin requirement and pay for securities purchased in a margin account.

(58) (B) The Depository Trust and Clearing Corporation.
The DTCC is responsible for the clearing and settlement processes of securities trading. It manages the transactions and transfer of securities from the seller's accounts to the buyer's.

(59) (D) The National Securities Clearing Corporation.
The NSCC is a subsidiary of the DTCC. It acts as a clearinghouse for payment settlements, records the deals and agreements, and sends settlement instructions to the DTCC.

(60) (B) Good delivery.
Good delivery requires that securities be in the proper form to transfer ownership from the seller to the buyer legally. It ensures that all necessary endorsements are present, securities are in the proper denominations, and no material alterations have been made.

(61) (D) All of the above.
Securities transferred from one party to another should comply with the market regulations, and proper documentation should be sent to meet the quality standards. These requirements must be met for good delivery.

(62) (A) Rights offerings.
A rights offering is made to the current shareholders of a particular company to purchase more stocks. The allocation of stocks is based on the current holdings of the shareholders. It is a method to raise capital by offering stocks at discounted prices.

(63) (A) Proxy holder.

Companies hold annual general meetings in which shareholders vote on important matters related to the company's future. If a shareholder cannot attend the meeting, another individual can be appointed to act on their behalf. That individual is called a proxy holder.

(64) (D) Both B and C.
Tender offers allow shareholders to sell their stocks to another company at a premium price. This results in a decent profit on the trade. Investors who might be stuck in a position or want to rebalance their portfolio can use this opportunity to exit with a decent offer and liquidity.

(65) (A) Both companies' stocks are often retired, and new stocks are issued for the merged entity.
When two companies merge, the stocks of the individual companies are often retired. The newly formed corporation issues new shares. This process consolidates the two companies' assets and capital structures.

(66) (B) The process in which a company creates a new, independent entity.
A spin-off establishes a new, independent firm from an existing company. A division or a subsidiary from the original company can separate to create a standalone entity with autonomous operations.

(67) (D) None of the above.
Legal tender is a currency that must be accepted if offered to pay a debt. In the United States, legal tender consists of Federal Reserve notes (paper money) and coins. A partial tender offer is the purchase of less than 100% of a company's outstanding shares. A reverse tender offer is when a company seeks to repurchase its shares from the market, often to consolidate ownership and potentially take the company private. A share exchange offer is where an acquiring company exchanges the target company's shares for shares in its company, often at a predetermined ratio. It is used during mergers and acquisitions.

(68) (D) Both A and B.
Companies buy back their stocks to decrease their total outstanding shares or support the share price of their stock to create more liquidity and market demand.

(69) (C) In forward stock splits, the company divides its existing shares into multiple shares. However, the company consolidates multiple shares into one in reverse stock splits.
Stock splits are a corporate action to increase or decrease the total outstanding shares of a company's stock. Forward stock splits increase the outstanding shares by dividing existing shares into multiple shares, whereas reverse stock splits reduce the outstanding shares by consolidating multiple shares into one.

(70) (B) Three business days.
US government securities and options are typically settled within three business days, known as T+3 settlement.

(71) (C) Firm members must send official information about securities to beneficial owners.
Under the rules of the SEC, member firms such as brokers must forward important official information about securities to their beneficial owners.

(72) (D) An annual report filed by publicly traded companies with the SEC.
Public companies file an annual report known as Form 10-K with the SEC. It comprehensively summarizes the company's business operations, risks, and financial performance.

(73) (B) A shareholder who refuses to disclose personal information to the company.
A shareholder who explicitly instructs their brokerage firm or intermediary not to disclose their personal information to the companies in which they hold securities is known as an objecting beneficial owner. This instruction ensures that their personal details remain confidential and are not shared with the relevant companies.

(74) (B) Interest payments are made directly to the bondholder.
Unregistered bearer bonds pay interest to the bearer or holder of the bond rather than a named registered owner. They may or may not provide a higher interest rate, which can vary by bond issuance. Bearer bonds do not grant voting rights, and the ownership details are not registered or publicly available.

(75) (B) A financial contract that allows the option holder to sell the underlying asset at a predetermined price.
A put option, or a seller's option, is a derivatives contract that gives the option holder the right to sell the underlying asset at a predetermined price within a specific period.

The option seller/writer must buy the asset if the option holder decides to exercise the option.

(76) (A) They may facilitate money laundering or other illicit activities.
From a regulatory standpoint, unregistered bearer bonds are a concern because there is no record of ownership. This makes them potentially valuable in money laundering, tax evasion, or other illicit activities. A default risk depends on the issuer, not the type of bond. Although there might be tax advantages for the individual holders, it is not necessarily beneficial for corporate entities. Credit ratings are based on the issuer's creditworthiness and not the registration status of the bond.

(77) (C) To offer a company's existing securities to holders in exchange for a different class of securities.
In an exchange offer, a company proposes to exchange the existing securities of current shareholders with new securities issued by the same company. It is a financial transaction that allows companies to modify the terms of their existing securities or replace them with new securities.

(78) (C) Sponsorship by a broker-dealer.
FINRA and other self-regulating authorities do not associate themselves with broker-dealers. Instead, associated persons are individuals who work with broker-dealers. To be associated with FINRA, it is essential to have a broker-dealer sponsor.

(79) (D) Both A and B.
The broker-dealer or the financial entity that sponsors an individual must ensure they are qualified to be associated with FINRA. One of these qualifications is to take and pass all the required exams. Moreover, the broker-dealer must also be registered with FINRA.

(80) (C) U4.
The U4 form, or the Uniform Application for Securities Industry Registration or Transfer, registers candidates and provides their personal information to FINRA, which includes records of any past criminal activity.

(81) (B) FINRA's Central Registration Depository.

Applicants who register with FINRA must submit the U4 form to FINRA's Central Registration Depository. They also must provide a fingerprint card to enable FINRA to run a background check.

(82) (C) A statutory disqualification barres a firm or financial entity from trading activities as they face disqualification.
A statutory disqualification is when a firm or broker-dealer is disqualified from engagement in financial activities.

(83) (D) Loan default.
Debtors tend to default on loans due to a shortage of funds, which is part of the financial risks incurred in securities investment. Securities fraud, market manipulation, and insider trading directly violate the terms and conditions defined by FINRA.

(84) (D) All of the above.
A securities and exchange officer must comply with federal laws established by the SEC, securities regulations defined by FINRA, and the Blue-Sky Rule, which asserts that every state has the right to create its own rules and regulations in regard to trading securities.

(85) (B) Uniform Investment Adviser Law Examination.
The Series 65 exam is also called the Uniform Investor Advisor Law Examination. It assesses candidates' command over state security laws that concern investment advisors.

Test 4: Questions

(1) What are the four main stages of a business cycle?
(A) Exploration, peak, contraction, and exploitation.
(B) Expansion, peak, contraction, and exploitation.
(C) Expansion, peak, exploitation, and trough.
(D) Expansion, peak, contraction, and trough.

(2) Economic indicators are a set of statistical parameters used to determine an economy's health and performance and make future projections.
Which factor is not considered an economic indicator?
(A) Consumer Price Index.
(B) Balance of trade.
(C) Geopolitical risks.
(D) Average prime rate.

(3) What is the federal funds rate?
(A) The interest credit unions and commercial banks charge other depository institutions to borrow funds.
(B) The interest rate the central bank charges other banks.
(C) The interest rate banks charge brokers to borrow money to fund investors' margin accounts.
(D) The introductory rate of interest banks charge their customers.

(4) Why are defensive stocks considered reliable investments during economic turmoil?
(A) They are offered by companies that provide essential goods or services for daily life.
(B) They are volatile.
(C) They have substantial market capitalizations, which make it hard to move their prices.
(D) None of the above.

(5) What is market capitalization?
(A) The total revenue generated by a company.
(B) The measure of a company's net value calculated by multiplying the market price per share with the total number of outstanding shares.
(C) The funds available to a company for investment endeavors.
(D) The total value of a company's assets.

(6) The policy central banks use to control the supply and demand of money and credit in the economy is known as _______.
(A) Fiat's policy.
(B) Fiscal policy.
(C) Monetary policy.
(D) Credit demand policy.

(7) Companies use a financial metric to measure how effectively their business generates profits over time. It is calculated by subtracting the company's total revenue from operating expenses.
What is this metric called?
(A) Earnings before interest and taxes.
(B) Net profit.
(C) Net revenue.
(D) Profit differentiator.

(8) Which statement correctly describes the contraction phase of a business cycle?
(A) A decrease in total income and consumer spending.
(B) A decrease in economic growth.
(C) A decrease in company expenditures through employee layoffs.
(D) All of the above.

(9) Market capitalization is a metric that classifies stocks into different categories. What is the market capitalization range of mid-cap stocks?
(A) $40 million to $250 million.
(B) $2 billion to $10 billion.
(C) $80 million to $450 million.
(D) $100 million to $480 million.

(10) Which point is correct about building permits?
(A) They help forecast future economic activity.
(B) They are legal documents issued by the government that allow contractors to start construction or demolition on a specific building or structure.
(C) An increased number of building permits can indicate economic growth.
(D) All of the above.

(11) What type of economic indicator is the index of industrial production?
(A) Lagging indicator.
(B) Leading indicator.
(C) Coincident indicator.
(D) None of the above.

(12) If an investor wants to purchase a currently undervalued stock with a share price projected to increase, they should invest in what type of stock?
(A) Growth stocks.
(B) Value stocks.
(C) Defensive stocks.
(D) Cyclical stocks.

(13) Which statement about interest rate spread is incorrect?
(A) It is an economic indicator.
(B) It measures the difference between long and short-term interest rates.
(C) A widening spread indicates growth in the future economy.
(D) All of the above.

(14) When the prices of goods or services rise over an extended period, it creates a phenomenon known as _________.
(A) Quantitative easing.
(B) Quantitative tightening.
(C) Inflation.
(D) Deflation.

(15) A prospectus contains several financial details of a company. One such report states that an investor paid the broker a commission on a specific investment in a mutual fund. This commission is a part of the ________.
(A) Investment objectives.
(B) Sales charge disclosure.
(C) Operating expenses disclosure.
(D) Exchange privileges.

(16) A fund on the market charges a front-end sales load of about 6% for investments up to $30,000. However, the front-end sales load drops to 5.25% for investments between $30,000 to $45,000.
Which concept explains this drop in the charged rate?
(A) Breakpoint.
(B) Up-charge.
(C) Down-charge.
(D) None of the above.

(17) Which of the following is the transfer agent's responsibility?
(A) To handle voting rights.
(B) To keep a record of every financial detail about securities.
(C) To offer services to support the client and act as a liaison.
(D) All of the above.

(18) Financial institutions or entities often incur financial risks for a fee. This process is known as _______.
(A) Trading by transfer agents.
(B) Principal underwriting.
(C) Mutual funding.
(D) None of the above.

(19) How can an investment company's net asset value (NAV) be calculated?
(A) (Fund assets – fund investments)/total value of shares.
(B) (Fund liabilities – fund assets)/total shares.
(C) (Fund assets – fund liabilities)/total shares.
(D) (Net capital loss)/total shares.

(20) Investors pay a fee when they buy a fund share. What is this fee called?
(A) Commission.
(B) Front-end load fund.
(C) Back-end load fund.
(D) None of the above.

(21) Which of the following would violate the sales practice of an individual or financial entity?
(A) Give sound investment advice.
(B) Work efficiently to earn the client the maximum return.
(C) Trade without authorization.
(D) Act as a facilitator between buyers and sellers.

(22) In which phase of an annuity does the investment provide regular income payments?
(A) Phase One.
(B) Phase Two.
(C) Phase Three.
(D) Phase Four.

(23) What is the difference between qualified and non-qualified annuities?
(A) Whether or not taxes must be paid.
(B) Whether or not they are listed.
(C) Whether the annuity is a certain value or not qualified.
(D) Whether the taxes are paid before or after payment withdrawal.

(24) What differentiates a moral obligation municipal bond from a general obligation municipal bond?
(A) Moral obligation bonds are backed by a state or municipality's taxing power.
(B) Moral obligation bonds are supported by the revenue of a specific project or source.
(C) Moral obligation bonds rely on an entity's moral commitment rather than a legal requirement to meet debt service.
(D) Moral obligation bonds cannot be issued by state governments.

(25) _________ allow investors to invest in an index fund to track its performance?
(A) Exchange-traded notes.
(B) Exchange-traded funds.
(C) Index funds.
(D) Hedge funds.

(26) Which of the following best describes a potential risk associated with investment in moral obligation municipal bonds?
(A) The issuer may legally default without repercussions.
(B) The interest rates are variable and can change every month.
(C) These bonds are more susceptible to market interest rate changes than other municipal bonds.
(D) They are backed by tangible assets, which may depreciate over time.

(27) How does a real estate investment trust (REIT) work?
(A) After registration, a REIT with high liquidity is listed on the exchange and traded publicly.
(B) After registration, a non-traded REIT can only be traded through broker-dealers and has certain restrictions.
(C) A REIT is not registered, so it is illiquid and only privately traded among certain investors.
(D) All of the above.

(28) What is the number of partners in a limited partnership?
(A) More than five.
(B) Five
(C) Less than five.
(D) Two or more.

(29) Which of the following correctly lists the disadvantages of a limited partnership?
(A) Limited liability, flow-through of income, and lack of control.
(B) Illiquidity, lack of control, limited liability, and flow-through of income.
(C) Illiquidity, lack of control, and increased tax complexity.
(D) Illiquidity, increased tax complexity, and limited liability.

(30) Which of the following is not true for a direct participation program?
(A) It grants management power to the general partner and limits the authority of the limited partners.
(B) The investments in a direct participation program are very liquid. Due to the ability to freely trade financial assets, capital can be lost.
(C) The inflow of capital from a DPP is quite unpredictable.
(D) In case of an unexpected cost, a limited partner is required to put in and invest more capital.

(31) What type of account does an investor typically open with an authorized broker?
(A) A discretionary account that grants the investor freedom to entrust the broker with decisions about the price and timing of security purchases.
(B) A checking account to provide a convenient avenue for financial transactions and cash management.
(C) A savings account to provide a secure place to accumulate funds and earn interest.
(D) A capital account to track and manage the investor's capital investments.

(32) What is the technical term for the contract of an investor with the right to purchase a financial asset at a specific price without an obligation to do so?
(A) A put option that entitles the investor to sell the underlying asset at the specified price.
(B) A call option that grants the investor the privilege to buy the underlying asset at the set price.
(C) A purchase contract that establishes the agreement to acquire the financial asset at the agreed-upon price.
(D) An equity contract that encompasses a broader scope of ownership interests in various assets.

(33) If an investor sells an option with a strike price of $120 and a premium of $5, that results in a breakeven value of $125, how would the investor realize a profit?
(A) The strike price falls below $125 before the option expires.
(B) The strike price surpasses $125 before the option expires.
(C) The strike price equals $125 as the option approaches its expiration date.
(D) The strike price fluctuates within the range of $115 to $125 over the option's life span.

(34) Which specific investment strategy does an investor employ when they foresee the price increase of a commodity and strategically acquire contracts to generate profits?
(A) Hedging.
(B) Speculation.
(C) Capital structure planning.
(D) Investment planning.

(35) In options contracts, which party typically initiates the presentation of the contract to the other party?
(A) A buyer who offers an option contract to a seller as a proposal for potential transactional arrangements.
(B) A seller who presents an option contract to a prospective buyer that outlines the terms and conditions for consideration.
(C) A seller who extends an option contract to another potential seller and seeks collaboration or partnership opportunities.
(D) A buyer who presents an option contract to another potential buyer to suggest a joint investment or shared interests.

(36) Which of the following is not a type of corporate bond?
(A) Income bond.
(B) Yankee bond.
(C) Euro bond.
(D) Call bond.

(37) A ________ holds a lien on the property of their debtor.
(A) Security creditor.
(B) General creditor.
(C) Subordinate creditor.
(D) Preferred stockholder.

(38) What is the difference between a common stockholder and a preferred stockholder?
(A) A common stockholder is the last priority in the case of asset distribution of the company, and a preferred stockholder is a top priority.
(B) Common stockholders do not carry voting rights in the company, and preferred stockholders do.
(C) Common stockholders carry voting rights in the company, and preferred stockholders do not.
(D) Both A and C.

(39) Which of the following is not true for a secured bond?
(A) A secured bond incorporates a certain value of the collateral.
(B) A mortgage bond is a type of secured corporate bond.
(C) A secured bond has a high interest rate.
(D) Secured bonds are low risk and readily available at smaller companies.

(40) In the context of a new securities issue, what is the primary purpose of the SEC's cooling-off period?
(A) It allows the SEC to review and approve the security's marketing materials.
(B) It provides investors with a break from volatile market conditions.
(C) It offers the issuing company time to revise its prospectus in response to SEC comments.
(D) It enables the issuer to adjust the offering price of the security.

(41) Which is not one of the three stages of the life of an option?
(A) Exercised.
(B) Invested.
(C) Expired worthless.
(D) Liquidated.

(42) Samantha decides to sell the options contract of a financial asset that has recently reduced in value.
What kind of trading strategy is this?
(A) Uncovered position.
(B) Covered position
(C) Pairs.
(D) None of the above.

(43) Which of the following best describes a systematic risk?
(A) It affects a firm or corporation.
(B) It impacts the return on investment of a corporation.
(C) It impacts a certain firm or corporation, an entire market, or a portion of a market.
(D) Both A and B.

(44) Which kind of investments are the most at risk from fluctuating interest rates?
(A) Long-term investments.
(B) Short-term investments.
(C) Medium-term investments.
(D) All of the above.

(45) Mary offered a borrower a loan. What kind of risk does Mary face if the borrower defaults and does not return Mary's capital or pay the interest?
(A) Capital.
(B) Credit.
(C) Legislative.
(D) Currency.

(46) Which factors result in unsystematic risks in companies and corporations?
(A) Management inefficiency, flawed business models, liquidity issues, and worker strikes.
(B) Interest rate fluctuation, management inefficiency, inflation, or liquidity issues.
(C) Inflation, flawed business models, liquidity issues, or worker strikes.
(D) Flawed business models, liquidity issues, inflation, or interest rate fluctuation.

(47) What trading strategy can help balance the potential returns and losses in business?
(A) Positions trading.
(B) Call options trading.
(C) Pairs trading.
(D) Asset allocation.

(48) Which party is most affected by a repayment risk?
(A) Investor.
(B) Bond issuing company.
(C) Broker.
(D) Clearinghouse.

(49) What is the purpose of indexing in passive strategic asset allocation?
(A) To prioritize long-term performance.
(B) To use a minimum fee to gain exposure to the broad market.
(C) To minimize the risks and losses incurred.
(D) To consolidate the remaining capital.

(50) Investors who adopt tactical asset allocation strategies base their investment decisions on ________.

(A) Short-term market trends.
(B) Long-term market trends.
(C) Inflationary expectations.
(D) Currency exchange rates.

(51) The hedging strategy prevents losses in investments caused by ________.

(A) Currency rate expectations.
(B) Political instability.
(C) Poor monetary and fiscal policies.
(D) Adverse price movements.

(52) A customer account that allows investors to buy securities for full price at the time of settlement is referred to as a ___________.

(A) Margin account.
(B) Trust account.
(C) Cash account.
(D) Health savings account.

(53) A group of friends pooled their savings and opened an account with a brokerage firm to purchase securities. They collected $800, but the desired securities cost $1,000. Their broker suggested opening an account that allows them to borrow funds.
What is this type of account called?

(A) Margin account.
(B) Education savings account.
(C) Cash account.
(D) None of the above.

(54) What is an agreement that contains specific provisions that address margin calls and the maintenance margin?
(A) A trust agreement that encompasses the legal framework for fiduciary relationships and asset management.
(B) An investment agreement that outlines the terms and conditions that govern investment activities and transactions.
(C) A trading agreement that establishes the rules and obligations associated with buying and selling securities.
(D) A margin agreement that specifies the requirements and responsibilities of margin trading and collateral.

(55) What is the definition of a put option in regard to financial instruments?
(A) A derivative contract that gives the holder the right to purchase securities at a predetermined price.
(B) A financial instrument that grants the holder the ability to buy and sell securities at a predetermined price.
(C) A contractual arrangement that enables the holder to sell securities at a predetermined price.
(D) None of the above.

(56) In investment management, which category of individuals is most ideally suited for a discretionary account?
(A) Experienced traders with a deep knowledge of market dynamics and investment strategies.
(B) Investors who prefer to manage their accounts directly without reliance on third-party professionals.
(C) Employees of the SEC who are intimately familiar with regulatory compliance and financial oversight.
(D) The board of directors.

(57) Anita intends to open an investment account that allows her to pay for investment management services based on a percentage of the assets under management. She should opt for which type of account?
(A) A margin account that facilitates borrowing against existing securities to finance additional investments.
(B) A fee-based account with fees calculated as a percentage of the value of managed assets.
(C) A trust account that provides a legal structure to administer and protect assets on behalf of beneficiaries.
(D) A cash account that does not borrow or leverage and uses available funds for transactions.

(58) If an investor wants to maximize his returns on a security purchase without adding more cash to his account, what is the most suitable strategy to achieve this objective?
(A) Use a margin account.
(B) Hold the shares for ten years.
(C) Sell a few shares every day.
(D) None of the above.

(59) Which type of traders are most suitable for options trading accounts?
(A) Inexperienced traders.
(B) Experienced traders.
(C) Traders with large sums of capital.
(D) Both B and C.

(60) A type of order in which brokers have the authority and flexibility to execute orders on behalf of their clients is known as a _______.
(A) Limit order.
(B) Not-held order.
(C) Held order.
(D) All of the above.

(61) What is liquidity in the securities market?
(A) The ability to quickly buy and sell securities without a significant effect on prices.
(B) The total value of securities held by an organization.
(C) The total revenue generated by a company.
(D) The ability of an individual to access credit.

(62) What is the maximum amount that can be contributed annually to a Coverdell Education Savings Account?

(A) $10,000.

(B) $1,000.

(C) $2,000.

(D) $5,000.

(63) Which of the following are tax-advantaged accounts?

(A) Individual retirement accounts.

(B) 529 savings plan.

(C) Both A and B.

(D) Individual brokerage account.

(64) In a 529 savings plan, how are the investment earnings treated for tax purposes?

(A) They are taxed annually.

(B) They grow on a tax-deferred basis.

(C) They are taxed at the time of withdrawal.

(D) They grow on a tax-free basis.

(65) What is the contribution limit for Roth IRAs for people under fifty?

(A) $8,000.

(B) $6,000.

(C) $7,000.

(D) $8,500.

(66) Issuers are not permitted to _______ in the SEC's cooling-off period for a new securities issue.

(A) Distribute a preliminary prospectus.

(B) Conduct a roadshow.

(C) Accept payments for the securities.

(D) Talk to potential investors about the offering.

(67) What is a profit-sharing plan?
(A) An employee benefit plan that guarantees equal distributions of profits among employees.
(B) An employee benefit plan in which companies share their profits with employees.
(C) A retirement plan in which employees receive a portion of the company's profits as additional income.
(D) None of the above.

(68) Under the SECURE Act, what is the age limit for required minimum distributions for 401(k) plans?
(A) Sixty.
(B) Fifty.
(C) Seventy and a half.
(D) Seventy-two.

(69) What does the Employee Retirement Income Security Act of 1974 (ERISA) prevent?
(A) Mismanagement of pension plans.
(B) Misuse of savings plans.
(C) Misuse of investment plans.
(D) All of the above.

(70) What is the limit of penalty-free withdrawals from retirement accounts permitted by the SECURE Act?
(A) $2,000.
(B) $3,700.
(C) $5,000.
(D) $3,500.

(71) What is the penalty for withdrawing funds from traditional IRAs before an individual turns fifty-nine and a half?
(A) Three percent.
(B) Ten percent.
(C) Twelve percent.
(D) Thirteen percent.

(72) What is the age limit for the required minimum distributions for a Roth IRA?
(A) Seventy-two.
(B) Sixty.
(C) Fifty-five.
(D) There are no RMDs for Roth IRAs.

(73) Which statement is correct about IRA rollovers?
(A) It is possible to roll over a Roth IRA to a traditional IRA.
(B) Traditional IRAs cannot be rolled over to Roth IRAs.
(C) Both A and B.
(D) None of the above.

(74) Before the introduction of the SECURE Act, were annuities disallowed in Roth IRAs?
(A) Yes.
(B) No.
(C) Yes, but only for certain types of annuities.
(D) No, but there were restrictions on the types of annuities that could be included.

(75) What is the maximum income threshold for single taxpayers to contribute to a Coverdell Education Savings Account?
(A) $100,000 in MAGI.
(B) $95,000 in MAGI.
(C) $150,000 in MAGI.
(D) $80,000 in MAGI.

(76) What type of income can be contributed to a Roth IRA?
(A) After-tax.
(B) Pretax.
(C) Both A and B.
(D) None of the above.

(77) What is the strike price?
(A) A set price at which the underlying asset can be bought or sold in options trading.
(B) A set price at which the underlying asset can be sold in futures trading.
(C) A set price at which the underlying asset can be bought in options trading.
(D) None of the above.

(78) How can you stay on top of developments in the finance industry?
(A) Frequently trade securities.
(B) Register with FINRA.
(C) Continue your education.
(D) Become an investor or creditor.

(79) What determines the frequency of regulatory element training for an individual in the financial industry?
(A) Their job title.
(B) Their number of years in the industry.
(C) The total amount of their investments.
(D) The date they first registered in the industry.

(80) Which elements deal with factors related to individual firms?
(A) Firm elements.
(B) Regulatory elements.
(C) Advisory elements.
(D) Both A and B.

(81) Which of the following correctly lists firm elements?
(A) Ethics, company culture, and regulations of the industry.
(B) Ethics, sales practices, policies, and procedures of the firm.
(C) Ethics, product knowledge, and regulations of the industry.
(D) Ethics, sales practices, and regulations of the industry.

(82) What is the U4 disclosure?
(A) It ensures an applicant fits the security industry well.
(B) It ensures an applicant is qualified to be a broker-dealer.
(C) It ensures that an applicant understands financial underwriting.
(D) It ensures an applicant's willingness to trade securities and get returns.

(83) Which of the following includes the disclosure reporting page?
(A) Prospectus.
(B) Mutual fund statement.
(C) Form U4.
(D) Investment report.

(84) What is the primary function of the disclosure reporting page?
(A) It helps candidates register complaints against certain financial entities.
(B) It discloses required information to potential employers before a project is undertaken.
(C) It discloses required information to past employers before a project is undertaken.
(D) None of the above.

(85) The pre-dispute arbitration agreement (PAA) is signed by the ________.
(A) Debtor and creditor.
(B) Investor and creditor.
(C) Employee and employer (broker-dealer).
(D) Employee and client.

Test 4: Answers and Explanations

(1) (D) Expansion, peak, contraction, and trough.
A country's economy goes through a series of fluctuations and creates a repeated pattern of contraction and expansion called a business cycle. A business cycle has four main phases: expansion, peak, contraction, and trough. Business cycles affect stock prices, bonds, profits, and earnings. It allows investors to evaluate when to invest.

(2) (C) Geopolitical risks.
Economic factors directly affect the economy and help determine the health and performance of a nation's economic growth. Geopolitical risks are a political factor not closely related to economics.

(3) (A) The interest credit unions and commercial banks charge other depository institutions to borrow funds.
The federal funds rate is the interest rate the Federal Open Market Committee sets, and commercial banks and credit unions charge other institutions to borrow reserved funds.

(4) (A) They are offered by companies that provide essential goods or services for daily life.
Defensive stocks perform very well even under extreme economic downturns. Defensive stocks are offered mainly by companies that produce products for daily, essential use. The demand for these products is high throughout the year, which makes them suitable investments in slowed economic times.

(5) (B) The measure of a company's net value calculated by multiplying the market price per share with the total number of outstanding shares.
Market capitalization determines the size and value of a publicly traded company compared with its competitors and the overall market. This metric is calculated by multiplying the price per share by the total number of outstanding shares.

(6) (C) Monetary policy.
Monetary policy refers to the set of economic measures the Federal Reserve takes to control the amount of credit and money in the system. This policy achieves macroeconomic objectives, such as inflation control, and promotes of sustainable economic growth.

(7) (A) Earnings before interest and taxes.

Earnings before interest and taxes (EBIT) measures a company's profitability over time and considers total revenue generated, expenses, and income tax costs. It is calculated by subtracting revenue from operating expenses, income tax costs, and other expenditures.

(8) (D) All of the above.
Economic growth decelerates in the contraction phase, which significantly impacts economic activities. Consumer spending declines, and companies lay off employees to save on running costs.

(9) (B) $2 billion to $10 billion.
Stocks are generally classified based on market capitalization. Some classifications include nano-cap, micro-cap, small-cap, mid-cap, and large-cap, with a defined market capitalization in a specified range. The range for mid-cap stocks is between $2 billion and $10 billion.

(10) (D) All of the above.
Building permits are part of a category of economic indicators called leading indicators. The government issues these legal authorizations, which allow companies and individuals to start or resume construction or renovation projects. The rise in the number of granted permits is a leading indicator of economic growth.

(11) (C) Coincident indicator.
The index of industrial production is a coincident indicator. A coincident indicator rises and falls with the economy. This action confirms and validates the current economic conditions. This index measures industries' production output of products and services.

(12) (B) Value stocks.
Value stocks have an extremely undervalued share price compared to their intrinsic value. Companies in emerging markets like energy, finance, and technology that are relatively new have stocks that are considered value stocks. Their share prices are projected to increase exponentially in the future.

(13) (D) All of the above.
Interest rate spread is the difference between the interest rates of two financial securities or instruments. It usually measures the difference between a long-term and a short-term interest rate. The wider the spread, the more likely it is for future economic growth.

(14) (C) Inflation.
Inflation causes the prices of goods and services to rise over an extended period, usually a year. Inflation negatively affects the economy.

(15) (B) Sales charge disclosure.
The commission given to the broker to trade financial instruments on behalf of the investor is called a sales charge. The sales charge disclosure document lists all expenses.

(16) (A) Breakpoint.
A breakpoint is an investment level that allows the investor to move into a bracket with a lower sales load. In this case, the investment level is $30,000. The investor needs to reach that value to receive a reduction in the front-end sales load.

(17) (D) All of the above.
A transfer agent can be any entity that handles financial affairs for an individual. The agent's responsibilities are to manage and maintain all financial records and facilitate trading.

(18) (B) Principal underwriting.
Principal underwriting is the assumption of risk in exchange for a specific consideration. This offer could be a fee in cash or capital.

(19) (C) (Fund assets – fund liabilities)/total shares
The value of net assets is calculated by subtracting the value of liabilities from the value of assets. Dividing that value by the total number of shares will give the net value of each asset in the investment company.

(20) (B) Front-end load fund.
A front-end load fund is a commission value an investor gives a broker. This fee is an up-front sales charge an investor must pay to buy a share fund. Often, this fee is directly deducted from the payment to purchase the fund.

(21) (C) Trade without authorization.
FINRA outlines rules and regulations for all brokers and firms that facilitate trading in the financial market. Brokers have the authority to deal with the client's financial instruments, but only to the extent the client allows. Any unauthorized trading will violate their sales practice.

(22) (B) Phase Two.
The annuitization phase is phase two. Annuitization is when an investment provides a return, and the investor receives regular payments. The nature of payments will depend on whether the annuity is fixed or variable.

(23) (D) Whether the taxes are paid before or after payment withdrawal.
Qualified annuities are funded with pre-tax money and require taxes to be paid upon withdrawal. In the case of non-qualified annuities, they are funded with after-tax money, and only the earnings portion of the withdrawal is taxed.

(24) (C) Moral obligation bonds rely on an entity's moral commitment rather than a legal requirement to meet debt service.
Moral obligation bonds come with a moral commitment to meet debt service obligations. However, there is no legal requirement to do so. General obligation bonds are legally backed by the full faith and credit (and taxing power) of the issuer. General obligation bonds are backed by a state or municipality's taxing power. A specific project or source supports revenue bonds. States cannot issue moral obligation bonds.

(25) (B) Exchange-traded funds.
Exchange-traded funds (ETFs) are a type of security that tracks an index, sector, or commodity. They can be bought or sold on a stock exchange like a regular stock. An ETF can be structured to track anything from the price of an individual commodity to a large and diverse collection of securities.

(26) (A) The issuer may legally default without repercussions.
The primary risk associated with moral obligation bonds is that the issuer has no legal requirement to repay the debt. Bondholders have no legal recourse if the issuer decides not to appropriate funds to cover a shortfall. Moral obligation bonds can have fixed or variable rates. Long-duration bonds are generally more susceptible to market interest rate changes. Moral obligation bonds are not backed by specific tangible assets.

(27) (D) All of the above.
A REIT with high liquidity is listed on the exchange after registration and is then traded publicly on the market. However, a non-traded REIT is not listed after registration. It is only traded through broker-dealers and has certain restrictions. Additionally, it can be dealt with privately, so it is illiquid and only traded among a certain group of investors.

(28) (D) Two or more.

A limited partnership has two or more partners, a general partner, and a limited partner. The better part of the authority lies with the general partner. Both or all partners have a share in the revenue of the business.

(29) (C) Illiquidity, lack of control, and increased tax complexity.
Limited liability and a guaranteed flow-through of income are advantages of limited partnerships. A limited partnership's disadvantages are a drop in liquid currency, a partner's lack of control, and sensitivity to volatile tax laws.

(30) (B) The investments in a direct participation program are very liquid. Due to the ability to freely trade financial assets, capital can be lost.
DPP investments are highly illiquid. It is the illiquidity that makes the investments highly risky. They cannot be traded on the market easily, and the investors must hold onto the investments until they are ready to sell.

(31) (A) A discretionary account that grants the investor freedom to entrust the broker with decisions about the price and timing of security purchases.
A broker is a person or an entity that can participate in financial activities on behalf of an investor. When an investor authorizes a broker to trade securities on their behalf, the broker opens a discretionary account, and both parties sign a discretionary disclosure.

(32) (B) A call option that grants the investor the privilege to buy the underlying asset at the set price.
A call option is a contract that does not require investors to purchase an asset but allows them the opportunity at a specific price.

(33) (A) The strike price falls below $125 before the option expires.
The seller of a call option makes a profit if the underlying asset's price falls below the breakeven point, which, in this case, is $125.

(34) (B) Speculation.
Speculation capitalizes on anticipated price movements to achieve financial gains. In this case, the commodity's price is expected to rise, so the investor will purchase it to sell later for a profit. Hedging utilizes derivative instruments to mitigate potential risks and losses. Capital structure planning optimizes the mix of debt and equity to maximize value for the business. Investment planning develops a comprehensive strategy to distribute capital across various assets and markets.

(35) (B) A seller who presents an option contract to a prospective buyer that outlines the terms and conditions for consideration.
An option contract is a contract between a buyer and a seller. A person looking to sell a commodity (seller) presents or offers an options contract to a person interested in its purchase (buyer).

(36) (D) Call bond.
There are several types of corporate bonds. Some of these include income bonds, Yankee bonds, and Eurodollar bonds. Euro bonds are international corporate bonds. Eurodollar bonds are also a type of Euro bond.

(37) (A) Security creditor.
A secured creditor can hold a lien on a debtor's property. That property can be used in case the debtor defaults on the loan. The lien provides interest from the debtor's property to the secured creditor.

(38) (D) Both A and C.
A common stockholder is the last priority in the case of asset distribution of the company, and a preferred stockholder is a top priority. Common stockholders carry voting rights in the company, and preferred stockholders do not. Even though common stockholders are not prioritized in asset distribution, they enjoy equity ownership.

(39) (C) A secured bond has a high interest rate.
A secured bond is a category of corporate bonds. A company provides collateral for the bond's security. It has a low risk, which indicates a low interest rate. A high interest rate would make the bond a higher return but increase the risk.

(40) (C) It offers the issuing company time to revise its prospectus in response to SEC comments.
The cooling-off period typically lasts twenty days. It is the period after the registration statement is filed with the SEC and before its effective date. At this time, the SEC reviews the registration statement, and the issuer may need to revise the prospectus based on the SEC's feedback. The issuer cannot sell the securities during this period.

(41) (B) Invested.
An option expires when an investor chooses not to sell the option or cash in on it in some other way. An investor can also liquidate the option contract through a sale before the expiration. Although one might "invest" in options by buying them, "invested" is not a stage like the other options listed.

(42) (B) Covered position.
A covered position trading strategy entails the sale of the option contract to limit the losses incurred if the prices drop further. However, the investor could miss out on any returns they might receive if the prices rose.

(43) (C) It impacts a certain firm or corporation, an entire market, or a portion of a market.
Systematic risks are market or non-diversifiable risks as they affect entire markets and industries due to their large-scale nature.

(44) (A) Long-term investments.
Long-term investments are prone to the effects of fluctuating interest risks. If the interest rate rises, the investor will get lower returns, but if the interest rate decreases, the investor's returns will increase.

(45) (B) Credit.
Currency risks relate to fluctuations in the exchange rate and capital risks to investment in a company. The attached risk to loan default is called a credit risk.

(46) (A) Management inefficiency, flawed business models, liquidity issues, and worker strikes.
Inflation rates and fluctuating interest rates impact entire financial markets, not just certain firms and companies.

(47) (D) Asset allocation.
The returns and losses on financial assets can only be regulated by allocating assets accordingly. Assets like equities and fixed income must be regulated to limit losses and maximize returns.

(48) (A) Investor.
An investor buys a bond from a company. If the company fails to pay the investor the amount due, the investor's income is at risk.

(49) (B) To use a minimum fee to gain exposure to the broad market.
Passive strategic asset allocation comprises three major components, one of which is indexing. Indexing primarily buys index funds, which offer exposure to the broad market and cost a minimum fee.

(50) (A) Short-term market trends.
Tactical asset allocation strategies entail the consideration of short-term market trends to decide on investment opportunities. These decisions are active and spontaneous, so investors must study current market trends.

(51) (D) Adverse price movements.
Hedging strategies help prevent investment losses due to adverse price movements. If asset prices are expected to fall, investors will use a put option to sell that asset if the value drops below the strike price to reduce their losses.

(52) (C) Cash account.
A cash account permits users to buy or sell securities strictly with the cash available in the account. Complete funds must be available at the time of settlement to purchase securities. Cash accounts cannot be used for loans to complete transactions.

(53) (A) Margin account.
A margin account permits investors to use loans to complete securities transactions. Funds are secured with collateral in cash, securities, or other investments.

(54) (D) A margin agreement that specifies the requirements and responsibilities of margin trading and collateral.
A margin agreement outlines the terms and conditions of the margin accounts. The contract contains all the relevant information, which includes interest rates, collateral requirements, maintenance margin, and margin calls. This account can only be opened if the investor agrees to the margin agreement.

(55) (C) A contractual arrangement that enables the holder to sell securities at a predetermined price.
A put option is a contract that allows the holder to sell an asset at a set price within a designated time frame.

(56) (A) Experienced traders with a deep knowledge of market dynamics and investment strategies.
Discretionary accounts are managed by a licensed broker or advisor with the authority to make trading decisions without the client's approval. They are typically suitable for experienced traders or individuals with significant capital and lack the time or expertise to manage their accounts.

(57) (B) A fee-based account with fees calculated as a percentage of the value of managed assets.
Fee-based accounts allow investors to pay fees based on the percentage of the assets under management to investment professionals for investment management services.

(58) (A) Use a margin account.
Investors can borrow funds to buy more shares to increase their buying power and maximize returns. A margin account holds funds that can be borrowed for the purchase or sale of securities without using more cash.

(59) (D) Both B and C.
Options trading accounts allow investors to buy or sell options contracts. These contracts are relatively complex for a novice trader since there are many moving parts in this type of trading, and a slight mistake can cause heavy losses. Large sums of capital are required to open options accounts, which makes them unsuitable for inexperienced traders.

(60) (B) Not-held order.
A not-held order gives brokers full authorization to execute the orders at their discretion.

(61) (A) The ability to quickly buy and sell securities without a significant effect on prices.
Liquidity measures the speed at which an asset, security, or other financial instrument can be bought or sold without a significant effect on its price or value. For instance, an investor wants to purchase 1000 shares of a stock at a particular price in a specified period. If the liquidity is high, the investor can quickly buy the shares without a pump or dump in the stock price.

(62) (C) $2,000.
$2,000 per year is the maximum contribution that can be made by an individual to a Coverdell Education Savings Account for every child under eighteen years old.

(63) (C) Both A and B.
Tax-advantaged accounts offer tax benefits to their holders. This allows individuals to reduce their tax liabilities and grow their savings. Individual retirement accounts and 529 savings plans are tax-advantaged accounts.

(64) (D) They grow on a tax-free basis.
The 529 savings plan produces tax-free earnings, provided the funds are used for qualified education expenses. This means that any interest, dividends, or capital gains generated by the investments in a 529 plan are not subject to federal (and often state) taxes when withdrawn to cover eligible education costs.
(65) (B) $6,000.
For people under fifty, the maximum contribution limit to a Roth IRA is $6,000 annually.

(66) (C) Accept payments for the securities.
In the cooling-off period, the issuer can distribute a preliminary prospectus (red herring), talk to potential investors about the offering, and conduct roadshows to promote interest in the offering. However, while these promotional activities are permitted, the issuer cannot accept any payments for the securities or make any sales until the cooling-off period has ended and the registration becomes effective.

(67) (B) An employee benefit plan in which companies share their profits with employees.
A profit-sharing plan awards employees a portion of the company's profits. This retirement plan provides additional retirement savings to the employees based on the company's profitability.

(68) (D) Seventy-two.
The SECURE Act raised the age limit for the required minimum distributions for traditional IRAs and 401(k) plans from seventy and a half to seventy-two.

(69) (A) Mismanagement of pension plans.
The sole purpose of the ERISA Act of 1974 was to eliminate the misuse and mismanagement of pension plans. The act set ground rules under which pension plans operate.

(70) (C) $5,000.
The SECURE Act permitted penalty-free withdrawals of up to $5,000 from retirement accounts to cover qualified expenses related to the birth or adoption of a child.

(71) (B) Ten percent.
If individuals withdraw funds from a traditional IRA before the age of fifty-nine and a half, they will be liable to pay a ten percent penalty to the IRS. This includes income taxes.

(72) (D) There are no RMDs for Roth IRAs.
Roth IRAs have no required minimum distributions (RMDs).

(73) (D) None of the above.
IRA rollovers transfer funds from one type of IRA to another. The rules stipulate that traditional IRAs can be rolled over to Roth IRAs, but Roth IRAs cannot be rolled over to traditional IRAs.

(74) (B) No.
Annuities were allowed in Roth IRAs before the SECURE Act. The SECURE Act does not pertain to whether Roth IRAs can offer annuities. Annuities are insurance products that can be held within accounts like IRAs (Roth or Traditional). The SECURE Act provisions impact the use of annuities within defined contribution plans like 401(k)s but do not directly affect the use of annuities within Roth IRAs. It is important to note that an individual could hold an annuity within a Roth IRA even before the SECURE Act.

(75) (B) $95,000 in MAGI.
Single taxpayers with a modified annual gross income of $95,000 or less are eligible to contribute to the Coverdell ESA.

(76) (A) After-tax.
Contributions to a Roth IRA are made with after-tax dollars, which means the contributions are not tax-deductible in the year they are made.

(77) (A) A set price at which the underlying asset can be bought or sold in options trading.
In options trading, a strike price is a fixed or agreed-upon price at which underlying assets can be bought or sold.

(78) (C) Continue your education.
Continued education allows an investor to stay updated with developments in the finance industry and regulatory changes.

(79) (D) The date they first registered in the industry.
The date an individual first registered in the industry determines the frequency of regulatory element training. The Financial Industry Regulatory Authority (FINRA) requires that registered securities professionals complete a Regulatory Element

Program on the second anniversary of their registration date and every three years thereafter. This requirement is irrespective of the individual's role or industry position.

(80) (A) Firm elements.
Firm elements only deal with factors related to companies. Regulatory elements are concerned with the regulations and laws of the entire financial industry.

(81) (B) Ethics, sales practices, policies, and procedures of the firm.
Industry regulations are related to the whole industry. However, each firm's ethics, sales practices, and procedures are unique.

(82) (A) It ensures an applicant fits the security industry well.
Form U4 is an official background check on all candidates who want to register with FINRA.

(83) (C) Form U4.
The U4 incorporates the disclosure reporting page to allow employers to check an applicant's suitability in the securities industry.

(84) (B) It discloses required information to potential employers before a project is undertaken.
The disclosure reporting page divulges information about the candidate to potential employers. This information includes any criminal charges, non-disciplinary actions, or customer complaints.

(85) (C) Employee and employer (broker-dealer).
The employee and employer sign a pre-dispute arbitration agreement to facilitate all activities in the respective financial institution. The employer is either a broker-dealer or a firm acting as a broker.

Test 5: Questions

(1) Which of the following statements about an initial public offering is incorrect?
(A) The process by which private companies make their shares available to the public for the first time.
(B) The process by which companies allow investors to purchase shares.
(C) The process by which companies raise capital by selling their assets to the public.
(D) The process by which a private company goes public and is listed on a stock exchange.

(2) What are private offerings?
(A) Exclusive invitations to select investors to participate in investments that are available to the public.
(B) Securities offerings presented to a small, private pool of investors who meet a specific eligibility requirement.
(C) Securities offerings designed for high-value accredited investors and require registration with the SEC.
(D) None of the above.

(3) Why are underwriting commitments important for companies to raise capital?
(A) They assure companies they can raise the funds they need to execute business plans.
(B) The underwriters agree to purchase securities from the company at a specified price and sell them to potential investors at a markup.
(C) They help establish a fair market price for securities, which creates high liquidity.
(D) All of the above.

(4) Which legal document provides investors with the necessary information about a company's operations and securities to make an informed investment decision?
(A) After-market prospectus.
(B) Underwriting commitments.
(C) Business continuity plan.
(D) Security offering prospectus.

(5) Which of the following are types of underwriting commitments?
(A) Best efforts, worst efforts, standby, and firm commitment.
(B) Best efforts, best efforts all-or-none, standby, and constitutional commitment.
(C) Standby, best efforts, best efforts mini-maxi, and constitutional commitment.
(D) Standby, best efforts, best efforts mini-maxi, and firm commitment.

(6) Which statement is correct about shelf registration with the SEC?
(A) Allows multiple securities to be registered.
(B) Requires a portion of profits from securities sales to be paid as a fee.
(C) Allows registered securities to be held for later sale.
(D) Both A and C.

(7) What is the role of syndicate members in an IPO?
(A) Work with underwriters to sell IPO shares to qualified investors.
(B) Register the IPO with the SEC.
(C) Promote the IPO to foreign markets.
(D) Establish compliance with the SEC rulings.

(8) A privately held company that creates and sells securities to raise capital is called a/an:
(A) Underwriting manager.
(B) Syndicate.
(C) Issuer.
(D) Selling Group.

(9) The difference between the price an underwriter buys a security and the price it is sold to the public is called the:
(A) Issuance fee.
(B) Underwriting spread.
(C) Distribution fee.
(D) Offering price markup.

(10) What best describes the main characteristic of the bidding process in a sealed bid auction for securities?
(A) All bids are made publicly and in real-time.
(B) Participants can adjust their bids based on others' bids.
(C) Bids are submitted privately and are not disclosed until the auction closes.
(D) Only the highest bidder is allowed to purchase the security.

(11) Why might an issuer choose a sealed bid auction to sell their securities?
(A) To foster competition among the largest institutional investors.
(B) To ensure that current market conditions influence all bids.
(C) To potentially obtain a higher price for their securities without bidders being influenced by each other.
(D) To facilitate faster transactions as bids are processed in real-time.

(12) A privately held company decides to go public. It publicly issues its shares to raise capital to achieve long-term business goals. The company aims to list stock on the NYSE, so it files after-market prospectus requirements.
How early should the prospectus be filed with the authorities?
(A) Within thirty days of the offering.
(B) After forty days of the offering.
(C) After fifty days of the offering.
(D) Within twenty-five days of the offering.

(13) A formal document required by and filed with the SEC is called a prospectus. There are several types of prospectuses. Which of the following is a type of prospectus?
(A) Surefire prospectus.
(B) Preliminary prospectus.
(C) Limited-time offer prospectus.
(D) None of the above.

(14) A prospectus in which an issuer discusses its securities during the waiting period of an IPO without being considered a prospect offering is known as a:
(A) Summary prospectus.
(B) Surefire prospectus.
(C) Free-writing prospectus.
(D) Statutory prospectus.

(15) What is the main difference between debt and equity financing?
(A) Equity financing involves the sale of ownership shares, whereas debt financing borrows money with repayment commitments.
(B) Equity financing awards ownership stakes, whereas debt financing necessitates interest payments.
(C) Loans or bonds are used for debt financing, whereas stocks or shares are used for equity financing.
(D) Equity financing generates ownership, whereas debt financing creates debt.

(16) Which of the following is incorrect about the ownership of common stocks?
(A) It does not confer voting rights.
(B) It does not entitle one to regular dividend payments.
(C) It does not confer priority in the event of bankruptcy.
(D) It does not entitle the holder to interest payments.

(17) What is the function of a lock-up agreement in terms of restricted securities?
(A) Permits the immediate sale of newly issued securities.
(B) Safeguards against excessive insider selling pressure.
(C) Makes the transfer of ownership rights easier.
(D) Ensures regulatory reporting compliance.

(18) How does debt financing help businesses raise money?
(A) Issues securities to investors.
(B) Provides fixed-income securities like bonds or notes.
(C) Repurchases shares from the market.
(D) Secures bank loans.

(19) What is rule 144?
(A) A set of rules that govern restricted and controlled securities trade.
(B) A document necessary for the formation of a corporation.
(C) A certificate that proves the holder's stock ownership in a foreign corporation.
(D) A document that grants common stockholders voting rights.

(20) What are American depositary receipts?
(A) Certificates that prove stock ownership in a foreign corporation.
(B) Shares of reputable blue chip companies.
(C) Procedures for shareholder voting.
(D) Documents that prove ownership of common stock.

(21) What is the primary attribute of blue chip stocks?
(A) They are well-known brands with successful track records.
(B) They provide regular dividend income.
(C) They provide consistent returns.
(D) They are expected to grow rapidly.

(22) What is the function of callable preferred stock?
(A) Provides the issuer a stable income stream in an economic downturn.
(B) Can be converted into a certain number of shares of common stock.
(C) Accumulates dividends until they are paid to common stockholders.
(D) Can be redeemed by the issuer for a predetermined price.

(23) What are preemptive rights?
(A) Allow stockholders to keep their ownership percentage.
(B) Allow stockholders access to corporate records.
(C) Allow stockholders to look into financial information.
(D) Allow stockholders to vote at annual meetings.

(24) What is a warrant?
(A) A certificate of stock ownership in a foreign corporation.
(B) A derivative that provides the right to buy a company's stock at a specified price.
(C) A document for corporate formation.
(D) A mandate that preferred shareholders must split additional dividends with common shareholders.

(25) What is a debt instrument?
(A) A contractual guarantee to raise money.
(B) A tangible financial asset.
(C) An intangible financial asset.
(D) A stock investment tool.

(26) Long-term debt is what kind of financial instrument?
(A) Treasury bill.
(B) Working loan given for less than one year.
(C) Payday loan.
(D) Bond.

(27) What is the main goal of bond issuance?
(A) To raise capital for government initiatives.
(B) To pay recurring interest payments.
(C) To remove the reinvestment risk.
(D) To receive a lump sum payment at maturity.

(28) What distinguishes term bonds from serial bonds?
(A) Serial bonds require a lump sum payment, whereas term bonds require installment payments.
(B) Serial bonds only require a single payment at maturity, whereas term bonds require payments in installments.
(C) Term bonds mature more quickly than serial bonds.
(D) Serial bonds are traded OTC, whereas term bonds are traded publicly.

(29) What is a zero-coupon bond?
(A) A bond with recurring interest payments.
(B) A bond sold at a significant discount.
(C) A bond with a maximum one-year maturity.
(D) A bond with a high risk of reinvestment.

(30) What is a bond's carrying value?
(A) The total face value plus the premium.
(B) The premium and face value subtracted from the purchase price.
(C) The interest compounded semi-annually.
(D) The amount set aside in a sinking fund.

(31) What is the market's method for trading bonds?
(A) Exchanges.
(B) Small broker-dealers.
(C) Bond dealers.
(D) Investors.

(32) Zero-coupon bonds are appropriate for investors who prefer:
(A) Regular interest payments.
(B) Short-term investments.
(C) Fixed nominal values in the distant future.
(D) High-yield bonds.

(33) Why do bond prices vary from par value?
(A) Because of changes in the issuer's credit rating.
(B) Because of a shift in the bond's supply or demand.
(C) Because of an increase in interest rates.
(D) All of the above.

(34) What is the risk of reinvestment?
(A) The potential for financial loss.
(B) The threat of bond issuer default.
(C) The possibility of interest rates falling.
(D) The possibility of reinvesting cash flow at a lower rate.

(35) What are the two categories of debt instruments?
(A) Short and long-term.
(B) Long-term and working capital.
(C) Long-term and T-bills.
(D) Medium-term and T-bills.

(36) Which debt instrument has a one-year or short-maturity term?
(A) Treasury notes.
(B) Treasury bonds.
(C) T-bills.
(D) T-STRIPS.

(37) What is a treasury bond's maturity range?
(A) Less than one year.
(B) One to Five years.
(C) Five to ten years.
(D) Ten to thirty years.

(38) Treasury inflation-protected securities serve as a vehicle for:
(A) Guarantee of return.
(B) Protection against inflation.
(C) Low-risk investment options.
(D) Tax-free income.

(39) Which of the following best describes the tax benefits of a 529 plan that is used for qualified educational expenses?

(A) Contributions are tax-deductible, and distributions are taxed as ordinary income.

(B) Both contributions and distributions are tax-free.

(C) Contributions are made with after-tax dollars, but qualified distributions are tax-free.

(D) Contributions receive a federal tax credit, and distributions are taxed at a reduced rate.

(40) Which of the following is mainly financed by municipal bonds?

(A) Public projects.

(B) Loans to farmers.

(C) Mortgage-backed securities.

(D) None of the above.

(41) What is the duration of a municipal note's maturity?

(A) More than one year.

(B) One year.

(C) Less than one year.

(D) No fixed maturity period.

(42) What type of municipal notes are repaid through upcoming tax receipts?

(A) Bond anticipation notes.

(B) Tax anticipation notes.

(C) Grant anticipation notes.

(D) Revenue anticipation notes.

(43) Which of the following best describes a trust fund?

(A) A mutual fund that mainly invests in government securities.

(B) An account managed by a trustee that is established for the benefit of another.

(C) An investment vehicle that exclusively invests in real estate properties.

(D) A bank account that earns higher interest than standard savings accounts.

(44) What kind of corporate bonds are supported by a particular collateral?
(A) Secured bonds.
(B) Income bonds.
(C) Eurodollar bonds.
(D) Debentures.

(45) Which type of liquidation is started by an insolvent company's directors or owners?
(A) Voluntary liquidation by creditors.
(B) Voluntary liquidation by members.
(C) Mandatory liquidation.
(D) Secured liquidation.

(46) What position do common stockholders hold in the allocation of corporate assets?
(A) First.
(B) Second.
(C) Third.
(D) Last.

(47) What is an option?
(A) A deal between a buyer and a seller.
(B) A commitment to buy an asset.
(C) A derivative instrument.
(D) Both A and C.

(48) What is a call option?
(A) A contract in which the buyer can sell an asset.
(B) A contract in which the buyer can purchase an asset.
(C) An agreement that grants the seller the authority to sell an asset.
(D) An agreement that grants the seller the option to purchase an asset.

(49) What is the long call option breakeven point?
(A) When the market price is less than the strike price.
(B) When the market price is greater than the strike price.
(C) When the market price equals the strike price plus the premium.
(D) When the market price equals the premium paid.

(50) Why is diversification in investment portfolios important?
(A) To increase prospective returns.
(B) To get rid of all possible dangers.
(C) To concentrate on one asset class for greater gains.
(D) To lessen exposure to random risks.

(51) What is the trustee's primary role in a trust fund?
(A) To contribute assets to the trust.
(B) To be the primary beneficiary of the trust.
(C) To manage and distribute the trust's assets per the grantor's wishes.
(D) To ensure the trust pays taxes at the highest rate possible.

(52) What is an institutional investor?
(A) An organization that makes investments for their accounts.
(B) An entity that makes investments on behalf of others.
(C) An individual who invests a substantial amount of money in financial markets.
(D) None of the above.

(53) What is suitability?
(A) To match investors with suitable brokers.
(B) To buy suitable securities that maximize the potential returns and minimize the underlying risks.
(C) To assess a financial product and determine if it is appropriate for investors based on their financial objectives and risk appetite.
(D) None of the above.

(54) Under Rule 17-3 of the SEA, which of the following is unnecessary for recordkeeping requirements?
(A) Employment history.
(B) Marital status.
(C) Source of income.
(D) Financial objectives.

(55) What is the primary purpose of Blue Sky Laws?
(A) To govern the structure and organization of the Securities and Exchange Commission (SEC).
(B) To protect investors from fraud at the federal level with regulated securities sales.
(C) To protect investors from fraud at the state level with regulated securities sales.
(D) To set the accounting standards for publicly traded companies.

(56) What is FINRA rule 2111?
(A) Broker-dealers must use a customer's complete investment profile as the basis to recommend suitable investment transactions or strategies.
(B) Security issuers must use a customer's risk tolerance as a reasonable basis to recommend securities.
(C) Security issuers must use a customer's demographic as a reasonable basis to recommend securities.
(D) None of the above.

(57) A law passed in 2001 to combat money laundering and terrorist financing is known as the:
(A) NCLB Act.
(B) EGTRRA.
(C) USA PATRIOT Act.
(D) None of the above.

(58) What is a customer identification program (CIP)?
(A) A regulatory requirement of the USA PATRIOT Act of 2001.
(B) A program for verification of a customer's identity.
(C) The procedure a financial institution uses to verify a client's information.
(D) All of the above.

(59) Which statement accurately defines money laundering?
(A) To cleanse physical cash of dirt or stains.
(B) To invest money into profitable ventures.
(C) To conceal the origin of illegally obtained money.
(D) To conceal the origin of legally obtained money.

(60) What can the company do in the post-registration period after a new security has been registered with the SEC?
(A) Solicit and accept money for the security.
(B) Advertise the security without any restrictions.
(C) Amend the registration statement with significant new information.
(D) Submit a new registration statement for a different security.

(61) What are the three stages of money laundering?
(A) Placement, fragmentation, and integration.
(B) Integration, investment, and fragmentation.
(C) Investment, placement, and layering.
(D) Placement, layering, and integration.

(62) The money laundering stage in which a series of transactions are made to hide the origin of funds is referred to as:
(A) Fragmentation.
(B) Layering.
(C) Integration.
(D) Placement.

(63) What happens in the integration stage of money laundering?
(A) The launderer moves illegally obtained funds to a legitimate financial institution.
(B) The launderer performs a series of transactions to hide the money's origin.
(C) The launderer places clean money in legitimate businesses or investments.
(D) The launderer transfers money from one country to another.

(64) What is the Financial Crimes Enforcement Network?
(A) A bureau that safeguards the financial system from money laundering.
(B) A department that combats financial scams in the securities market.
(C) A federal agency that oversees the US stock market.
(D) None of the above.

(65) In which scenario are broker-dealers allowed to disclose customer information?
(A) To market or advertise products.
(B) A court order to provide specific information.
(C) A client's relative asks for particular information.
(D) Both A and C.

(66) What is regulation S-P?
(A) The restriction of broker firms from collecting specific customer information.
(B) The requirements for the use of customer information for business solicitation.
(C) The protection of an investor's real estate investments from confiscation.
(D) The privacy requirements for financial institutions to use or disclose private customer information to third parties.

(67) The theft of an individual's private information to commit fraud, which damages the victim's reputation, is known as:
(A) Identity theft.
(B) ID fraud.
(C) Identity misappropriation.
(D) Identity hacking.

(68) Which red flags can result in identity theft?
(A) Suspicious documents.
(B) Notifications from customers or law enforcement about identity theft.
(C) Lost or stolen wallets.
(D) All of the above.

(69) What are the conditions in which FINRA members can hold customer mail?
(A) When a customer provides written instructions with a stated reason for the hold.
(B) When a customer provides written consent without a stated reason.
(C) When a customer provides written consent with "inconvenience" as the stated reason for the hold.
(D) All of the above.

(70) What is the customer protection rule?

(A) A regulation that protects customer information, such as residential addresses.

(B) A regulation that protects customers' funds and securities held by broker-dealers.

(C) A regulation that protects customers from financial scams.

(D) Both A and C.

(71) What measures should firms take to safeguard customers' assets under the customer protection rule?

(A) Advise customers to take full custody of their assets.

(B) Refrain from phone communication with customers.

(C) Delay the delivery of securities to their owners.

(D) Separate customer funds from the assets of broker-dealers.

(72) A type of insurance that protects employers against losses due to the fraud or misconduct of employees is called:

(A) Employee theft insurance.

(B) A fidelity bond.

(C) Business fraud insurance.

(D) None of the above.

(73) What is a business continuity plan?

(A) An outline of strategies to maximize profitability.

(B) An insurance for minimizing financial losses because of business interruptions.

(C) A documented strategy to protect business operations because of disruptive events.

(D) None of the above.

(74) Under FINRA rule 4511(b), records that do not have a specified retention period must be retained for:

(A) At least one year.

(B) At least six years.

(C) At least two years.

(D) At least four years.

(75) What is the first stage of the money laundering process?
(A) Fragmentation.
(B) Layering.
(C) Integration.
(D) Placement.

(76) A report that is filed by financial institutions when suspicious activity is detected is called a:
(A) Suspicious activity report.
(B) Criminal activity report.
(C) Supervisory activity report.
(D) Fraud report.

(77) Reports of a suspicious cash transaction should be made by financial institutions if the transaction exceeds:
(A) $4,000.
(B) $10,000.
(C) $6,000.
(D) $12,000.

(78) Meghan is associated with FINRA and works for a broker-dealer. She and the broker-dealer had a disagreement.
Which of the following agreements can help her resolve the issue?
(A) Disclosure reporting agreement.
(B) Pre-dispute arbitration agreement.
(C) Pre-dispute reporting agreement.
(D) Disclosure arbitration agreement.

(79) Which statement is true about the post-registration period with the SEC?
(A) Issuers can only distribute a preliminary prospectus to investors.
(B) The security can be sold, but no advertising or sales literature can be used.
(C) The final prospectus must accompany or precede the delivery of the security to investors.
(D) The issuer cannot accept any payment for the security until the end of the post-registration period.

(80) Which form is filed to terminate the registration of an individual with a broker-dealer?
(A) U4.
(B) U6.
(C) U5.
(D) U7.

(81) How long should you wait before filing Form U6 after disciplinary action has been taken?
(A) Forty-five days.
(B) Forty days.
(C) Thirty days.
(D) Twenty days.

(82) Which of the following can you use to conduct background research into brokers and brokerage firms associated with FINRA?
(A) Broker check.
(B) Investor check.
(C) Broker financial check.
(D) None of the above.

(83) What is the difference between Forms U5 and U6?
(A) Form U5 must be submitted to FINRA, but Form U6 does not.
(B) Form U5 terminates an individual's employment, whereas Form U6 reports any disciplinary action taken against an individual or financial entity.
(C) Form U5 reports any disciplinary action taken against an individual or financial entity, whereas Form U6 terminates someone's employment.
(D) Form U5 does not have to be submitted to FINRA, whereas Form U6 does.

(84) What is the main function of Forms U5 and U6 in the securities industry?
(A) To facilitate transparency and uphold investor confidence in the market.
(B) To provide an advantage to one firm over the others.
(C) To regulate the financial market independently.
(D) To resolve creditor-investor disputes directly.

(85) Which rule requires members to provide investors with information about underlying investments?

(A) Rule 144.

(B) Rule 206.

(C) FINRA Investor Education Rule.

(D) FINRA Continuing Education Rule.

Test 5: Answers and Explanations

(1) (C) The process by which companies raise capital by selling their assets to the public.
An IPO allows privately held companies to trade their shares publicly for the first time. They can sell their company's stocks to potential investors and raise capital for business endeavors.

(2) (B) Securities offerings presented to a small, private pool of investors who meet a specific eligibility requirement.
A private offering sells securities to a small group of authorized investors. These securities are not available to the general public, and registration with the SEC is not required. Investors in private offerings are generally accredited institutional investors who can evaluate the risks involved with such securities.

(3) (D) All of the above.
Underwriting commitments are important to securities offerings, especially for companies looking to raise funds through the sale of securities. Underwriters buy the securities at a specified price and sell them for a profit. Companies can leverage underwriting commitments to reduce their risk and raise capital, which ensures the prompt sale of the securities.

(4) (D) Security offering prospectus.
A security offering prospectus provides investors with information about a company's operations and securities. This includes financial statements, management background, legal problems, where the money will be used, and whether the founders are keeping a stake in the company. It helps potential investors make informed investment decisions.

(5) (D) Standby, best efforts, best efforts mini-maxi, and firm commitment.
Underwriting commitments are a set of liabilities under which underwriters are responsible for the sale of securities to investors on time to help companies raise capital. Many underwriting commitments include firm commitment, best efforts, best efforts all-or-none, best efforts mini-maxi, and standby.

(6) (D) Both A and C.

Shelf registration is a provision of the SEC that permits issuers to register new securities in advance without any obligation to sell the entire inventory immediately. This allows issuers to get registration statements approved in advance and sell securities later when market conditions are more favorable.

(7) (A) Work with underwriters to sell IPO shares to qualified investors.
The syndicate members are key components of the primary market. Syndicates and underwriters sell securities to qualified investors. Syndicate members also provide market research, distribution, and other services to security issuers.

(8) (C) Issuer.
Issuers are private companies that go public for the first time to raise capital with the sale of their securities.

(9) (B) Underwriting spread.
Underwriters help companies to raise money with the sale of securities. Underwriters, like investment banks, purchase securities from the company at a specific price. This price is usually lower than the public sale price. Underwriters sell the purchased securities to public investors for a profit. This price difference is called an underwriting spread.

(10) (C) Bids are submitted privately and are not disclosed until the auction closes.
In a sealed bid auction, participants submit their bids privately. The bids are not disclosed to other participants or the public until after the auction has closed. This ensures that each bid is made without the influence of the other participant's bids.

(11) (C) To potentially obtain a higher price for their securities without bidders being influenced by each other.
In a sealed bid auction, bids are not disclosed. The bidders are more likely to bid based on their genuine assessment of the security's value rather than to outbid competitors. This can result in a higher price for the securities, as the bidders cannot strategize based on the others' bids.

(12) (D) Within twenty-five days of the offering.
If a company wants to get listed on the NYSE or the Nasdaq, then the requirements prospectus must be filed within twenty-five days of the securities offering.

(13) (B) Preliminary prospectus.
Types of prospectuses include a preliminary prospectus, statutory prospectus, and summary prospectus.

(14) (C) Free-writing prospectus.
A Free-writing prospectus provides additional information to potential investors during the waiting period of an IPO without being considered a formal offer. It supplements the preliminary prospectus and provides flexibility in the type and amount of information that can be shared.

(15) (A) Equity financing involves the sale of ownership shares, whereas debt financing borrows money with repayment commitments.
The source of the funding is the main difference between equity and debt financing. In equity financing, the investor obtains a company stake after the purchase of its shares or stocks. Debt financing simply means to borrow money from lenders in the form of bonds or loans. However, the money is repaid to the lender with interest, which ends the commitment.

(16) (A) It does not confer voting rights.
Common stockholders often have voting rights, usually on a one-vote-per-share basis.

(17) (B) Safeguards against excessive insider selling pressure.
The lock-up agreement in an IPO usually restricts the sale of securities by company insiders, such as executives or major shareholders. This prevents the negative effect on stock prices due to the pressure of insider selling.

(18) (B) Provides fixed-income securities like bonds or notes.
Debt financing is a complex process whereby investors acquire fixed-income securities issued by businesses to safeguard their funds. This method grants the company access to capital, which enables smooth day-to-day operations. In exchange for their financial support, investors receive regular interest payments and the complete repayment of the principal amount upon maturity. This serves as a means for companies to secure vital funds and allows investors to accrue returns through interest payments and eventual principal redemption.

(19) (A) A set of rules that govern restricted and controlled securities trade.
Rule 144 outlines specific conditions that govern the sale of restricted and controlled securities. It was established by the SEC and provides guidelines about how securities holders can engage in transactions within the secondary market. Additionally, this rule promotes transparency and accountability, which safeguards investor interests.

(20) (A) Certificates that prove stock ownership in a foreign corporation.
American depositary receipts are certificates issued by US banks that prove stock ownership in a foreign corporation.

(21) (A) They are well-known brands with successful track records.
A main feature of blue chip stocks is a proven track record of consistent performance. These stocks represent valuable ownership stakes in firmly established, financially secure companies with dominant positions in their respective industries.

(22) (D) Can be redeemed by the issuer for a predetermined price.
The company that issues callable preferred stock can repurchase the shares from owners at a predetermined price. The issuer may return or withdraw the stock before the maturity date. Callable preferred stock enables a company to manage its capital structure more efficiently and change its financing arrangements in response to shifts in market conditions.

(23) (A) Allow stockholders to keep their ownership percentage.
Preemptive rights enable stockholders to safeguard their ownership interest in a company. It gives them priority to purchase additional shares before they are made available to the public. This ensures that their percentage ownership does not decline by the issuance of new shares.

(24) (B) A derivative that provides the right to buy a company's stock at a specified price.
A warrant grants the holder the right, but not the duty, to buy shares of a company's stock within a given time frame and at a certain price. It is a derivative because the underlying stock is the basis for its value. In securities offers, warrants are frequently utilized as incentives or extra benefits.

(25) (A) A contractual guarantee to raise money.

A debt instrument is a financial contract. It allows a business to borrow money to raise capital. The investor lends the business at an agreed-upon interest amount over a specific period.

(26) (D) Bond.
Bonds are fixed-income securities issued by the government, municipalities, or corporations to raise capital. Long-term debt refers to any financial obligation with a maturity of more than one year. This includes various types of bonds, loans, and lease obligations.

(27) (A) To raise capital for government initiatives.
The government usually issues bonds to fund infrastructure projects, public initiatives, or other government expenditures. The government can access a large pool of capital from investors in exchange for regular interest payments and the return of the principal when the bond matures.

(28) (B) Serial bonds only require a single payment at maturity, whereas term bonds require payments in installments.
The difference between term and serial bonds is their payment structures. Term bonds require the issuer to make installment payments until the bond matures. A serial bond requires a single payment of the principal amount on the date of the bond's maturity.

(29) (B) A bond sold at a significant discount.
Zero-coupon bonds are fixed-income securities. They are sold at a discounted price compared to their face value and provide a return on the investment at maturity.

(30) (A) The total face value plus the premium.
A bond's carrying value is its face value with the addition of unamortized premiums and the deduction of any unamortized discounts.

(31) (C) Bond dealers.
Decentralized, dealer-based, over-the-counter markets handle most bond transactions, especially Treasury and corporate bonds.

(32) (C) Fixed nominal values in the distant future.
Zero-coupon bonds provide a return on the date of maturity and are ideal for long-term financial planning, like retirement. They are suitable for investors who require a fixed nominal value at a future mature date without regular interest payments.

(33) (D) All of the above.
Bond prices can shift because of a change in the issuer's credit rating. This can affect the riskiness of the bond and cause price fluctuations. A change in the demand and supply curve and interest rates can also cause price fluctuations.

(34) (D) The possibility of reinvesting cash flow at a lower rate.
The risk of reinvestment is the possibility that an investor might reinvest the interest gained from a bond at a lower rate of return. This usually happens when the interest rates decline over time, which reduces the return on reinvested funds.

(35) (A) Short and long-term.
Debt instruments have two types: short or long-term, based on their maturity period. Short-term debt instruments have a maturity period of one year or less. Long-term debt instruments have a maturity period of longer than one year.

(36) (C) T-bills.
Treasury bills have maturities of one year or less. They are short-term debt instruments the government issues to raise money. T-bills frequently finance short-term government debts because they are considered low-risk investments.

(37) (D) Ten to thirty years.
The maturity of treasury bonds ranges from ten to thirty years. These are long-term debt instruments the government issues. They continue to pay bondholders periodic interest until they mature. T-bills and treasury notes are shorter-term investment options.

(38) (B) Protection against inflation.
Treasury inflation-protected securities (TIPS) are a means of protection against inflation. The principal value rises and falls along with inflation. This allows investors to keep pace with price increases as their investment's purchasing power remains unchanged.

(39) (C) Contributions are made with after-tax dollars, but qualified distributions are tax-free.
A 529 plan allows contributions to be made with after-tax dollars. However, the earnings grow tax-deferred, and distributions for qualified educational expenses are not subject to federal income tax.

(40) (A) Public projects.
Municipal bonds fund public projects, such as new roads, bridges, schools, and other public facilities. Individuals can help finance local projects with investment in municipal bonds.

(41) (C) Less than one year.
The maturity period of municipal notes is less than one year. Municipalities issue these short-term debt instruments to meet their immediate financial needs. Municipal notes frequently finance projects or fill short-term budget gaps.

(42) (B) Tax anticipation note.
Upcoming tax revenues repay municipal notes, also called tax anticipation notes (TAN).

(43) (B) An account managed by a trustee that is established for the benefit of another.
A trust fund is a fiduciary arrangement that allows a third party or trustee to manage assets on behalf of a beneficiary. It provides financial security to individuals, most often to children, grandchildren, or nonprofits.
(44) (A) Secured bonds.
Secured bonds are corporate bonds supported by a particular form of collateral, like assets or real estate. In the event of a default, bondholders are given additional security with these kinds of bonds. Debentures, income bonds, and Eurodollars are not secured by collateral.

(45) (B) Voluntary liquidation by members.
If a company is insolvent, the business's shareholders or directors can initiate member-prompted voluntary liquidation. This enables the company to repay its debt.

(46) (D) Last.

Common stockholders do not have priority to receive any assets that remain in the event of liquidation or bankruptcy. The company compensates bondholders, preferred stockholders, and other creditors first. Common stockholders have the highest risk and potential reward compared to other stakeholders.

(47) (D) Both A and C.
An option represents a contractual arrangement between a buyer and a seller. It gives the buyer the right, but not the obligation, to buy or sell an asset at a set price, commonly called the strike price. It derives its value from the underlying asset. Options provide a flexible tool that can be utilized in various hedging and investment strategies.

(48) (B) A contract in which the buyer can purchase an asset.
A call option gives the purchaser the right to buy an asset at a set price, commonly called the strike price. When a call option is acquired, the buyer expects the underlying asset's value to rise. This allows them to exercise the option and obtain the asset at a price lower than its market value.

(49) (C) When the market price equals the strike price plus the premium.
The long call option breakeven point is the price at which the market value of the underlying asset equals the strike price plus the option premium. The option holder does not experience a gain or loss at this point. The holder begins to make money if the asset's market value exceeds the breakeven point.

(50) (D) To lessen exposure to random risks.
Diversification in investment portfolios decreases exposure to random or unsystematic risks. Investors can lessen the impact of unfavorable events that might affect a single investment or a particular industry by the distribution of their investments across various asset industries and geographical regions. Diversification also helps reduce the risk connected to any given investment.

(51) (C) To manage and distribute the assets of the trust per the grantor's wishes.
The trustee's main responsibility is to administer the trust fund, manage its assets, and distribute them to beneficiaries as specified in the trust agreement. This ensures the trust's terms and conditions are followed and the beneficiary's best interests are considered.

(52) (B) An entity that makes investments on behalf of others.
An institutional investor is an organization or an entity that pools substantial funds from various sources and invests them on behalf of others. Pension funds, hedge funds, and endowments are some examples of institutional investors.

(53) (C) To assess a financial product and determine if it is appropriate for investors based on their financial objectives and risk appetite.
In the securities market, suitability refers to the proper assessment of investment strategies and financial advice from broker-dealers to their investors. Brokers should analyze their customers' investment profiles to provide the most suitable financial advice.

(54) (B) Marital status.
Marital status is not required to maintain recordkeeping. The SEC requires information relevant to the customer's financial history, investment objectives, and personal information, such as ID, contact number, and address.

(55) (C) To protect investors from fraud at the state level with regulated securities sales.
Blue Sky Laws are state laws that protect the public from fraud. They regulate the offering and sale of securities. They are enacted on a state-by-state basis and help to ensure sufficient disclosure and prevent deceitful practices in the sale of securities within their jurisdictions.

(56) (A) Broker-dealers must use a customer's complete investment profile as the basis to recommend suitable investment transactions or strategies.
FINRA rule 2111 states that broker-dealers must have a reasonable basis to recommend investments. The investors' objectives, risk tolerance, time horizon, and other relevant factors should be analyzed to form a foundation to provide the most appropriate financial advice.

(57) (C) USA PATRIOT Act.
Congress passed the USA PATRIOT Act of 2001 to combat terrorism and money laundering in the US.

(58) (D) All of the above.
The Customer Identification Program is a regulatory procedure introduced in the USA PATRIOT Act. Financial institutions must verify clients' personal information to prevent crimes like identity theft and money laundering.

(59) (C) To conceal the origin of illegally obtained money.
Money laundering uses a series of financial transactions to conceal the origin and source of illegally obtained money.

(60) (A) Solicit and accept money for the security.
The post-registration or after-market period begins after the SEC registration becomes effective. At this time, issuers can solicit orders and accept payments for the securities.

(61) (D) Placement, layering, and integration.
Placement, layering, and integration are the three stages of the money laundering process.

(62) (B) Layering.
The layering stage involves the movement of money through a series of transactions to hide the funds' origin.

(63) (C) The launderer places clean money in legitimate businesses or investments.
The final stage of the money laundering process is called integration. In this stage, the launderer uses the laundered or cleaned funds to purchase goods or participate in investment activities that require legitimately obtained money.

(64) (A) A bureau that safeguards the financial system from money laundering.
The key role of the Financial Crimes Enforcement Network is to combat financial crimes like money laundering.

(65) (B) A court order to provide specific information.
Financial institutions are only allowed to disclose the private information of their clients at the behest of the court or a government entity. Broker-dealers can also provide the required information if the client brings written consent from an authorized entity.

(66) (D) The privacy requirements for financial institutions to use or disclose private customer information to third parties.
Regulation S-P enacted by the SEC requires all investment companies, brokers, or financial advisors to follow privacy rules to disclose their clients' personal information to third parties. Clients must be informed and allowed to opt out before any information is disclosed.

(67) (A) Identity theft.
Identity theft occurs when a victim’s personal identifying information, such as name or credit card number, is stolen to commit crimes or fraud in the victim's name.

(68) (D) All of the above.
Suspicious documents, notifications from customers or law enforcement about identity theft, and lost or stolen wallets can be potential red flags or causes for identity theft.

(69) (A) When a customer provides written instructions with a stated reason for the hold.
FINRA has strictly advised member firms not to hold customer mail unless the customer gives a written request and a valid reason for the hold. The period for a hold should be mentioned, and if it is over three months, a valid reason must be provided. This cannot include reasons like “inconvenience.”

(70) (B) A regulation that protects customers’ funds and securities held by broker-dealers.
The customer protection rule is a regulation of the SEC. It aims to protect the customers’ funds held by broker-dealers.

(71) (D) Separate customer funds from the assets of broker-dealers.
The customer protection rule instructs firms to ensure the funds and securities of the customers are separate from the assets of the broker-dealers.

(72) (B) A fidelity bond.

A fidelity bond is a type of insurance designed to protect employers from potential losses caused by the fraud or misconduct of employees. Monetary and physical losses are both covered in fidelity bonds.

(73) (C) A documented strategy to protect business operations because of disruptive events.
A business continuity plan ensures that a business's everyday operations remain active in the events of disruption or disasters like natural disasters or cyber-attacks.

(74) (B) At least six years.
Under FINRA rule 4511(b), books or records with no stated retention period must be kept for at least six years.

(75) (D) Placement.
The first stage of money laundering is placement, in which the launderer introduces the dirty money into the financial system.

(76) (A) Suspicious activity reports.
If financial institutions detect suspicious activity, they must report it within thirty days of detection. This type of report is called a suspicious activity report.

(77) (B) $10,000.
Financial institutions are obligated under the Bank Secrecy Act to report any suspicious transaction that exceeds $10,000.

(78) (B) Pre-dispute arbitration agreement.
A pre-dispute arbitration agreement facilitates relations between an employer and an employee. They can sign this agreement to resolve the issue and avoid going to court.

(79) (C) The final prospectus must accompany or precede the delivery of the security to investors.
Once the SEC registration becomes effective, securities can be sold to the public. In the post-registration period, the final prospectus must be delivered to investors before or with the security. The prospectus provides comprehensive details about the investment offering and helps ensure transparency and protection for investors.

(80) (C) U5.
Form U5 is filed to terminate an individual's agreement with an employer. This revokes the individual's registration as an associated member of FINRA.

(81) (C) Thirty days.
If a firm takes disciplinary action against an employee, they must file Form U6 within thirty days of the conflict. FINRA needs to be informed of the incident.

(82) (A) Broker check.
A broker check can confirm the registration of a broker or brokerage firm with FINRA and conduct a background check before an investor enters a business arrangement.

(83) (B) Form U5 terminates an individual's employment, whereas Form U6 reports any disciplinary action taken against an individual or financial entity.
The U5 is filed to revoke the registration of an individual with a broker-dealer. The U6 is filed in case of disciplinary action.

(84) (A) To facilitate transparency and uphold investor confidence in the market
Forms U5 and U6 are important in maintaining transparency in the securities industry. The Form U5 reports the termination of a registered individual. The Form U6 reports disciplinary actions against a person or entity in the securities industry. These forms help uphold investor confidence and satisfaction. Potential investors and the public can access this information, which enables them to make informed decisions.

(85) (C) FINRA Investor Education Rule.
FINRA Investor Education Rule requires all members to share information about investment opportunities with their investors so they can make informed decisions.

Test 6: Questions

(1) Which of the following is a type of exempt security?
(A) Municipal.
(B) Short-term corporate debt.
(C) US government and agency.
(D) All of the above.

(2) What types of securities offerings are exempt from registration with the SEC?
(A) Private placement.
(B) Public placement.
(C) Unregistered stock offering.
(D) Private stock offering.

(3) Rule 504 of Regulation D is a provision that exempts certain security offerings from registration requirements.
Rule 504 stipulates which of the following?
(A) The sale of at least $10 million worth of securities within twelve months.
(B) The sale of at least $8 million worth of securities within twelve months.
(C) The sale of at least $10 million worth of securities within six months.
(D) The sale of at least $12 million worth of securities within six months.

(4) What is the difference between general obligation and revenue bonds?
(A) Revenue bonds are backed by the full faith of the state or local governments, whereas general obligation bonds are backed by the projects that they fund.
(B) General obligation bonds and revenue bonds are both backed by the local governments.
(C) General obligation bonds are supported by the credit of the issuing government, and revenue bonds are secured by the income generated from the specific projects they fund.
(D) Both A and B.

(5) What method involves a public announcement to sell securities?
(A) Confidential offering.
(B) Public offering.
(C) Private placement.
(D) Direct listing.

(6) What is Electronic Municipal Market Access (EMMA)?
(A) An online portal operated by the MSRB to provide public access to information related to the municipal securities market, such as trading data and official disclosures.
(B) A website designed by the MSRB to sell valuable municipal market information at a fixed cost.
(C) A trading platform for municipal securities traders to buy and sell securities.
(D) An interactive tool for information about primary and secondary markets.

(7) A regulation passed by the SEC that permits securities buyers to resell them to qualified institutional buyers is known as:
(A) Rule 5250.
(B) Rule 2269.
(C) Rule 144A.
(D) Rule 506.

(8) Municipal documents contain valuable legal information about municipal securities provided to the investors at the time of securities issuance.
Which of the following are municipal documents?
(A) Legal opinions and new issue confirmations.
(B) Legal opinions and legal briefs.
(C) Official statements and legal briefs.
(D) New issue confirmations and legal briefs.

(9) What is SEC rule 145?
(A) It defines the recordkeeping requirements of financial institutions.
(B) It defines the conditions under which companies can sell securities without a registration process.
(C) It states the regulations about the underwriting process of the securities offerings.
(D) None of the above.

(10) Which rule allows small companies to raise funds locally without registering with the SEC?
(A) Rule 145.
(B) Rule 147.
(C) Rule 144A.
(D) Rule 507A.

(11) A provision that allows underwriters to cancel agreements without a penalty is referred to as:
(A) Shelf registration.
(B) Firm commitment.
(C) Market-out clause.
(D) Both A and B.

(12) The Securities Act of 1933 was enacted to regulate:
(A) Sale of real estate.
(B) Sale of securities.
(C) Sale of cryptocurrencies.
(D) Sale of commodities.

(13) When should a company file a prospectus to issue securities to the public if they are not listed on the stock exchange but had an IPO?
(A) Within forty days.
(B) Within seven days.
(C) Within ten days.
(D) None of the above.

(14) What are agency securities?
(A) Municipal securities issued by state governments.
(B) Debt securities issued by municipal committees.
(C) Debt securities issued by government-sponsored enterprises or federal agencies.
(D) None of the above.

(15) Which of the following are types of equity securities?
(A) Common and preferred investments.
(B) Common and preferred stock.
(C) Common preferences and preferred stock.
(D) Common stock and preferred investments.

(16) What is the difference between common and preferred stocks?
(A) Common stock incorporates company ownership, whereas preferred stock deals with the company's cash stream.
(B) Preferred stock incorporates company ownership, whereas common stock deals with the company's cash stream.
(C) Both A and B.
(D) None of the above.

(17) In which financing process does an investor provide funds to a corporation for a return on the investment but does not share in potential company losses?
(A) Equity financing.
(B) Convertible debt financing.
(C) Debt financing.
(D) Participative financing.

(18) What is the similarity between equity financing and debt financing?
(A) Bond markets use them as trading strategies.
(B) Corporations use them as strategies to raise money.
(C) They deal with municipal securities.
(D) They finance debts related to mortgages.

(19) Marcus acquired a type of security that he cannot transfer until he meets a specific list of conditions.
What type of security did Marcus acquire?
(A) Preferred stock.
(B) Restricted securities.
(C) Lock-up securities.
(D) Controlled stock.

(20) How long do lock-up periods usually last?
(A) Thirty to fifty days.
(B) Fifty to 100 days.
(C) 100 to 150 days.
(D) Ninety to 180 days.

(21) Which of the following best defines restricted stock awards?
(A) An award of company stock with restricted rights that are lifted after a specified time or certain shares are vested.
(B) An award of company stock with unrestricted rights and room to invest more shares.
(C) An award of company shares with no voting rights until the restrictions are lifted or certain shares are invested.
(D) An award of company stock with unrestricted rights until shares are sold.

(22) Which of the following legalizes the relationship between an ADR and a foreign company?
(A) Unsponsored ADR.
(B) Sponsored ADR.
(C) Restricted ADR.
(D) International ADR.

(23) On what does a bond's price sensitivity to interest rate fluctuation depend?
(A) A bond's maturity period and coupon rate.
(B) A bond's maturity period and bond type.
(C) A bond's coupon rate and bond type.
(D) A bond's maturity period and market inflation.

(24) Which of the following correctly lists the three types of credit risk?
(A) Default, city, and concentration.
(B) Credit, country, and distribution.
(C) Interest rate, credit default, and concentration.
(D) Credit default, country, and concentration.

(25) What are the features of government securities?
(A) They are issued at face value with no default risk or tax deductions.
(B) They are issued at the asking price with a default risk but no tax deductions.
(C) They are issued at the asking price with no default risk or tax deductions.
(D) They are issued at face value with a default risk and tax deductions.

(26) Call provisions are a feature of:
(A) Government bonds.
(B) State bonds.
(C) US Treasury bonds.
(D) Corporate bonds.

(27) What is the primary difference between sinking funds and extraordinary call provisions?
(A) A sinking fund requires all bonds to be redeemed by the issuer on a set schedule, whereas an extraordinary fund allows certain bonds to be redeemed after the conditions are met.
(B) A sinking fund is a type of put provision, whereas an extraordinary fund is a call provision.
(C) A sinking fund is a type of call provision, whereas an extraordinary fund is a put provision.
(D) A sinking fund requires a certain number of bonds to be redeemed by the issuer on a set schedule, whereas an extraordinary fund allows the bonds to be redeemed after the conditions are met.

(28) Which of the following is true about credit ratings?
(A) Investment grades are higher than speculative grades.
(B) Speculative grades are higher than investment grades.
(C) Investment grades indicate credit risk as the creditors are at risk of default.
(D) Speculative grades help make investments and lend capital.

(29) Which of the following is a short or medium-term debt instrument?

(A) Mortgage.

(B) Debentures.

(C) Treasury bills.

(D) Leases.

(30) Which debt instruments have a two to ten-year maturity period and a fixed interest rate?

(A) Treasury notes.

(B) Treasury bills.

(C) Treasury bonds.

(D) Treasury cash.

(31) Which securities trade principal and coupon payments separately?

(A) Separate trading inflation-protected securities.

(B) Treasury inflation-protected securities.

(C) Separate trading of registered interest and principal securities.

(D) Treasury principal securities.

(32) In what do buyers compete when placing bids?

(A) Trading market.

(B) Financial entity.

(C) Auction.

(D) Clearinghouse.

(33) Which authority issues agency securities?

(A) Government-sponsored enterprise.

(B) Stock exchange.

(C) Financial Investment Regulation Authority.

(D) Security and Exchange Commission.

(34) Which is not a component of the Farm Credit System?
(A) Federal Land Bank System.
(B) Banks for Cooperatives.
(C) Government National Mortgage Association.
(D) Production Credit Associations.

(35) What is a mortgage-backed security?
(A) Asset-backed security.
(B) Mortgage security.
(C) Loan security.
(D) Short-term security.

(36) Which does not issue municipal bonds?
(A) School districts.
(B) Local governments.
(C) Transit authorities.
(D) Private creditors.

(37) What type of a bond is a private activity bond?
(A) Corporate bond.
(B) Revenue bond.
(C) Exchange-traded fund.
(D) Green bond.

(38) Why are grant anticipation notes issued?
(A) To provide cash to maintain and construct highways.
(B) To provide long-term bonds to construct and maintain highways.
(C) To provide grants for the federal government and its authorities to construct and maintain highways.
(D) To provide long-term bonds for the federal government and its authorities to construct and maintain highways.

(39) Which is the best quality rating assigned to municipal notes by Moody's?
(A) MIG 1.
(B) MIG 2.
(C) MIG 3.
(D) MIG 4.

(40) Which debt instrument allows a financial entity to possess an asset, use it, and pay for it over time?
(A) Certificate bonds.
(B) Collateral trust bonds.
(C) Equipment trust certificate.
(D) Mortgage bonds.

(41) Which type of liquidation allows a company to pay off its liabilities once it liquidates its assets?
(A) Creditors' voluntary liquidation.
(B) Members' voluntary liquidation.
(C) Compulsory liquidation.
(D) Forced liquidation.

(42) James decides to loan money to a business colleague. He transfers the amount agreed upon to his colleague. James does not sign a legal agreement that would allow him to hold his business colleague's assets as collateral for failure to repay the stipulated amount.
What kind of creditor is James?
(A) Secured creditor.
(B) Administrative expense claims creditor.
(C) General creditor.
(D) Subordinated creditor.

(43) Which type of investment company deals with publicly issued fund shares?
(A) Management investment companies.
(B) Unit investment trusts.
(C) Face amount certificate companies.
(D) Investment certificate companies.

(44) Which of the following is not true for closed and open-end mutual funds?

(A) Open-end mutual funds do not have a fixed maturity date, unlike closed-end mutual funds.

(B) Open-end mutual funds have a flexible fund size, whereas closed-end mutual fund sizes are fixed.

(C) Open-end mutual funds include unlimited shares, whereas closed-end mutual funds could have a limited number.

(D) Open and closed-end mutual funds' prices depend on the market's demand and supply of shares.

(45) Which annuity guarantees payment over the owner's entire life and is then passed onto the beneficiary in case of the owner's death?

(A) Guarantee annuity.

(B) Life annuity with a specific period.

(C) Bond annuity.

(D) Life annuity with a refund clause.

(46) What is the purpose of a separate account held by insurance companies?

(A) They keep a clear record of assets backed by variable annuities and ensure efficient management of any financial issue.

(B) They distinguish between the inflows and outflows of capital.

(C) They help manage and reconcile all the discrepancies related to the assets and liabilities.

(D) They are general accounts that deal with investment portions of life insurance products.

(47) Which of the following is true for inverse ETFs?

(A) It provides an investor with a return that is inverse to the asset's performance.

(B) It produces a positive return on an asset when its index is up.

(C) It produces a return for foreign investors only.

(D) It produces a negative return on an asset when its index is down.

(48) What type of Real Estate Investment Trust (REIT) provides investors with regular income and the possibility for capital appreciation?
(A) Equity REIT.
(B) Mortgage REIT.
(C) Hybrid REIT.
(D) Retail REIT.

(49) Which of the following is not required to become an accredited investor?
(A) Creditor's default risk.
(B) Risk of ROI.
(C) Discretionary account.
(D) Investor certification.

(50) Susan expects that the value of security A will rise soon. She wants to purchase it now to limit her losses and maximize profits.
Susan employs which kind of strategy?
(A) Medium hedging.
(B) Long hedging.
(C) Short hedging.
(D) Hybrid hedging.

(51) By hedging, an investor can risk:
(A) An investment opportunity.
(B) Incurred losses.
(C) A potential return.
(D) The purchase of faulty assets.

(52) Which organization established the anti-intimidation/coordination interpretation to curb manipulative practices during a securities offering?
(A) Financial Industry Regulatory Authority (FINRA).
(B) Securities and Exchange Commission (SEC).
(C) US Department of the Treasury.
(D) Federal Reserve.

(53) Which legislation regulates securities trade on secondary financial markets and ensures transparency for investors?

(A) The Securities Exchange Act of 1934.

(B) Regulation M.

(C) Rule 10b-5.

(D) Rule G-30.

(54) What prohibited trading practice involves the manipulation of a security's price with false or misleading information?

(A) Interpositioning.

(B) Churning.

(C) Market rumors.

(D) Front-running.

(55) Which rule strongly prohibited trading ahead of customer orders?

(A) Rule 5210.

(B) Rule 5320.

(C) Rule G-27.

(D) Rule 6370.

(56) What is the purpose of the New Issue rule that FINRA introduced?

(A) To promote transparency and fairness in the allocation and distribution of new securities issues.

(B) To prevent manipulation by entities or individuals in securities offerings.

(C) To regulate compensation arrangements between broker-dealers and registered representatives.

(D) To prohibit financial exploitation of vulnerable adults and older adults.

(57) Which regulatory authority actively monitors firms for compliance with Regulation M during securities offerings?

(A) The Securities and Exchange Commission.

(B) The Financial Industry Regulatory Authority.

(C) The Municipal Securities Rulemaking Board.

(D) The Federal Reserve Board.

(58) Which federal law requires institutions to report financial exploitation of vulnerable and older adults?
(A) Senior Safe Act.
(B) Bank Secrecy Act.
(C) Securities Exchange Act of 1934.
(D) Investment Company Act of 1940.

(59) What does the anti-intimidation/coordination interpretation of the Securities Exchange Act of 1934 regulate?
(A) Compensation arrangements.
(B) Insider trading.
(C) Intimidation or coordination as a means to manipulate security prices.
(D) Trading ahead of customer orders.

(60) Under FINRA rule 3210, what must registered financial advisors do with their outside brokerage accounts?
(A) Report their external accounts to their affiliated brokerage firm.
(B) Maintain their outside accounts without employer notification.
(C) Hide their outside accounts from clients.
(D) Violate the rule and not obtain written consent.

(61) Which rule requires municipal security dealers to charge fair and reasonable prices in securities transactions?
(A) Rule G-30.
(B) Rule G-18.
(C) Rule G-26.
(D) Rule G-27.

(62) What is Regulation M designed to prevent?
(A) Insider trading.
(B) Market manipulation in securities offerings.
(C) Customer account churn.
(D) Compensation rules violations.

(63) Which of the following involves taking advantage of another person's financial resources for personal gain?
(A) Market manipulation.
(B) Securities fraud.
(C) Financial exploitation.
(D) Interpositioning.

(64) Which rule prohibits the manipulation of a security's price with false information?
(A) Rule 5320.
(B) Rule G-27.
(C) Rule 10b-5.
(D) None of the above.

(65) Which activity is prohibited in the restricted period under Regulation M?
(A) Churning.
(B) Trading ahead of the customer.
(C) Both A and B.
(D) Short selling.

(66) What is a forgery?
(A) To accurately reflect the finances and transactions in the records.
(B) To alter or falsely documents to deceive or defraud.
(C) To create solid policies and procedures for the management of registered representatives.
(D) To provide clear disclosure of compensation arrangements, which include conflicts of interest.

(67) What is a guarantee in the securities industry?
(A) A legal agreement between joint account holders.
(B) A disclosure document that describes the advantages and drawbacks of joint accounts.
(C) Both A and B.
(D) A document that guarantees coverage of a borrower's credit exposure in case of default.

(68) What is the difference between front-running and insider trading?

(A) Retail investors practice insider trading, whereas institutional investors practice front-running.

(B) Insider trading is an illicit act, and front-running is a legal act for brokers.

(C) Front-running executes trades based on advanced knowledge of pending orders, whereas insider trading trades securities based on non-public information.

(D) Both A and B.

(69) Which statement about Regulation M is incorrect?

(A) Regulation M allows underwriters to engage in activities that may artificially inflate the price of a security.

(B) Regulation M does not impose any penalties for non-compliance.

(C) Regulation M applies only to institutional investors and does not affect individual investors.

(D) All of the above.

(70) Kazak purchased securities with loans to cover fifty percent of the transaction price. The price of the security declined thirteen percent the following night. Kazak is anxious because he does not have more funds to fulfill the maintenance margin requirement. The brokerage firm will issue a Reg T call if the security price falls a further five percent. What will happen after the Reg T call?

(A) The brokerage firm will give Kazak ten days to add funds.

(B) The broker-dealer may sell his securities.

(C) The broker-dealer will ban his account.

(D) None of the above.

(71) What is an individual who receives insider information from another person or entity called?

(A) Third party.

(B) Insider friend.

(C) Tippee.

(D) None of the above.

(72) Which rule of FINRA allows member firms to temporarily restrict the release of funds or securities from specific accounts due to financial exploitation concerns?
(A) Rule 6370.
(B) Rule 2165.
(C) Rule 2020.
(D) Rule 5210.

(73) What information does FINRA require brokers to collect from customers before they open an account?
(A) The customer's favorite color and hobbies.
(B) The customer's name and business address.
(C) The customer's name and residential address.
(D) All of the above.

(74) What is the main objective of institutional suitability?
(A) To guarantee investment profitability for institutional investors.
(B) To provide sound financial advice to institutional investors.
(C) To shield institutional investors from market volatility.
(D) To regulate the trading behavior of institutional investors.

(75) According to FINRA rule 2111, what are the three main suitability obligations for firms and associated people?
(A) Fancy-basis, specific-customer, and quantitative obligations.
(B) Reasonable-basis, customer-specific, and quantitative obligations.
(C) Suitability-basis, risk-specific, and quantitative obligations.
(D) Compliance-basis, customer-specific, and financial obligations.

(76) According to FINRA rule 2330, what risks are associated with joint accounts?
(A) Potential loss of funds if one account holder withdraws all funds.
(B) Potential exposure to fraudulent practices by brokers.
(C) Potential restriction on further credit extensions.
(D) Potential violation of anti-intimidation/coordination interpretation.

(77) What consequences are imposed by the SEC for insider trading?
(A) Monetary fines, repayment of profits, and imprisonment.
(B) Suspension of trading activities and loss of securities accounts.
(C) Penalties imposed on brokers for non-compliance with Regulation M.
(D) Liquidation of securities and restriction on credit extensions.

(78) What does expungement mean?
(A) To add information to broker records.
(B) To remove details from broker records.
(C) To edit details from broker records.
(D) To archive sections of broker records.

(79) What measures has FINRA taken to deal with issues related to expungement?
(A) Increased the efficiency of expungement.
(B) Prohibited expungement in all cases by a broker.
(C) Introduced rule 2080.
(D) Both A and C.

(80) What are the duties of the MSRB?
(A) To trade securities, monitor trading activities, and facilitate financial activities.
(B) To trade securities, educate investors, and monitor their trading decisions.
(C) To educate investors, monitor their activities, and regulate their accounts.
(D) To educate investors, provide them with helpful material, and encourage informed decisions.

(81) What is the correct protocol to respond and deal with a customer complaint?
(A) Investigate, respond to the customer, record the complaint, recognize the issue, and follow up on it.
(B) Respond to the customer, record the complaint, recognize the issue, and follow up.
(C) Recognize the issue, investigate, inform the customer of your findings, record the complaint, and follow up.
(D) Recognize the issue, investigate, record the complaint, respond to the customer, and follow up.

(82) The reporting requirements of FINRA ensure the protection of:
(A) FINRA.
(B) The financial market.
(C) Broker-dealers.
(D) Investors.

(83) Which is not a red flag per the rules of the SEC?
(A) Unknown sources who provide unsolicited tips to investors.
(B) Brokers not registered with the SEC/FINRA.
(C) Investors with a high credit score.
(D) Unexplained account discrepancies and unauthorized transactions.

(84) What action is taken in response to a red flag?
(A) To investigate the account to confirm suspicions.
(B) To freeze the account.
(C) To halt all transactions.
(D) Both B and C.

(85) Which policies prohibit political contributions to be used for a dealer's gain?
(A) Rule G-37.
(B) Rule G-20.
(C) EMMA.
(D) G-7.

Test 6: Answers and Explanations

(1) (D) All of the above.
Exempt securities can be sold without filing a statement with the SEC. Municipal securities, short-term corporate debt, and US government and agency securities are some of the most common types of exempt securities.

(2) (A) Private placement.
Regulation D exempts certain security offerings from registration with the SEC. Security offerings exempt from such requirements are also called private placements.

(3) (A) The sale of at least $10 million worth of securities within twelve months.
Rule 504 states that certain companies and issuers are exempted from the registration requirements of the federal securities law under two conditions: the issuer must sell at least $10 million worth of securities, and it must be done within twelve months.

(4) (C) General obligation bonds are supported by the credit of the issuing government, and revenue bonds are secured by the income generated from the specific projects they fund.
General obligation and revenue bonds are both issued by municipalities or government entities. They are differentiated by how they are secured and the source of their repayment. The issuing governments protect general obligation bonds, whereas revenue bonds rely upon the revenue generated by the projects they fund.

(5) (B) Public Offering.
A public offering is the sale of securities via public announcements or advertisements. Companies normally use this type of offering to raise capital. Both institutional and individual investors purchase these securities.
(6) (A) An online portal operated by the MSRB to provide public access to information related to the municipal securities market, such as trading data and official disclosures.
The MSRB operates an online system called the Electronic Municipal Market Access (EMMA). It provides information about municipal securities and other related financial data and contains interactive tools for investors and entities.

(7) (C) Rule 144A.

Rule 144A is an SEC regulation that allows investors to buy securities and resell them to qualified institutional buyers.

(8) (A) Legal opinion and new issue confirmation.
Municipal documents provide investors with important legal information at the issuance of municipal securities. These documents include official statements, legal opinions, new issue confirmation, and the Committee on Uniform Securities identification procedures.

(9) (B) It defines the conditions under which companies can sell securities without a registration process.
Rule 145 allows companies to sell specific securities without participating in the registration process under certain conditions. The specific securities include stocks the investor accumulates due to a merger, reclassification, or acquisition.

(10) (B) Rule 147.
Rule 147 is also known as the safe harbor rule. It allows companies to raise capital without registering with the SEC. It applies especially to small-scale companies that want to raise funds locally and save on expensive registration fees.

(11) (C) Market-out clause.
This particular provision within the underwriting agreement allows the underwriters to cancel agreements without a penalty. Underwriters can activate this clause when they find it difficult to sell the company's stocks or when they cannot withstand a decline in market conditions.

(12) (B) Sale of securities.
The Securities Act of 1933 is a federal law that regulates the sale of securities. This act requires stock issuers to disclose all stock information to the public. It creates transparency and prevents fraudulent activities.

(13) (A) Within forty days.
All companies must file a prospectus before the deadline to publicly issue securities. Some companies make an initial public offering (IPO) but are not listed on the stock

exchange. If those companies desire to list on a particular stock exchange to issue securities to the public, they are obligated to file a prospectus within forty days of the offering.

(14) (C) Debt securities issued by government-sponsored enterprises or federal agencies.
Agency securities are debt securities issued by federal agencies or government-sponsored enterprises like Fannie Mae and Freddie Mac. They are less risky than corporate bonds but provide lower yields.

(15) (B) Common and preferred stock.
Equity securities have two main types: common and preferred stock. These stocks have several types, including callable and consumable shares.

(16) (A) Common stock incorporates ownership of the company, whereas preferred stock deals with the company's cash stream.
There are many differences between common and preferred stock, as they represent different ownership levels and voting rights within a company. Common stock has voting rights and greater ownership of shares. Preferred stock has greater priority but no voting rights. Preferred stocks more commonly deal with the company's cash stream.

(17) (C) Debt financing.
Investors who use debt financing provide funds to a corporation with the expectation that the corporation will repay the loan amount with interest. However, the investor does not take on any ownership stake in the company, and their potential loss is capped at the loan amount, regardless of the company's performance.

(18) (B) Corporations use them as strategies to raise money.
When a corporation runs short on funds, it must raise money to meet its obligation. It can use debt financing or equity financing. The choice will depend on the level of risk the cooperation is ready to take and the extent of resources they have on hand.

(19) (B) Restricted securities.
Restricted securities can only be sold when certain conditions are met. If Marcus cannot sell his security due to the limitations of the conditions, it is a restricted security.

(20) (D) Ninety to 180 days.

Most conditions or trading restrictions wane in ninety to 180 days. This is the usual range of lock-up periods.

(21) (A) An award of company stock with restricted rights that are lifted after a specified time or certain shares are vested.
A restricted stock award is a gift to a stockholder. These stocks have limited rights due to restrictions. The rights are restored after the end of the restriction period, fulfillment of conditions, or vesting of specific shares.

(22) (B) Sponsored ADR.
A sponsored American depository receipt creates a legal relationship between the ADR and a foreign company. Sponsored ADRs include the world's largest stock exchanges like the NYSE and Nasdaq.

(23) (A) A bond's maturity period and coupon rate.
The bond's price is sensitive to market interest rates. The market interest rate fluctuations cause the bond price to rise or fall. However, this sensitivity will depend on the bond's maturity time and coupon rate.

(24) (D) Credit default, country, and concentration.
Credit risks are assumed by creditors as there is a chance that borrowers might be unable to repay their debt security. There are three types of credit risk. Default risk is the uncertainty that a borrower may not meet their loan terms. Country risk is the uncertainty of investing in a particular country. Concentration risk is assumed by investors with portfolios focused on single investment areas.

(25) (A) They are issued at face value with no default risk or tax deductions.
Government securities are state securities that usually fund public welfare operations and projects. They are unlikely to default, have no tax deductions, and are always issued at face value.

(26) (D) Corporate bonds.

Corporate bonds have call provisions that allow them to be repurchased or retired. Corporate and municipal bonds also have this feature. However, government securities issued by the US Treasury do not.

(27) (D) A sinking fund requires a certain number of bonds to be redeemed by the issuer on a set schedule, whereas an extraordinary fund allows the bonds to be redeemed after the conditions are met.
Sinking funds and extraordinary call provisions are both call provisions. The type of fund determines how these bonds are issued and redeemed.

(28) (A) Investment grades are higher than speculative grades.
The investment grade is used to make investments and lend money to a borrower. The speculative grade is lower than the investment grade as it is based on speculations and carries risk.

(29) (C) Treasury bills.
Short or medium-term debt instruments are based on short-term returns. Mortgages, debentures, and leases are long-term instruments. Treasury bills can finance short-term requirements.

(30) (A) Treasury notes.
Treasury notes are the only debt instrument with a maturity period of two to ten years and a fixed interest rate.

(31) (C) Separate trading of registered interest and principal securities.
Separate trading of registered interest and principal securities are bonds known as STRIPS. These are the only government-issued securities that treat principal and coupon payments as individual and distinct entities.

(32) (C) Auction.
Auctions are a method to sell assets. Buyers place competing bids with each other to acquire them.

(33) (A) Government-sponsored enterprise.
A government-sponsored enterprise issues debt obligations known as agency securities. These enterprises include FNMA and SLMA.

(34) (C) Government National Mortgage Association.
The Government National Mortgage Association (Ginnie Mae) is a government-owned corporation within the US Department of Housing and Urban Development. It is not a component of the Farm Credit System but instead guarantees mortgage-backed securities of government-insured loans.

(35) (A) Asset-backed security.
A mortgage-backed security is an asset-backed security formed by a collection of mortgages sold as a package. They are secured with collateral. They use mortgages as assets to generate cash.

(36) (D) Private creditor.
A private creditor cannot issue municipal securities. Government entities issue municipal bonds and include transit authorities, school districts, and the state.

(37) (B) Revenue bond.
A revenue bond is a private activity bond. These municipal bonds deal with privately developed public projects and include municipal authorities and state entities.

(38) (A) To provide cash to maintain and construct highways.
Grant anticipation notes are a form of municipal financing for the construction and maintenance of highways. These notes provide immediate cash related to those projects.

(39) (A) MIG 1.
Moody's assigns three ratings to municipal notes. MIG 1 is the best quality rating.

(40) (C) Equipment trust certificate.
An equipment trust certificate is a type of secured corporate bond. It grants a company authority to possess and make use of an asset. The trustee of the investment pays for those rights over time.

(41) (B) Members' voluntary liquidation.

Members' voluntary liquidation is a type of liquidation that occurs with consent. Businesses can be closed after the repayment of all liabilities and liquidation of their assets.

(42) (C) General creditor.
A general creditor is the only creditor without the legal right to hold the property or asset of the debtor as collateral in case of default. If James's colleague fails to repay the loan, he cannot hold anything as collateral.

(43) (A) Management investment company.
A management investment company helps manage fund shares that are publicly issued. They are either open-end or closed-end companies.

(44) (D) Open and closed-end mutual funds' prices depend on the market's demand and supply of shares.
The prices of open-end mutual funds do not depend on the market's demand and supply of shares. Their prices are calculated by the NAV divided by the number of shares. The prices of closed-end mutual funds depend on the supply and demand of shares in the market.

(45) (D) Life annuity with a refund clause.
A life annuity with a refund clause guarantees payment for the annuitant's entire lifetime. It passes the residual amount or payments onto a beneficiary in the event of the annuitant's death.

(46) (A) They keep a clear record of assets backed by variable annuities and ensure efficient management of any financial issue.
Separate accounts hold all the assets backed by variable annuities. Each investment policyholder is assigned a separate account to help deal with any financial discrepancies.

(47) (A) It provides an investor with a return that is inverse to the asset's performance.
Inverse ETFs give a positive return when the underlying index of that asset drops in the financial market. It shows an inverse relationship between the index and the asset.

(48) (A) Equity REIT.

Equity REITs invest in and own properties. Their revenue comes predominantly from rental income. This makes them an attractive option for investors who seek a regular income stream. As property values potentially increase over time, Equity REITs can also provide the opportunity for capital appreciation.

(49) (D) Investor certification.
There are financial requirements to become an accredited investor in the United States. An investor must have a net worth of at least $1 million, which excludes the value of their primary residence, or have an income of at least $200,000 each year for the last two years. If married, their combined income must be $300,000, with the expectation of the same amount in the current year. There is no specific investor certification.

(50) (B) Long hedging.
If the value of a security is expected to rise, and an investor purchases the security to limit losses and maximize profits, they are long hedging.

(51) (C) A potential return.
Hedging is used to increase profits and limit losses. However, the early sale or purchase of an asset could result in the loss of potential gains. The price could fluctuate in the future and result in a higher return.

(52) (A) FINRA.
FINRA's rule 5240 established the anti-intimidation/coordination interpretation. This makes it illegal for firms registered with FINRA to coordinate their activities. It prohibits the threat, harassment, and intimidation of members of other firms or any person to perform specific actions.

(53) (A) Securities Exchange Act of 1934 (SEA).
The SEA fosters transparency and fairness within securities transactions, safeguards the interests of investors, and imposes regulations on the securities industry. The SEC is the regulatory authority entrusted with the responsibility to oversee and enforce the provisions outlined within the act.

(54) (C) Market rumors.

Market rumors disseminate false or misleading information about securities with the intent to manipulate their price. This practice is prohibited as it can distort the market and harm investors.

(55) (B) Rule 5320.
Rule 5320 strongly prohibits the practice of trading ahead of customer orders. This is the unethical practice of a broker-dealer who executes trades before a customer submits an order. The broker uses non-public information about the customer's intention to buy or sell.

(56) (A) To promote transparency and fairness in the allocation and distribution of new securities issues.
FINRA introduced the New Issue rule to ensure transparency and fairness in the allocation and distribution of new securities offerings. It sets guidelines for member firms to participate and handle new issue securities.

(57) (A) The Securities and Exchange Commission.
The SEC actively monitors firms for compliance with Regulation M. This regulation governs the activities of securities issuers. It prohibits artificial influence on the market for an offered security.

(58) (A) Senior Safe Act.
The Senior Safe Act is a federal law. It requires financial institutions to report cases of suspected financial exploitation of vulnerable adults and older adults to relevant authorities for investigation and protection.

(59) (C) Intimidation or coordination as a means to manipulate security prices.
The anti-intimidation/coordination interpretation of the Securities Exchange Act of 1934 prohibits the manipulation of security prices through the tactics of intimidation or coordination.

(60) (A) Report their external accounts to their affiliated brokerage firm.
FINRA Rule 3210 requires registered financial advisors to disclose their outside brokerage accounts to their member firms to promote transparency and accountability.

(61) (A) Rule G-30.

The MSRB established Rule G-30, which requires municipal security dealers to charge fair and reasonable prices in securities transactions to ensure fairness and protect investor interests.

(62) (B) Market manipulation in securities offerings.
Regulation M prevents market manipulation during securities offerings, which include IPOs and secondary offerings. It regulates stabilizing bids and purchases.

(63) (C) Financial exploitation.
Financial exploitation is the manipulation or misuse of someone's financial resources for personal gain. It targets vulnerable individuals like older adults or those who lack financial literacy. It involves various fraudulent activities, which include embezzlement, identity theft, and undue influence over financial decision-making.

(64) (C) Rule 10b-5.
The Securities Exchange Act of 1934 established Rule 10b-5 to preserve the integrity of the securities market and combat fraudulent practices. This rule prohibits the use of false or misleading information to manipulate the price or trade of a security. Rule 10b-5 explicitly forbids fraudulent misrepresentation, omission of material facts, or the use of deceptive devices. It safeguards investors and maintains a fair and transparent marketplace.

(65) (D) Short selling.
Short selling is prohibited in the restricted period under Regulation M as it involves the sale of borrowed securities only to repurchase them at a lower price for a profit. It is seen as a potentially manipulative practice that can negatively impact the market during an offering period as it can put downward pressure on the stock price.

(66) (B) To alter or falsely documents to deceive or defraud.
Forgery is the alteration or amendment of documents, signatures, or records to deceive or defraud others. It is an illegal and fraudulent practice.

(67) (D) A document that guarantees coverage of a borrower's credit exposure in case of default.

In the securities industry, a guarantee refers to a document that provides assurance or coverage of a borrower's credit exposure in the event of default. It ensures repayment to the lender in such circumstances.

(68) (C) Front-running executes trades based on advanced knowledge of pending orders, whereas insider trading trades securities based on non-public information.
Front-running is an unethical practice that executes trades for personal gain based on advanced knowledge of pending orders. Insider trading involves the illegal trade of securities based on material non-public information.

(69) (D) All of the above.
Regulation M prevents the manipulation of the market by investors to affect the outcome of an offering. FINRA monitors investors for compliance.

(70) (B) The broker-dealer may sell his securities.
After a Reg T call, if Kazak fails to meet the additional funds' requirement, the broker-dealer may sell his securities to cover the margin deficiency.

(71) (C) Tippee.
A tippee is an individual who receives insider information from another person or entity. This individual may be liable for insider trading if they trade securities based on non-public information.

(72) (B) Rule 2165.
FINRA implemented Rule 2165 to enable member firms to temporarily restrict the transfer of securities or funds from the accounts of vulnerable adults (such as older investors) in cases with a chance of financial exploitation.

(73) (C) The customer's name and residential address.
When brokers open accounts, they must collect the customer's name and residential address, among other required information. This helps to establish the customer's identity and comply with regulatory obligations.

(74) (B) To provide sound financial advice to institutional investors.
Institutional suitability ensures that the investment advice provided by brokers or financial advisors aligns with the risk tolerance, investment goals, and specific

requirements of institutional investors. Institutional investors may include large entities like mutual funds, pensions, and insurance companies. This advice helps them make informed decisions that further their financial objectives.

(75) (B) Reasonable-basis, customer-specific, and quantitative obligations.
Per FINRA rule 2111, firms and associated people have three main suitability obligations: reasonable-basis obligation ensures a reasonable basis for investment recommendations, customer-specific obligation considers the customer's investment profile, and quantitative obligation accounts for the number of recommended transactions.

(76) (A) Potential loss of funds if one account holder withdraws all funds.
Per FINRA rule 2330, a risk associated with joint accounts is the potential loss of funds if one account holder withdraws all funds without the consent of the other account holder(s).

(77) (A) Monetary fines, repayment of profits, and imprisonment.
Per SEC regulations, the consequences of insider trading can include monetary fines, repayment of illicit profits, and imprisonment. These penalties aim to deter and punish individuals engaged in illegal insider trading activities.

(78) (B) To remove details from broker records.
Brokers often erase details from their records to present a cleaner record to investors. This process is known as expungement.

(79) (C) Introduced rule 2080.
Rule 2080 limits the expungement authority of brokers. It requires them to explain and report their expungement actions to FINRA. Due to this rule, brokers may not use expungement to their advantage and mislead investors.

(80) (D) To educate investors, provide them with helpful material, and encourage informed decisions.

The MSRB is a securities rulemaking board that oversees security trading and helps facilitate its actions. It provides investors with informational materials about municipal securities that enable them to make well-informed decisions.

(81) (C) Recognize the issue, investigate, inform the customer of your findings, record the complaint, and follow up.
The correct protocol for customer complaints is first to recognize the issue at hand. Next, investigate the matter and respond to the customer with the investigation results. Then, officially record the complaint and follow up with the customer.

(82) (D) Investors.
The reporting requirements ensure that investors stay protected.

(83) (C) Investors with a high credit score.
Red flags are factors or actions that raise investor concerns. They include brokers not registered with the SEC/FINRA, unknown sources who make unsolicited offers to investors, unexplained account discrepancies, and unauthorized transactions. A high credit score is not a red flag.

(84) (D) Both B and C.
If a red flag is detected, all transactions must be stopped immediately. The accounts must be frozen to allow an investigation into any unauthorized transactions. The matter should also be taken up with law enforcement agencies.

(85) (A) Rule G-37.
The MSRB regulates municipal securities and monitors financial activities. Rule G-37 prohibits the use of political advantage to influence the distribution of municipal securities.

Access the Bonus Audiobook and Flash Cards!

Scan the QR code below with your phone and you will be given a link to google drive, where you can download the audiobook and flash cards.

If the QR code does not work for you, please contact us at info@newstonetestprep.com

1. Roth IRA & Roth 401(k)
2. Margin - cash deposit
3. index funds - benefit
4. selling away
5. interest on treasury notes
6. insider trading laws
7. AML program
8. low period of inflation
10) 529 savings plan
11. U4 form

Made in the USA
Coppell, TX
05 February 2024

28626399R00221